Remembraunces at my next goyng to the Courte

First for redresse of suche riottes as be in the Northe parties.

Item for lres to be writen to Sir John Wallop.

Item for to declare the matiers of Ireland to the kynge highnes, and to devise what shalbe done there.

Item to send lres into Ireland and to advise the Deputey of the kynges pleasure, and to send lres for money.

Item to advertise the kyng of the orderyng of Master ffissher, and to shewe hym of the Indenture whiche Gans delyuyd to the Solicitour.

Item to knowe his pleasure towchyng Master More

Item to declare vnto his highnes the procedynges in his cause of vses and willes.

Item to declare vnto his grace theffect of Master Pates lres.

Item to remember specially Master Shelley.

Item to remember Brothers for his consyderment and his mater towchyng Sir Water Hungerford in his well doynges.

Item when Master ffissher shall go to execucion & also the other.

Item what shalbe done farther towching Master More

Item towching the conuencion for my Lord of Suffolke.

Item to send vnto the kyng by taske the behauiour of Master ffissher.

Item towching the Sermond made in London vpon Sunday next

Item towching the surge is well broght out of Almayne.

Item speciall lres to be drawen to Justices of assise throughout the realme towching the vnyte of the people.

Item to seke out the first Commyssion for the first fruites in Ciuill and to delyver the same to Danster.

Item to take an end in the warr of Halifax for his fyne that

'THE KING'S GOOD SERVANT'

Sir Thomas More after Hans Holbein the Younger (no. 26)

'The King's Good Servant'
Sir Thomas More
1477/8–1535

J. B. Trapp and
Hubertus Schulte Herbrüggen

The Boydell Press
Rowman and Littlefield

Published for the exhibition held at
the National Portrait Gallery from
25 November 1977 to 12 March 1978

Exhibition Organiser Richard Ormond
Exhibition Designer Michael Haynes

Catalogue edited by Mary Pettman
Designed by Paul Sharp
Printed by Westerham Press
© J. B. Trapp and Hubertus Schulte Herbrüggen, 1977
ISBN (UK) 0 85115 095 0

Cloth edition published by The Boydell Press,
PO Box 24, Ipswich IP1 1JJ, and
Rowman and Littlefield, 81 Adams Drive,
Totowa, NJ 07512, USA

Front cover: Detail from *Sir Thomas More, his father, his household and his descendants* by Rowland Lockey, 1593 (no. 1)
Inside front cover: Thomas Cromwell's *Remembrances*, [June] 1535 (no. 245)
Back cover: Letter from Sir Thomas More to Cardinal Wolsey, [1523] (no. 120)
Inside back cover: Fragment B from William Rastell's *Life of Sir Thomas More* (no. 235)

Contents

Foreword 6

Acknowledgements 7

Genealogy 8

Chronology 10

Abbreviations 15

Catalogue note 16

CATALOGUE

I   Sir Thomas More and his kings   17

II   Early life in London: birth, schooldays, humanism, the law and the Church   23

III   Humanism and royal service   30

IV   Sir Thomas More and the defence of the Church:
     i Luther and the Continental Reformers   63
     ii The English Reformers   73

V   Sir Thomas More and his household   85

VI   Politics at home and abroad   98

VII   Sir Thomas More in the Tower   114

VIII   Succession, Supremacy and execution   120

IX   The posthumous reputation of Sir Thomas More   132

List of Lenders   141

Index   142

Foreword

'The king's good servant, but God's first.' By extension these famous words, uttered by More on the scaffold, might be those of an Einstein, or any modern thinker concerned with universals, with the destiny of man, rather than the practical politics of the day. So much about More's life and work is relevant to our own times. He was a perfect gentleman who moved serenely in what Professor Hugh Trevor-Roper has aptly called a 'splendid, cannibal Court', one so typical of a fledgling dynasty of the Renaissance. He was a man of the most diverse accomplishments and interests: trained as a lawyer, he was a humanist scholar, a writer and philosopher of the first consequence, a brilliant diplomat and a statesman who was able to hold his own with anyone and knew the ways of the great as well as Talleyrand. Succeeding Wolsey as first minister of the Crown, his career was shattered by Henry VIII's demand for a divorce from Catherine of Aragon, and the subsequent breach with Rome. For on this issue there could be no compromise as far as More was concerned: the unity of Christendom was sacrosanct. His integrity and courage, the humour and sense of irony which tempered the rigour of his mind, the total absence of pretentiousness that marked his public life, the love of family – all combine to make More one of the most appealing figures in English history and the very epitome of the purpose for which this Gallery was founded, an inspiration 'to mental exertion, to noble actions, to good conduct on the part of the living', as Lord Palmerston put it in his speech winding up the debate on the National Portrait Gallery.

The exhibition is one of a sequence devoted to the lives of great historical figures which have been mounted at the National Portrait Gallery in recent years. It was preceded by *The Winter Queen*, 1963, the first specially designed exhibition to be held at the Gallery, *Mr Boswell* in 1967, *Samuel Pepys* in 1971, and most recently, *Richard III* in 1973. All these exhibitions set the characters concerned in the context of their times, and this we have attempted to do in the case of Sir Thomas More. His career is documented by such manuscripts and objects as still survive, and the works of art assembled, many of them of the highest quality, reflect the best in the art and culture of the early sixteenth century. Indeed the exhibition is one of the most comprehensive biographical surveys of a great man ever to be staged.

The presence of so many rare and valuable loans is a testimony both to the generosity of countless owners and to the strength of the feelings inspired by the memory of More himself. Her Majesty The Queen has graciously lent all the great Holbein drawings of More and his family from Windsor, together with a group of important paintings, including the Holbein portrait of the Duke of Norfolk. We are equally privileged to be allowed to show Holbein's magnificent but terrifying portrait of Henry VIII, so generously lent by Baron Thyssen-Bornemisza, which is one of the most exquisitely painted of all Renaissance portraits. The Earl of Radnor has lent the portrait of Peter Gillis by Quentin Massys, one part of a diptych (the other part containing a portrait of Erasmus) which was sent to More. And the City of Bristol Museum and Art Gallery has lent the fine Cranach of Martin Luther. We are also indebted to many of the world's great libraries. Extensive loans of books and manuscripts have come from the Bodleian Library, Oxford, the British Library, Cambridge University Library, Guildhall Library and the Public Record Office. Stonyhurst College has lent an important group of relics, and other items personally associated with More have been lent by his descendant, Thomas More Eyston. The only surviving manuscript of any importance in More's own hand, *De Tristitia Christi*, has been lent by the Real Colegio de Corpus Christi in Valencia; the Beinecke Library at Yale has lent More's prayer-book; and the Vatican has lent Henry VIII's presentation copy of the *Assertio septem Sacramentorum*.

The organisation of such an exhibition as this has been a complex task. The Trustees are particularly indebted to Professor J. B. Trapp, Director of the Warburg Institute, who has given so freely of his time and knowledge; they are also immensely grateful to Professor Hubertus Schulte Herbrüggen of Düsseldorf University. These two scholars, in association with my colleague, Richard Ormond, have selected the exhibits, and they are responsible for the illuminating and scholarly catalogue, which will remain a lasting contribution to our knowledge and understanding of More long after the exhibition has closed. Professor Schulte Herbrüggen has prepared the chronology, the genealogy and the entries for documents, letters and More's works; all other entries are by Professor Trapp. The evocative setting for the exhibition we owe to the imagination and practical skill of Michael Haynes, who has thrown himself whole-heartedly into the enterprise, and has been at special pains to recreate the atmosphere of places associated with More, most notably Hampton Court and the Tower. We earnestly hope that the combination of so many generous and apposite loans, distinguished scholarship, and appropriate and convincing design, will prove to be a worthy celebration of the quincentenary of the birth of one of the greatest Englishmen of all time.

JOHN HAYES
Director, National Portrait Gallery
July 1977

Acknowledgements

We would like to thank the following people on the Gallery staff for their contribution to the exhibition: Jacquie Meredith, who shouldered the immense burden of arranging and transporting the loans; Angela Cox, who organised the lectures and educational visits; Heather Tilbury, the Public Relations Adviser; and Mary Pettman, editor of the catalogue.

In putting on the exhibition we received help from individuals and institutions too numerous to list, but we owe a special debt of thanks to the following: Dr Charles Avery, Mr N. J. Barker, Dr Bruce Barker-Benfield, Mr C. B. L. Barr, Mr John Barr, Mr M. D. K. Baxandall, Professor S. T. Bindoff and the Tudor Section of the History of Parliament Trust, Mr C. Blair, Mr David Brown, Sir Alan Campbell, Dr Lorne Campbell, Professor F. A. Carreres, Signor R. E. Cavaliero, Mr E. Chamberlain, Dr D. S. Chambers, Mr A. Darr, Dr A. C. de la Mare, Dr James Diggle, Dr A. I. Doyle, Signor Roberto Ducci, Mr K. Garside, Mr J. W. Goodison, The Countess of Halsbury, Archbishop Bruno Heim, Mr K. Hempel, Mr Michael Hirst, Mr J. H. Hopkins, Mr W. H. Hutton, Professor J. IJsewijn, Miss Jean M. Imray, Mrs H. Jones, Dr C. M. Kauffmann, Mr William Kellaway, Mr and Mrs R. W. Lightbown, Dr C. Ligota, Dr Elizabeth McGrath, Mr D. J. McKitterick, M. l'abbé G. Marc'hadour, Miss A. M. Meyer, Miss Helen Miller, Dr Jennifer Montagu, Mr J. C. Moss, Miss Marie Ney, Dr J. D. North, Mr J. C. T. Oates, Mr S. G. Parker-Ross, Mr J. G. Pollard, Mr M. Powell-Jones, Miss Elizabeth Poyser, the Hon Mrs Jane Roberts, Mr R. J. Roberts, Mr D. Robinson, Dr D. M. Rogers, Mr J. K. Rowlands, Dr C. B. Schmitt, Miss Anna E. C. Simoni, Miss A. Somers Cox, Dr Roy Strong, Professor R. S. Sylvester, the Reverend C. E. Leighton Thomson, Dr Pamela Tudor-Craig, Mr D. H. Turner, Mr D. G. Vaisey, Mr Oliver van Oss, Mr R. J. B. Walker, Dr N. G. Wilson, Mr T. H. Wilson, Mr H. J. R. Wing.

H. SCHULTE HERBRÜGGEN, J. B. TRAPP, R. L. ORMOND

Genealogy

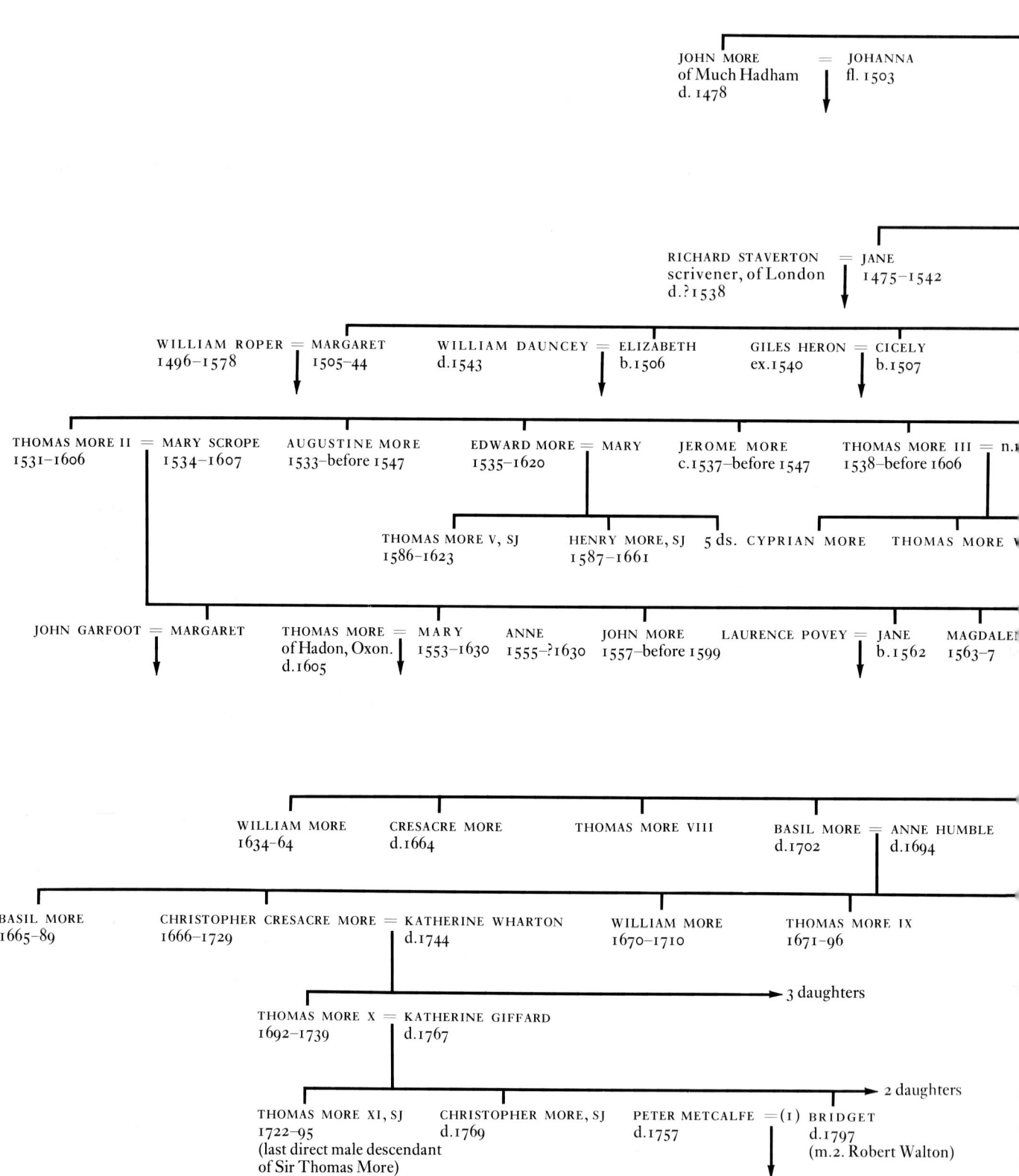

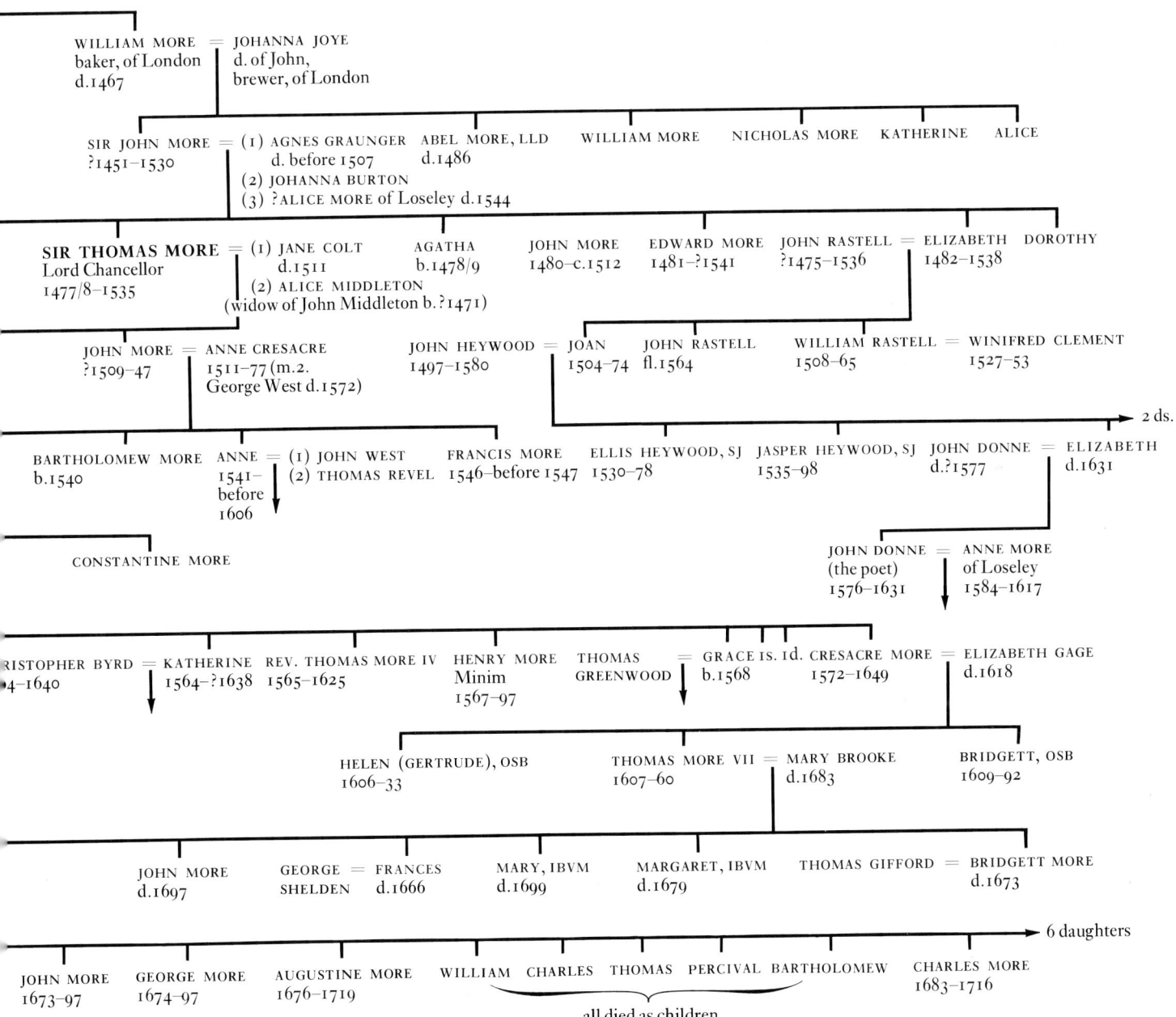

Chronology

1477/8	6/7 February	Thomas More born in Milk Street, Cripplegate, the second child and eldest son of John More (*c*.1451–1530) and Agnes, daughter of Thomas Graunger (d. 1510), skinner, alderman and sheriff of London.
–*c*.1490		Thomas attends St Antony's School, Threadneedle Street, under Master Nicholas Holt.
c.1490		His father finds him a place, as page, in the household of Archbishop Morton, Lord Chancellor (d.1500), at Lambeth Palace.
c.1492		Morton, recognising More's promise, sends him to Oxford University.
c.1494		Recalled from Oxford by his father to embark on a legal career, beginning at New Inn.
1496		Admitted to Lincoln's Inn.
c.1497		Contributes Latin verses to John Holt, *Lac puerorum*.
1499		First meeting with Erasmus, whom he takes on a visit to the royal children at Eltham.
c.1499–1503		Practising as a barrister and living, without vow, in the London Charterhouse.
1501		Lectures at William Grocyn's church, St Lawrence Jewry, on St Augustine, *City of God*; studies Greek with Grocyn and Thomas Linacre; translates from the *Greek Anthology*, with William Lily. Called to the bar; Reader at Furnivall's Inn for three years.
c.1503		Writes English poems: *A merry Jest*, *Nine Pageants*, verses for the *Book of Fortune*, *A Rueful Lamentation*.
1504		MP for unknown constituency; opposes Henry VII's demand for subsidy for marriage of his daughter Margaret.
1505	by January	Marries Jane, eldest daughter of Sir John Colt, MP (1465–1521), of Netherhall, nr Roydon, Essex. Lives at The Old Barge, Bucklersbury, in the parish of St Stephen Walbrook. About October, Margaret, his eldest daughter, born. Translates Gianfrancesco Pico's *Life* of his uncle, Giovanni Pico della Mirandola.
1505–6		Erasmus, staying in the house at Bucklersbury, and More translate Lucian.
1506		Elizabeth, More's second daughter, born.
1507		Cicely, third daughter, born.
?1508		Visits Paris and Louvain and their universities.
1509	21 March	More's only son, John, born. Granted freedom of Mercers' Company. Composes Latin epigrams on the coronation of Henry VIII (24 June).
	5 July	More's first Royal Commission
	6–13 September	Conducts negotiations on behalf of Mercers with the Pensionary of Antwerp.
	October	Erasmus, back from Italy, writes the *Praise of Folly* under More's roof and dedicates it to his host.
1510		MP for London in the first Parliament of Henry VIII.
	3 September	Appointed Under-Sheriff of the City of London. Autumn Reader at Lincoln's Inn. *Life of Picus* printed by John Rastell.
1511	summer autumn	Jane More dies, aged 23. Marries Alice Middleton (b.*c*.1471), widow of John Middleton (d.1509), citizen and mercer of London and merchant of the Staple at Calais. Governor of Lincoln's Inn. Host to Andrea Ammonio at Bucklersbury.

1512	1 April	Elected by Merchants of the Staple to negotiate with Merchants Adventurers.
	12 August	Naval battle between English and French, on which writes Latin epigrams, later subject of controversy with Germanus Brixius.
	16 November	Accompanies City delegation to Council.
	7 December	With father, on legal committees.
1513	20 January	Appears before Council on City matters.
	13 September	With others to have care of London Bridge.
1514		Lent Reader at Lincoln's Inn.
	3 December	Admitted to Doctors' Commons.
	11 December	Rewarded by the City.
1514–18		Writes Latin and English versions of his *History of Richard III*.
1515	7 May–22 October	First mission abroad, to Flanders. Meets Erasmus at Bruges, Peter Gillis at Antwerp and Jerome Busleyden at Malines. Begins to write *Utopia*.
	21 October	Enters controversy with Martin Dorp.
1516		Completes *Utopia* in London by addition of Book I.
	February	Frequents court.
	10 June	Assists City's committee on price of victuals.
	c. December	*Utopia* published at Louvain.
		Wins case of the pope's ship against the Crown and is pressed to enter royal service.
1517	10–17 March	Concerned with London office of gaugership and tithes.
	1 May	Intervenes at Evil May Day riots.
	28 May	On commission to enquire about enclosed lands.
	17 June	Present at Court of Star Chamber.
	29 June	Address on behalf of City, to Cardinal Lorenzo Campeggio, Papal Legate.
	by August	Member of the King's Council.
	26 August–December	More's second embassy, to Calais.
	16 September	Erasmus sends More portraits of himself and Peter Gillis by Quentin Massys.
1518	February	Acting as royal secretary.
	March	*Utopia* and *Epigrammata* printed at Basel.
	29 March	More's *Letter to the University of Oxford*, reproving their opposition to the study of Greek.
	21 June	More granted £100 annuity for life.
	23 July	Resigns as Under-Sheriff.
	18 September	Venetian ambassador reports on More's diplomatic silence about Anglo-French negotiations.
	19 September	On Commission of Peace for Kent.
	2–4 October	More co-signatory of peace treaty with France.
1519	5 March	Gives legal advice to Mercers' Company.
	summer	Follows court, acting as royal secretary.
		Visits his sister, Elizabeth Rastell, at Coventry, where a dispute with a friar prompts his *Letter to a Monk*.
	23 July	Erasmus gives portrait of More in letter to Ulrich von Hutten.
1520	27 February	Champions Erasmus in letter to Edward Lee.
	April	Publishes rejoinder to Brixius's *Antimorus*.
		Attends Henry at visit of Charles V to Canterbury and London.
	11 April	On commission to negotiate with Charles V.
	May–June	Attends king to Field of the Cloth of Gold, where meets Guillaume Budé and Francis Cranevelt.
	19 July–12 August	At Bruges, settles dispute with German Hansa.
	24–29 July	Charles V visits Bruges; More meets members of his entourage: Erasmus, Hutten, Peutinger, Vives.
	28 November	Granted keepership of the Change and Exchange in England.
		Praised by Robert Whittinton in his *Vulgaria* and John Constable in his *Epigrammata*.

1521		Sits as judge in the Star Chamber.
	9 February	Paid 20 marks by Merchants Adventurers for services.
	2 May	Sub-Treasurer of England, in succession to Sir John Cutte; knighted.
	21 May	Henry VIII confirms his authorship of the *Assertio septem Sacramentorum*, and receives title of *Fidei defensor* (October).
	2 July	Margaret More marries William Roper.
	5 July	Present on the king's behalf at the London Court of Aldermen.
	August	Accompanies Wolsey on mission to Calais and Bruges.
	12 September–8 October	Negotiates with the Hansa at Bruges; meets Erasmus and Vives.
	8–14 October	With Wolsey at Calais.
1522		Writes unfinished *Treatise of the Four Last Things*.
	23 March	Receives grant of the Manor of South, Kent.
	27 May	Attends king to Canterbury for meeting with Charles V.
	6 June	Welcomes Charles V to the City in formal oration.
	14 June	Wolsey notified that the king desires to have, besides More, 'noble and wise persons' about him.
	14 October	Tunstall's *De arte supputandi* published and dedicated to More.
1523	January	Begins to write *Responsio ad Lutherum*.
	15 April	Chosen Speaker of the House of Commons.
	1 June	Buys lease of Crosby Place, St Helen's, Bishopsgate.
	September–October	With the court at Woodstock; meets Thomas Murner.
	after 3 December	Publishes *Responsio ad Lutherum*.
1524	9 January	Nicolaus Leonicus sends More his translation of Aristotle, *Parva naturalia*, 1523.
	20 January	Sells lease of Crosby Place to Antonio Bonvisi.
	20 June	High Steward of Oxford University.
		Buys land at Chelsea.
		Margaret Roper's English translation of Erasmus on the Paternoster published.
1525	16 January	Receives grant of manors of Ducklington, Fringford and Barleypark, Oxon.
	6 June	At reception of Leonardo Orio, the new Venetian ambassador.
	18 June	Reads decree creating Henry's bastard son, Henry Fitzroy, Earl of Nottingham and Duke of Richmond and Somerset.
	29 June	Steward of the Duchy of Lancaster in Hertfordshire and Middlesex, for life.
	end July and 14 August	Present at peace talks with French envoys.
	28 August	On commission to treat with France for peace; signs, with others, Treaty of the More, and receives pension of 150 crowns from French.
	29 September	Chancellor of Duchy of Lancaster in succession to Sir Richard Wingfield; on the same day as his daughter Elizabeth is married to William Dauncey (d.1543) and his daughter Cicely to Giles Heron (executed 1540).
	c.November	Steward of Cambridge University.
1526	17 January	'Eltham Ordinances' decree that More, as one of the Council, is always to be 'about the King'.
	26–27 January	Visits the Steelyard, London house of the Hansa merchants, about Lutheran books.
	5 February	Judge in the Star Chamber.
	c.February	Receives dedication of Johann Eck's *Enchiridion*.
		John Clement and his wife Margaret Gigs set up house at The Old Barge.
	autumn	Receives visit of Hans Holbein the Younger, who stays in household and makes drawings and paintings of its members singly and together.
		Concerned with the king's answer to Luther's letter.
		Controversy with Johann Bugenhagen Pomeranus.
1527	March–April	On commission to treat with France.
	20 March	More's lands and fees assessed for subsidy at £340.
	26 May	Commissioned, with Stephen Gardiner, to treat with France.
	July–September	Accompanies Wolsey to Calais and Amiens.
	c.October	On return, consulted about 'the King's great matter', ie the divorce.

1528	7 March	Licensed by Tunstall to read and retain heretical books in order to defend the Catholic faith.
	11 November	Receives dedication of Cochlaeus's Cassiodorus.
		Installs More chapel in his parish church at Chelsea.
1529	25 May	The king's and More's orations to the Star Chamber on heresy.
	June	*Dialogue concerning Heresies* published.
	30 June	On commissions, with Tunstall and others, to treat for peace and alliance with imperial, French and Venetian ambassadors.
	1 July	Departs from England to be present 5 August at promulgation of 'Ladies' Peace' at Cambrai.
	September	More's barns at Chelsea burned down.
		Two editions of *Supplication of Souls* published.
	17–18 October	At Westminster, Wolsey delivers Great Seal.
	25–26 October	Receives Seal, and takes oath as Lord Chancellor.
	3 November	Opens 'Reformation Parliament'.
	1 December	Signs 44 articles against Wolsey.
	uncertain date	John More marries Anne Cresacre, More's ward.
1530	23 February	Fraternity letter to Sir Thomas and Lady More from Christ Church, Canterbury.
	24 May	Member of commission drawing up 'Publick Instrument' listing heresies.
	?1 December	Death of Sir John More, aged 79; will proved 5 December.
1531	16 January	Opens second session of Parliament.
	11 February	Convocation of Canterbury: submission of the clergy to Henry's claim to Supremacy 'as far as the law of God permits'.
	11 March	Charles V writes to More.
	30 March	Delivers Henry's message about his divorce to Parliament, but refuses to disclose his opinion.
	May	Visited by Simon Grynaeus; 2nd edn of *Dialogue on Heresies* published.
1532	January	Opens third session of Parliament.
		First part of the *Confutation of Tyndale's Answer* published.
	1 January	Receives New Year's gifts from king and queen – gilt goblet and walking staff wrought with gold.
	15 May	Submission of Clergy.
	16 May	Resigns chancellorship on grounds of ill health.
		Writes his Latin epitaph and sends it to Erasmus.
		Refuses reward offered by the clergy.
	7 December	*Letter to John Frith* against Frith's views on the Eucharist (published early 1533).
1533	?February	Second part of *Confutation of Tyndale's Answer* published.
	Easter	*Apology* published.
		John More's translation from Fridericus Nausea published.
	1 June	Refuses to attend Anne Boleyn's coronation.
	2 July	Asks Fitzwilliam to intervene for him with Cromwell.
	autumn	Enquires into the case of Elizabeth Barton, the Nun of Kent (executed 1534).
	1 November	*Debellation of Salem and Bizance* published.
	December	Finishes his *Answer to ... a poisoned Book*, published January 1534.
1534	January	Accused of having written an answer to the Council's *Book of IX Articles*, justifying the royal marriage.
	1 February	Rebuts the charge to Cromwell.
	January–March	'Cromwell's Remembrances' to know the king's pleasure regarding More.
	21 February	Bill of attainder concerning Elizabeth Barton and others; Fisher's name included; More's struck out.
	February–March	Letters to Cromwell and the king.
	6 March	Examined by Council.
	25 March	Indenture granting lands at Chelsea to John Clement and others.
	30 March	Act of Succession.
	13 April	'Before the Lords at Lambeth' refuses the Oath, though willing to swear to the succession.
	17 April	Sent to Tower of London.

		Writes *Treatise on the Passion*, *Treatise to receive the Blessed Body*, *Dialogue of Comfort*, *De Tristitia Christi* with *Instructions and Prayers* interspersed.
	3 November	Acts of Attainder of Fisher and More; Act of Supremacy.
1535	January	Lady More's letter supplicating for More's release.
	16 January	More's manors of Ducklington, etc, granted to Sir Henry Norris.
	April	Manor of South granted to George Boleyn.
	30 April	Interrogated by Council in Tower.
	May	Lady More, forced to sell her wardrobe to pay for More's board and lodging in the Tower, supplicates Cromwell.
	4 May	More and Margaret in Tower watch Reynolds and the Carthusians brought down to execution.
	7 May	Second interrogation of More and first of Fisher by Cromwell.
	3 June	Third interrogation of More in Tower.
	11 June	Further interrogation of More, Fisher and servants.
	12 June	Visit by Richard Rich who tries to trap More.
	14 June	Further interrogation: More keeps silence.
	c.18 June	Final letter to Antonio Bonvisi.
	19 June	Martyrdom of the Carthusians.
	22 June	Martyrdom of John Fisher.
	26 June	Special commission of *oyer and terminer* to try More.
	1 July	More indicted at Westminster Hall, pleads not guilty and is condemned on perjured testimony of Richard Rich. Returned to the Tower.
	5 July	Last letter to Margaret.
	6 July	Before 9 am, executed on Tower Hill.
	4 August	'Paris News Letter' on More's trial and execution, available in Rome on 12 August.
	23 August	Cromwell instructs English ambassador to justify Fisher's and More's execution to Francis I.
	31 August	Henry instructs envoy to Germany to spread word that Fisher and More were traitors condemned 'by due course of law'.
	before 6 October	*Expositio fidelis de morte D. Thomae Mori* printed on Continent and soon translated.
1536	4 February	Act of Parliament annulling transfer by More of his Chelsea lands.
	26 April	Grant of More's Chelsea property to Sir William Poulet.
1551		Ralph Robynson's English translation of *Utopia* published.
1557		More's *English Works* published by William Rastell in London.
1563		More's *Lucubrationes* published in Basel.
1565/6		More's *Omnia Latina Opera* published in Louvain.
1588		Thomas Stapleton's *Tres Thomae* published in Douai.
1592		Fernando de Herrera, *Tómas Moro* published in Seville.
		(The biographies by William Roper, Nicholas Harpsfield and Ro.Ba. remained in MS until 1626, 1932 and 1950 respectively.)
1631		Cresacre More's *Life and Death of Thomas More* published in Douai.
1652		John Hoddesdon, *Tho. Mori Vita et Exitus*... published in London.
1675		Domenico Regi, *Della Vita di Tommaso Moro*, published in Milan.
1689		More's *Opera omnia* published in Frankfurt a.M.
1886	29 December	Beatification of John Fisher and Thomas More.
1935	19 May	Canonisation of John Fisher and Thomas More.

Abbreviations — List of works referred to in abbreviated form

Adams	H. M. Adams, *Catalogue of Books printed on the Continent of Europe 1500–1600 in Cambridge Libraries*, Cambridge 1967
Allen	P. S. and H. M. Allen, eds., completed by H. W. Garrod, *Opus epistolarum D. Erasmi Roterodami*, Oxford 1906–58 (cited by letter number)
Armand	A. Armand, *Les médailleurs italiens des XVe et XVIe siècles*, 1883–7
Bartsch	A. Bartsch, *Le peintre-graveur*, nouvelle édn., Leipzig 1854–76
Basel, *Malerfamilie Holbein*	*Die Malerfamilie Holbein in Basel. Ausstellung im Kunstmuseum Basel zur Fünfhundertjahrfeier der Universität Basel*, 1960
BFAC	Burlington Fine Arts Club
BM British Catalogue	E. Croft-Murray and P. Hulton, *British Museum: Catalogue of British Drawings...*, 1960
BMC	*Catalogue of Books printed in the XVth Century now in the British Museum*, 1908–
Bridgett	T. E. Bridgett, *The Life and Writings of Blessed Thomas More*, 3rd edn., 1913
Chambers	R. W. Chambers, *Thomas More*, 1935
Chelsea, 1929	*Catalogue of the Memorial Loan Exhibition ... of Sir Thomas More...*, Chelsea 1929
CMA	E. Bernard, *Catalogi Librorum Manuscriptorum Angliae et Hiberniae*, Oxford 1697
CW	*The Yale Edition of the Complete Works of St Thomas More*, New Haven, Conn.: II *Richard III*, ed. R. S. Sylvester, 1963 III, 1 *Translations of Lucian*, ed. Craig R. Thompson, 1974 IV *Utopia*, ed. E. Surtz and J. H. Hexter, 1965 V *Responsio ad Lutherum*, ed. J. M. Headley, 1969 VIII *The Confutation of Tyndale's Answer*, ed. L. A. Schuster, R. C. Marius, J. P. Lusardi and R. J. Schoeck, 1973 XII *A Dialogue of Comfort against Tribulation*, ed. L. L. Martz and F. E. Manley, 1976 XIII *A Treatise on the Passion; A Treatise to receive the Blessed Body; Instructions and Prayers*, ed. G. E. Haupt, 1976 XIV *De tristitia Christi*, ed. C. H. Miller, 1976
Dodgson II	Campbell Dodgson, *Catalogue of early German and Flemish Woodcuts ... in the British Museum*, II, 1911
EETS, OS and ES	*Early English Text Society*, Original and Extra Series
EHR	*English Historical Review*
Emden, *Cambridge*	A. B. Emden, *A biographical Register of the University of Cambridge to 1500*, Cambridge 1963
Emden, *Oxford*	A. B. Emden, *A biographical Register of the University of Oxford to 1500*, Oxford 1957–9
Emden, *Oxford 1540*	A. B. Emden, *A biographical Register of the University of Oxford, 1501–40*, Oxford 1974
Erasmus, 1969	*Erasmus en zijn Tijd* (catalogue of the exhibition in commemoration of the 500th anniversary of the birth of Erasmus), Rotterdam, Museum Boymans-van Beuningen, 1969
EW	*The Workes of Sir Thomas More Knyght, sometyme Lorde Chancellour of England, wrytten by him in the Englysh tonge*, 1557
Ganz, *Handzeichnungen*	Paul Ganz, *Handzeichnungen H. Holbeins d. J. Kritischer Katalog*, 1937
Ganz, *Paintings*	Paul Ganz, *The Paintings of Hans Holbein. Complete edn.*, 1956
Gibson	R. W. Gibson, *St Thomas More: a preliminary Bibliography of his Works and of Moreana to the Year 1700...*, New Haven and London 1961
GKW	*Gesamtkatalog der Wiegendrucke*, Leipzig 1925–
Goff	F. R. Goff, *Incunabula in American Libraries*, New York 1964
Habich	G. Habich, *Die deutschen Schaumünzen des XVI Jahrhunderts*, Munich 1929–35
Hain	L. Hain, *Repertorium bibliographicum* and continuations, Stuttgart-Paris 1826ff.
Harpsfield	Nicholas Harpsfield, ed. Elsie Vaughan Hitchcock, *The Life and Death of Sr Thomas Moore, knight...*, EETS, OS, CLXXXVI, 1932
Hill, *Corpus*	Sir George F. Hill, *A Corpus of the Italian Medals of the Renaissance before Cellini*, 1930
Hill-Pollard	Sir George F. Hill, revised by Graham Pollard, *Renaissance Medals from the Samuel H. Kress Collection*, 1967
Hollstein	F. W. H. Hollstein, *German Engravings, Etchings and Woodcuts, c 1400–1700*, Amsterdam 1954–
James, *Corpus Christi* (etc)	M. R. James, *A descriptive Catalogue of the Western MSS in Corpus Christi College* (etc), Cambridge
JW(C)I	*Journal of the Warburg (& Courtauld) Institute(s)*
Koepplin-Falk	D. Koepplin and T. Falk, *Lukas Cranach. Gemälde, Zeichnungen, Buchgraphik. Ausstellung im Kunstmuseum Basel*, 1974
LP	J. S. Brewer, James Gairdner and R. H. Brodie, eds., *Letters and Papers, foreign and domestic, of the Reign of Henry VIII*, 1862–1932
McKerrow-Ferguson	R. B. McKerrow and F. S. Ferguson, *Title-page Borders used in England and Scotland, 1485–1640*, 1932

Marc'hadour, *Bible*	G. Marc'hadour, *The Bible in the Works of Thomas More*, Nieuwkoop 1969–71	Rogers	Elizabeth Frances Rogers, ed., *The Correspondence of Sir Thomas More*, Princeton 1947 (cited by letter number)
Medallic Illustrations	*Medallic Illustrations of the History of Great Britain and Ireland*, compiled by E. Hawkins, ed. A. W. Franks and H. A. Grueber, 1885–1909	Roper	Elsie Vaughan Hitchcock, ed., *The Lyfe of Sir Thomas Moore, knighte, written by William Roper, Esquire...*, EETS, OS, CXCVII, 1935
Millar	Sir Oliver Millar, *The Tudor, Stuart and early Georgian Pictures in the Collection of H.M. the Queen*, 1963	Routh	E. M. G. Routh, *Sir Thomas More and his Friends*, 1934
Moreana	*Moreana. Bulletin Thomas More*, Angers 1964–	Rymer	T. Rymer, *Foedera...*, 1704–35
		SC	*A Summary Catalogue of the Western MSS in the Bodleian Library at Oxford*, Oxford 1895–1933
Morison-Barker	S. Morison, supplemented by N. Barker, *The Likeness of Thomas More*, 1963	Schmid, *Holbein*	H. A. Schmid, *Hans Holbein d. J. Sein Aufstieg zur Meisterschaft und sein englischer Stil*, Basel 1948
Neue Briefe	H. Schulte Herbrüggen, ed., *Sir Thomas More: Neue Briefe*, Münster 1966		
NK	W. Nijhoff and M. E. Kronenberg, *Nederlandse Bibliographie van 1500 tot 1540*, The Hague 1923–61	*SL*	Elizabeth Frances Rogers, ed., *Selected Letters of St Thomas More*, New Haven 1961
NPE, 1866	*Catalogue of the First Special Exhibition of National Portraits...*, 1866	Special Exhibition, 1862	*Special Exhibition of Works of Art... on loan at the South Kensington Museum*, 1862
N & Q	*Notes and Queries*	Stapleton	Thomas Stapleton, *Vita Thomae Mori*, quoted after English trans. by P. E. Hallett, ed. E. E. Reynolds, 1966
Panofsky	E. Panofsky, *Albrecht Dürer*, 3rd edn. Princeton 1948		
Parker	Sir Karl T. Parker, *The Drawings of Hans Holbein in the Collection of H.M. the King at Windsor Castle*, 1945	*STC*	A. W. Pollard and G. R. Redgrave, *A Short Title Catalogue of Books printed in England, Scotland and Ireland and of English Books printed abroad 1475–1640*, 1926
RA, *Holbein*	Royal Academy, *Exhibition of Works by Holbein and other Masters*, 1950–1	*STC2*	*A Short Title Catalogue...*, 2nd edn. revised and enlarged. Begun by W. A. Jackson and F. S. Ferguson, completed by K. F. Pantzer, vol II, I–Z, 1976
RA, *King's Pictures*	Royal Academy, *The King's Pictures: an Exhibition*, 1946–7	Strong, *Catalogue*	Roy Strong, *National Portrait Gallery: Tudor and Jacobean Portraits*, 1969
RGG3	*Religion in Geschichte und Gegenwart*, 3rd edn., Tübingen 1957–65	Strong, *English Icon*	Roy Strong, *The English Icon: Elizabethan and Jacobean Portraiture*, 1969

Catalogue note

No attempt has been made to give a full bibliography for each item. Earlier literature is subsumed under later, and, where feasible, a recent book or article has been cited for each person or topic represented. General references have been kept to a minimum, and R. W. Chambers's *Thomas More*, still far the best general treatment of its subject, is hardly mentioned. Place of publication, unless otherwise stated, is London for books in English, Paris for books in French, Rome for books in Italian.

Measurements are given in centimetres and (in brackets) inches, height before width.

I *Sir Thomas More and his Kings*

Hans Holbein's great group portrait of Sir Thomas More and his household is tragically lost to us. It was made during the painter's first visit to England from 1526 to 1528, the first such picture painted north of the Alps. Some compensation remains. From Holbein's own hand we have eight superb preliminary drawings, a painting of the chief member of the family, and a small sketch of the whole group. There are also later full-size and miniature copies and composites.

Holbein's preliminary drawings at Windsor (nos. 9, 176–9, 182–4) are of Sir John More, Sir Thomas's father; Sir Thomas More himself; his son John, and his wife Anne Cresacre; his daughters Elizabeth Dauncey and Cicely Heron; and his foster-daughter Margaret Gigs (Mistress Clement). The finished portrait of Sir Thomas More himself is in the Frick Collection, New York; a fine sixteenth-century version is shown in this exhibition (no. 26). The little sketch of the whole group (no. 169) is in Basel, where it has been since it was taken there to Erasmus in 1528, probably by Holbein himself. A full-size copy, made later in the century, is at Nostell Priory, Yorkshire.

The group portrait presents the most familiar and sympathetic of our images of Sir Thomas More, at the centre of a family united in the common pursuit of piety and learning, serious but not solemn, ever ready to extend itself by welcoming others of like mind.

Sir Thomas is shown in full maturity and dignity at the age of about fifty, filially deferential still to his father, the judge, whom he has already surpassed in his career. Half a century after the cruel and senseless execution of Henry VIII's former lord chancellor, Sir Thomas More's grandson commissioned two composite groups (nos. 1 and 170), adding two further generations to emphasise the unbroken allegiance of the family to the Catholic faith.

Sir Thomas More's life was lived under five English kings: he was born under Edward IV; was a child under Edward V and Richard III (no. 2), whose history he was to write; grew to manhood and began his career under Henry VII (nos. 3, 4), on the death of whose queen, Elizabeth of York (no. 5), he was to write an elegy. In 1517 he entered the service of Henry VIII (no. 6), under whom he was to experience eminence, disgrace and death.

1
Sir Thomas More, his Father, his Household and his Descendants
(Front cover)
Rowland Lockey, 1593
Oil on canvas, 227.4 × 330.2 (89½ × 130)

Provenance Seen by William Burton (1575–1645) in artist's studio; Thomas More II (1531–1606); Cresacre More (1572–1649); borrowed and retained *c.*1642 by William Lenthall, Speaker of the House of Commons; seen by John Aubrey at Lenthall family house, Besselsleigh; seen at Burford Priory by George Vertue 1721, 1727, 1741; Lenthall sale Christie's 21 May 1808 (12); 1833 Walter Strickland; C. W. Cottrell-Dormer; sold Christie's 26 February 1910 (105); Sir Hugh Lane; Lord Lee of Fareham; E. J. Horniman; NPG 1935.
Exhibition Erasmus, 1969 (68).
Bibliography Morison-Barker, no. 404; Strong, *Catalogue*, 345–51, pl 679; id. *English Icon*, no. 238; O. Kurz, 'Rowland Locky', *Burlington Magazine*, XCIX, 1957, 13–16; E. E. Reynolds, *Moreana*, LIII, 1977, 11–14 (coats of arms); A. Lewi, *The Thomas More Family Group*, 1974; *Essex Recusant*, IV, 1962, 1–5 and XII, 1974, 55–8.

National Portrait Gallery, London (2765)

Thomas More among his household is the most familiar image of the man, in prosperous, patriarchal, domestic harmony. The image is the creation of Hans Holbein the Younger (1497/8–1543) during his first visit to England (1526–8), but the only surviving record of the whole from his own hand is the sketch now in Basel (no. 169). A replica of Holbein's large painting, made by Rowland Lockey (d. 1616), is now at Nostell Priory, Yorkshire.

Lockey executed two other versions of the household group: the present full-size oil (the Burford Priory version), and a miniature (no. 170). Like the Nostell Priory picture, they were commissioned by Sir Thomas More's grandson, Thomas More II, son of John More by his wife Anne Cresacre. By his wife Mary Scrope this Thomas More had thirteen children, and the family was already living at Barnborough, Yorkshire, in 1557, on Anne Cresacre's family estates. In 1577 the Mores began to appear on the lists of known recusants. They moved south to Lower Leyton, Essex, about 1581. Thomas More II fell under suspicion, and a raid by Richard Topclyffe, the priest-catcher (no. 272), led to his confinement in the Marshalsea prison until 1586.

Two of the pictures commissioned by Thomas More II from Lockey explicitly emphasise his family's unbroken allegiance to the Catholic faith. In this one, there are seven of the figures shown in the Nostell Priory picture. Those not of the More blood have been excluded: Margaret Gigs, More's foster-daughter (no. 184); Dame Alice More; Henry Patenson, the jester; and John Harris, More's secretary. An exception is naturally made in favour of Anne Cresacre (1511–77; no. 179), mother of Thomas More II. She appears twice, once in her place in the group and once in a portrait of her as she was in later life, directly above Cresacre More on the wall behind her sons and grandsons. The right of the picture is occupied by Thomas More II and his family: his wife, Mary, and his two sons, Thomas More III and Cresacre More.

Colour plate I *Henry VII* by Pietro Torrigiano (no. 3)

2

**2
Richard III** (1452–85; reigned 1483–5)
Unknown artist, 16th century
Oil on panel, 63.8 × 47 (25½ × 18½)

Provenance Presented to NPG by James Gibson Craig of Edinburgh 1862; 'formerly in General Stibbard's collection, and afterwards in the collection of Mr. Brown of Newhall'.
Exhibitions Manchester, 1857 (7); Edinburgh, 1859; NPG, *Richard III*, 1973 (P 18).
Bibliography Strong, *Catalogue*, 262–4, pl 516.

National Portrait Gallery, London (148)

This portrait, inscribed RICARDUS. III. ANG. REX. on a crimson brocade background below gold spandrels, is a late descendant of what is probably the earliest surviving likeness of the king. This is now in the collection of Her Majesty the Queen at Windsor Castle (exhibited NPG, *Richard III*, 1973 (P44)), and dates 'almost certainly' from before 1542. 'There is no reason to disbelieve' that it goes back to an authentic lost portrait from life (Strong, loc. cit.). The present portrait, in all but its lack of a full architectural framework, is very close to the Windsor version. Richard, half-length, to right, plays with a third ring on the little finger of the right hand. There is no trace of the hostile image of the king projected by More (nos. 109, 110), among others, or of the physical and moral deformity attributed to him.

**3
Henry VII** (1457–1509; reigned 1485–1509)
(Colour plate I, page 19)
Pietro Torrigiano, ?1508–9
Terracotta bust, painted and gilded, height 60.6 (23⅞)

Provenance Perhaps from the Holbein Gate of Whitehall Palace, demolished 1759; a Mr Wright, coachbuilder in Long Acre; repaired at his order by John Flaxman 1769; at Hatfield Peverel Priory, Wright's house in Essex, 1779–1928; Arthur Watson Filmer, from whose widow bt. Victoria and Albert Museum 1935.
Exhibitions Special Exhibition, 1862; Royal Academy, *British Portraits*, 1956–7 (28).
Bibliography A. Higgins, 'On the Work of Florentine Sculptors in England in the early Part of the Sixteenth Century', *Archaeological Journal*, II, 1894, 129–220; A. E. Popham, 'Hans Holbein's Italian Contemporaries in England', *Burlington Magazine*, LXXXIV, 1944, 12–17; F. Grossmann, 'Holbein, Torrigiano and some Portraits of Dean Colet', *JWCI*, XIII, 1950, esp. 208–9, 223; Sir John Pope-Hennessy, *Catalogue of the Italian Sculpture in the Victoria and Albert Museum*, 1964, 399–401, fig 415; Strong, *Catalogue*, pl 292.

Victoria and Albert Museum, London (49–1935)

Pietro Torrigiano was the first to arrive and the most important of the Italian artists employed by Henry VIII. If this bust was taken from the life, he must have been in the country by April 1509 at the latest, though his presence is not documented before November 1511. Less majestic than Torrigiano's recumbent full-length bronze of Henry VII in the king's chapel in Westminster Abbey, this is an impressive portrait. Torrigiano also executed the painted terracotta busts of Henry VIII(?) and the unknown ecclesiastic, called John Fisher, now in the Metropolitan Museum, New York, and the bust of John Colet (no. 11) has been convincingly attributed to him.

The bust of Henry VII has recently been restored and layers of overpainting removed to reveal the original colouring: the robe black instead of crimson, the hat black, the hair reddish-brown, the complexion fresh. This is its first public appearance since restoration.

4

5

4
Henry VII
Master Michiel (Michiel Sittow), 1505
Oil on panel, arched top, 42.5 × 30.5 (16¾ × 12)

Provenance Commissioned 20 October 1505 by Hermann Rinck, envoy of Maximilian I; sent to Maximilian's daughter Margaret at Malines; recorded there in inventories, 1516, 1523; Julian of Le Mans; Emile Barré, Paris; E. G. Muller, London; from whom bt. NPG 1876.
Exhibitions NPG, *Richard III*, 1973 (P 43); NPG, *Dendrochronology*, 1977 (1).
Bibliography Strong, *Catalogue*, 149–52, pls 290–1; J. Trizna, *Michel Sittow, peintre revalais de l'école brugeoise (1468–1525/6)*, (Les primitifs flamands. Contributions, VI), Brussels 1976, 31–4, 36–7, 96.

National Portrait Gallery, London (416)

The king is shown bust-length, turned to the left, with a red rose of Lancaster in his right hand, wearing the collar of the Golden Fleece over a cloth-of-gold surcoat, lined with white fur. According to its inscription, the picture was commissioned by Hermann Rinck: *Anno 1505 20 Octobre ymago Henrich VII Francieque regis illustrissimi ordinata per Hermann Rinck Ro[manorum] Regis [Com]missiarium*. It was almost certainly intended as an exchange for two portraits of Margaret of Austria (no. 196), daughter of Maximilian, King of the Romans, later the Emperor Maximilian I, brought over by Rinck. Henry VII, a widower since 1503, had only one surviving son to carry on the dynasty, and was seeking a second wife. Maximilian wanted military aid and offered marriage with Margaret, a widow since 1504. Negotiations were abandoned in 1508.

The painter Michiel Sittow, born in Tallinn, Estonia, entered service with Philip of Burgundy and Castile on 26 November 1504 and seems to have been in England in 1505.

5
Elizabeth of York (1465–1503)
Unknown artist, late 16th century
Oil on panel, 56.5 × 41.6 (22¼ × 16⅜)

Provenance Bt. NPG from S. Willson & Son, 1870; previous history unknown.
Bibliography Strong, *Catalogue*, 97–8, pl 182.

National Portrait Gallery, London (311)

A late version, once probably part of a set of kings and queens, of the standard painted portrait of Elizabeth of York, Queen of Henry VII, daughter of Edward IV and Elizabeth Woodville. Her funeral effigy by Torrigiano in Henry VII's Chapel at Westminster Abbey is a more splendid likeness.

Thomas More wrote an English elegy for her (no. 19) and celebrated her goodness in his Latin verses for the coronation of Henry VIII (no. 37).

6

**6
Henry VIII** (1491–1547; reigned 1509–47) as a Young Man
Unknown artist, c.1525
Oil on panel, 51 × 38 (20 × 15)

Provenance c.1920 in possession of 'a Haileybury master'; H. Clifford Smith 1924; Sotheby's 7 July 1967 (10); bt. NPG from S. F. Sabin 1967.
Exhibitions Royal Academy, *British Primitive Paintings from the twelfth to the early sixteenth century*, 1923–4, 44–5; NPG, *Dendrochronology*, 1977 (6).
Bibliography Martin Conway (Lord Conway), 'A Portrait of King Henry VIII', *Burlington Magazine*, XLV, 1924, 42; Strong, *Catalogue*, 157–8, pl 301; John Fletcher, 'Tree-ring Dates for some Panel Paintings in England', *Burlington Magazine*, CXVI, 1974, 258.

National Portrait Gallery, London (4690)

This is the young king into whose service Thomas More entered in 1517. The image, Strong's Type I, was probably created about 1520, some fifteen years before Holbein established the predominant type (nos. 70, 71). The NPG panel is a workshop production under French influence. The costume, though less dazzling than in the later assertions of sovereignty, is rich and bejewelled, with an opulent brocade in the background and the Tudor dynastic badges, rose and portcullis, at the upper corners. The king wears his hair longer than he was later to do, but he has the reddish beard which he grew in imitation of Francis I's French fashion (according to the Venetian ambassador, Sebastiano Giustinian, in 1519). The handsome face spoken of by another Venetian ambassador, Francesco Cornaro, in 1521, is also apparent and the 'well-proportioned body' may be deduced.

II *Early Life in London: Birth, Schooldays, Humanism, the Law and the Church*

Thomas More was born a Londoner on 6 or 7 February 1477 or 1478, and was 'brought up in the Latin tongue' at St Antony's School, one of two rival establishments in the City (the other was St Thomas of Acre; John Colet's revitalised St Paul's School was not founded until 1509). At about twelve he left St Antony's for the household of John Morton, Archbishop of Canterbury and later Lord Chancellor, where his precocity won from his master the prediction 'This child here waiting at table, whosoever shall live to see it, will prove a marvellous man'. This is the first testimony to the power possessed by Thomas More, lasting long beyond the grave, to win respect, admiration and affection from rich and poor, from family, friends, fellow humanists, men of affairs, mitred, noble and crowned heads, not only in his own country but in the whole of Europe. Reaction from it, as in Henry VIII's case, was correspondingly violent.

Morton placed his protégé at Oxford, probably intending him for the clergy, a direction to which he seems himself then to have inclined. When, a couple of years later, in 1494, John More called his son back to London to the study of the law at England's third university, the Inns of Court, Thomas was still undecided about his fitness for the religious life. He tested his vocation while practising his profession, living for four years the austere life of the Carthusian order, in their house in East Smithfield. With William Grocyn and later John Colet as his spiritual guides, he learned Greek, translated from the *Greek Anthology* together with William Lily, lectured on St Augustine in Grocyn's church and translated the Latin *Life* of Pico della Mirandola, with some short devotional pieces, into English. 'For his pastime' he wrote English poems.

7
Four Views from a Panorama of London
Anthonis van den Wyngaerde (?1510–?72)
Pen and brown ink over traces of black chalk, mid-16th century
a London, showing Westminster Abbey and Palace
  24.2×43 $(9\frac{1}{2} \times 16\frac{7}{8})$
b London, with Old St Paul's Cathedral
  25.6×40.3 $(10 \times 15\frac{7}{8})$
c Old London Bridge
  25.3×42.2 $(10 \times 16\frac{5}{8})$
d North Bank of the Thames with the Tower
  24.5×42.6 $(9\frac{11}{16} \times 16\frac{11}{16})$

7d

EARLY LIFE IN LONDON

Provenance ?Harding, Triphook & Lepard, London booksellers
1826 (cf N. Dalloway in H. Walpole, *Anecdotes of English Painting*,
I, 1862 edn., 184); Colnaghi; Sutherland Collection – bt. 1823 from
Colnaghi by widow of Alexander Hendras Sutherland (d.1820)
according to J. Livingston Jay in Hasted's *History of Kent*, ed.
H. H. Drake, 1886, I, 67 n. 2, and presented by her to Bodleian
Library 1837; deposited there 1839; transferred to Ashmolean
Museum 1950.
Exhibitions Victoria and Albert Museum, *The Growth of London
A.D. 43–1964*, 1964, D2, p 30 (all); *Erasmus*, 1969 (1, 3, 4; 162–4);
Bodleian Library, *Erasmus*, 1969 (3–4).
Bibliography Facsimile, London Topographical Society, I, 1882;
G. E. Mitton, *Maps of Old London*, 1908; I. Darlington and J. E.
Howgego, *Printed Maps of Old London c.1553–1850*, 1963, 6–8;
Susan E. Booth, unpublished typescript, *Check-List of the Drawings
of Anthonis van den Wyngaerde in the Department of Western Art, the
Ashmolean Museum, Oxford*, April 1974; E. Haverkamp-Begemann,
'The Spanish Views of A. van den Wyngaerde', *Old Master
Drawings*, VII, 1969, 375–99.

The Visitors of the Ashmolean Museum, Oxford

These views belong to a panorama of London, formerly
rolled and now mounted as fourteen separate drawings,
showing the city north of the river in great detail, from a high
vantage-point in Southwark. It may have been made as early
as 1544–5.

Little is known about the artist, whose reputation rests
almost exclusively on his topographical drawings and
engravings. In 1557 he accompanied the Spanish troops on
campaign against the French, and was Painter in Ordinary to
Philip II, with whom he may have visited England, 1557–8.
He seems to have shuttled between this country and the
Netherlands from 1558 to 1562.

8
Old St Paul's (Henry Farley's Dream)
John Gipkym or Gipkyn, 1616
Oil on panel in two leaves, pointed top, 110.5 × 86.4
(43½ × 34)

Provenance Tooke family, three of whom successively rectors of
Lambourne, Essex, 1704–76; a Mr Webster of Chigwell from whom
bt. 23 May 1781 by Mr Brigden for Society of Antiquaries.
Bibliography STC, 10688–90; *Gentleman's Magazine*, L, 1780,
179–81; Sir George Scharf, *Catalogue of Pictures belonging to the
Society of Antiquaries*, 1865, XLIII, pp 32–8; Pamela Tudor-Craig,
unpublished description in possession of Society of Antiquaries,
1977; Millar MacLure, *The Paul's Cross Sermons*, Toronto 1958.

The Society of Antiquaries of London

This triptych in the form of a diptych shows:
a A procession led by King James I crossing London
Bridge. Ships bring materials for the restoration of the
cathedral and carpenters are working. The border inscription begins with a quotation from 2 Chronicles xxiv 4, 5, 9:
'And when it came into the King's mind to renew the house of
the Lord . . .', and ends 'Amore, veritate et reverentia. So
invented, and at my costs, made for me H. Farley 1616.
Wrought by John Gipkyn. Fiat voluntas Dei.'
b James, the queen and officials in a gallery listening to a
sermon from St Paul's Cross, with a quotation from Haggai
i 2, 4 on the border.
c St Paul's refurbished. In its tower, with its Jacobean spire,

8b

the statued apotheosis of James I, with angel trumpeters and
Farley's verses to the side and the dove of the Holy Ghost
hovering above in rays of divine light. On the frame a
quotation from Ezra vii 27; with *Vivat, vincat, regnatque
Jacobus, Amen.*

When the diptych was painted, Old St Paul's had for many
years been in a dilapidated condition and Henry Farley, who
commissioned the work, had been importuning James to see
to the cathedral's repair. The paintings are illustrations of a
dream Farley purports to have had. He published a written
account of it, *St Paules Church her Bill for the Parliament*, in
1621. The painter was John Gipkym or Gipkyn, probably a
naturalised Dutchman, of whom next to nothing is known.

The cathedral is in something like the condition that
Thomas More would have known, especially as regards the
pulpit cross. This was an octagonal roofed structure on a
stepped pedestal, erected about 1449 in the churchyard
under the north-east wall of the old cathedral choir. It survived until 1643. 'Paul's Cross' was the place of ecclesiastical
proclamation and ceremony for the City of London. The
chief current preoccupations of the clergy – the spread of
heresy and the illicit translations of Scripture (nos. 140–67) –
were reflected in sermons and demonstrations there from the
early fifteenth century to More's day.

9
Sir John More (?1451–1530)
Hans Holbein the Younger, 1526–7
Coloured chalks on white paper, 35.4 × 27.6 (13 15/16 × 10 7/8)

Provenance As for other Windsor Holbein drawings, see no. 176.
Exhibition RA, *Holbein* (118).
Bibliography Parker, no. 1; Schmid, *Holbein*, 83, 281, 289f, pl 43;
Harpsfield, 303–5.

Her Majesty the Queen (Windsor Castle 12224)

EARLY LIFE IN LONDON

Iudge More Sr Tho: Mores Father.

9

Sir John More was probably born in 1451, son of William More, baker (d. 1467), by his wife Johanna. John More married first Agnes Graunger, daughter of Thomas Graunger, a well-to-do citizen of London and later sheriff, 'in the parish of St Giles outside Cripplegate, London', on 24 April 1474. By her he had six children, of whom Thomas was the second. There were two other sons and three daughters. Though he thought matrimony a 'perilous choice', as if 'ye should put your hand into a blind bag of snakes and eels together, seven snakes for one eel', he married three times in all. The remarriages seem to have been childless, and his last wife survived him. John More was butler of Lincoln's Inn and later a barrister, Serjeant at Law (1503), Judge of the Court of Common Pleas (1518) and of the King's Bench (1523). It is not known when he was knighted. He died in 1530.

Holbein's splendid drawing, preparatory to his lost group portrait, of this 'man very virtuous, and of a very upright and sincere conscience ... a companionable, a merry and pleasantly conceited man' (Harpsfield) was made during his first visit to England, 1526–8. The inscription 'Iudge More Sr Tho: More's Father' is of a later date.

10
Memorandum of Thomas More's Birth, 1477/8
Geoffrey of Monmouth, *Historia regum Britanniae*, etc
Manuscript on vellum, 13th–14th century

Bibliography James, *Trinity*, 1900–4, III, 113–15; Chambers, 48–50; id. in Harpsfield, 298–303; id. *Place of St Thomas More in English Literature and History*, 1937, 119–24; G. Marc'hadour, *L'Univers de Thomas More*, 1963, 34–41, and in *Moreana*, LIII, 1977, 5–10.

The Master and Fellows of Trinity College, Cambridge (MS 0.2.21, ff. 139v–140v)

John More used this manuscript to record family history: his marriage to Agnes Graunger (24 April 1474), and the births of six children: Joan (11 March 1475), Thomas, Agatha (31 January 1479), John (16 June 1480), Edward (3 September 1481) and Elizabeth (22 September 1482). For Thomas, he noted:

Memorandum quod die veneris proximo post Festum purificationis beatae Mariae virginis inter horam secundam et horam tertiam in mane Natus fuit Thomas More filius Johannis More Gent. anno Regni Regis Edwardi quarti post conquestum Anglie decimo septimo.
(Memorandum that on Friday next after the feast of Purification of the blessed Virgin Mary (ie Candlemas), between the second and the third hour of the morning, Thomas More was born, son of John More, Gent. in the seventeenth year of King Edward the Fourth after the Conquest of England.)

If John More had left it at that, all would be clear: Thomas, his eldest son, was born on Friday, 6 February 1478. But he later added the interlinear note: 'videlicet septimo die Februarii'. In the seventeenth year of Edward IV the Friday next after Candlemas was 6, not 7 February, so that three dates are possible for More's birthday: Friday 6 February 1477, Friday 6 February 1478, Saturday 7 February 1478. Internal evidence favours 1478; external evidence (the age given on Holbein's sketch of the household (no. 169) and Erasmus's letter to Hutten (no. 265)) favours 1477.

11

11
John Colet (?1466–1519)
Pietro Torrigiano, ?1518
Plaster cast, height 74 (29)

Bibliography Emden, *Cambridge*, 148; id. *Oxford*, 462–3; J. H. Lupton, *Life of John Colet*, 1909; F. Grossmann, 'Holbein, Torrigiano, and Portraits of Dean Colet: a Study of Holbein's Work in Relation to Sculpture', *JWCI*, XIII, 1950, 202–36.

National Portrait Gallery, London (4823)

John Colet was the first of twenty-two children born to Sir Henry Colet, a wealthy mercer, twice Mayor of London, and

25

EARLY LIFE IN LONDON

his wife Dame Christian (no. 190). Little is known of his early life, except that he went up to Oxford about 1483. In 1492 or 1493 he journeyed to France and Italy, returning to Oxford in the spring of 1496. There he lectured on the Pauline Epistles and made the acquaintance of Erasmus. In 1505 he returned to London as Dean of St Paul's. He died of the sweating sickness in 1519.

Colet and Thomas More were friends for many years. One of the few surviving letters from More's first thirty years was written to Colet in 1504, naming Colet and William Grocyn (nos. 90, 91, 92) as the guides of his life. In 1512, More wrote a few lines in praise of Colet's newly established St Paul's School, and he praises the Dean's learning in his *Letter to a Monk* (no. 102). Colet returned this admiration. Erasmus reports that he thought More England's one great genius.

Erasmus also describes Colet as endowed by fortune with a tall and handsome figure. The bust ascribed to Pietro Torrigiano (1472–1528) probably shows him as he was a year or two before his death. It is the basis for Holbein's portrait drawing of *c*.1527, now at Windsor, and is the only authentic portrait of Colet, the kneeling figure of the miniatures in his New Testament manuscripts (no. 38) being a nondescript. The bust was originally part of Colet's second monument (no. 12) in Old St Paul's; several casts are extant.

12
John Colet
Sir William Segar, 1585–6
Water-colour on vellum, 26.5 × 20.5 (10½ × 8)

Provenance Perhaps St Paul's School; Mercers' Hall, probably from third quarter of 16th century.
Bibliography Grossmann, loc. cit. (no. 11) 211–13; E. Auerbach, *Tudor Artists*, 1954, 121; id. *Nicholas Hilliard*, 1961, 271–81; Strong, *English Icon*, 17–19, 215–24; Jean Imray, unpublished report, *History of Dean Colet's Statutes for St Paul's School*, 1963; J. B. Trapp, 'John Colet, his MSS and the ps.-Dionysius', *Classical Influences in European Culture 1500–1700*, ed. R. R. Bolgar, Cambridge 1976, 210–11.

The Worshipful Company of Mercers, London

Inside this decorated vellum cover are the statutes of Colet's new foundation, St Paul's School, as drafted in 1512, but in a transcript made in 1517 or 1518, together with the additional statutes of 1602 and 1841. This is probably the earliest extant transcript.

The design on the cover is a reduced and embellished version of the elaborate tomb erected during the sixteenth century in the choir of Old St Paul's to replace an earlier and more modest 'lytel monyment' designed by Colet himself. The water-colour is our earliest surviving record of the tomb, which was destroyed in the Great Fire of 1666. The inscription below the skeleton reads *Istuc recidit gloria carnis* (To this the glory of the flesh returns) and the label *Io. Colet Deca. S. Pauli* (John Colet, Dean of St Paul's). The arms of Colet himself are below his portrait, those of the Mercers' Company at upper right and those of the Deanery of St Paul's at upper left. In 1585–6 one Segar, who is either Sir William Segar, Garter King of Arms (d. 1633), or his brother Francis, was paid by the Mercers for 'drawing the picture of Mr. Dr. Collette vpon the cover of vellom of the book of ordinaunce very fair in cullors'.

12

13
John Colet's Supplication to Pope Julius II, 1512
Manuscript on vellum, first quarter of 16th century

Provenance Mercers' Company.
Bibliography M. F. J. (Sir Michael) McDonnell, *Annals of St Paul's School*, 1959, 33–45; Jean Imray, loc. cit. (no. 12).

The Worshipful Company of Mercers, London

In 1512 Colet handed over to the Mercers' Company, whom he had made the overseers of his school, the title deeds to the lands of the school's endowment. A transcript of these and of other documents relating to the school was made for the company by William Newbold, Colet's servant, who was later registrar to the company and, later still, clerk. The transcript, known as the *Book of Evidences of Dean Colet's Lands*, contains the text of Colet's formal supplication to Rome for certain privileges for his school.

14
The Statutes of St Paul's School, London
Manuscript on paper, second half of 16th century

Provenance William Hamper of Birmingham 1818; presented by him to British Museum 1820.
Bibliography Jean Imray, loc. cit. (no. 12); J. B. Trapp, loc. cit. (no. 12).

The British Library Board (MS Add. 6274)

According to its inscriptions, this is the attested copy of the statutes of St Paul's School handed over by Colet to his first High Master, William Lily (no. 15), in 1518. It is, in fact, a transcript of the later sixteenth century.

Colet provided for a Master, a Sur-Master and a Chaplain, at salaries generous for the day, to ensure the increase of 'knowledge and worshipping of god and oure lorde Crist Jesu and good Cristen lyff and maners in the Children', through the reading of 'good litterature both laten and greke'. 'That fylthynesse and all such abusyon', he goes on, 'which the later blynde worlde brought in whych may rather be called blotterature thanne litterature I vtterly abbanysh and exclude oute of this scole...'.

Set books were to be the Catechism, the Accidence which he himself had compiled, two works specially written by Erasmus for the school (*The Institution of a Christian Man* (no. 16) and *Copiousness of Words and Thought*), as well as certain Christian Latin authors.

More and Erasmus had to defend their friend's new school. Erasmus says that he has heard a bishop call it 'a home of idolatry because, I believe, the poets are taught there'.

15
Grammar Books for St Paul's School by William Lily
Libellus de constructione octo partium orationis, London, R. Pynson, 1513, and *Guilelmi Lilii Angli Rudimenta. Parvulorum Lilii nuper impressa & correcta*, [York, U. Mylner, ?1516]

Bibliography Emden, *Oxford*, 1147; *STC2* 15601.3, 15609.3 and p 62, s.v. Lily's Grammar.

Bodleian Library, Oxford (Bodley C.23 Art B/S; Rawl. 206)

William Lily (?1468–1522), Colet's first High Master of St Paul's School, was Thomas More's friend from at least the time he returned to England from study abroad. The two translated from the Greek in friendly rivalry, but Lily is perhaps best known for his grammar books.

'Lily's Grammar' was the current school-book from about 1540, and consists of a number of works by Lily and others combined into one. It was composed of two parts: the first part for elementary instruction (Colet's *Aeditio*, Lily's Grammar in English, the *Rudimenta*, of which the first extant separate edition is shown here, and Lily's *Carmen de moribus*); the second part, for more advanced students, includes the *Libellus de constructione* written by Lily, revised by Erasmus and thereafter denied by both, of which the first surviving edition is also shown here.

16
Erasmus's Idea of Christian Upbringing
Desiderii Erasmi Institutum christiani hominis, in Erasmus, *Lucubrationes*, Louvain, Thierry Martens, 1514

Bodleian Library, Oxford (Douce C.259)

The *Institutum christiani hominis*, written by 'lernyd Erasmus' at John Colet's request, for St Paul's School, was first published in this volume of Erasmus's miscellaneous works. It was later translated into English.

17
Photograph: **Thomas More's Admission to Lincoln's Inn, 1496**
Photograph of Lincoln's Inn, Black Book, vol. II, part ii, f.34v

Bibliography Records of the Hon. Society of Lincoln's Inn, I: Admission Register, 1420–1789, 1896, 27; D. Walker and W. P. Baildon, eds., *The Records of the Hon. Society of Lincoln's Inn:*

The Black Books..., I, 1897, 105; Sir Ronald Roxburgh, ed., *The Records of the Hon. Society of Lincoln's Inn: The Black Books*, V, A.D. 1845–1914, 1968, passim.

Private Collection

After preliminary training at New Inn from about 1494, Thomas More was admitted to Lincoln's Inn on 12 February 1496 at the instance of his father and pardoned four vacations: 'Thomas More admissus est in Societatem xij die Februarii anno supradicto [11 H.VII = 1496] et pardonatur ei quatuor vacationes ad instanciam Johannis More patris sui'. Immediately following this entry in the register there is the admission on the same day, also at John More's instance, of Richard Stafferton, who married Thomas's sister Joan.

Later entries in the Black Book record More's successful legal career at the Inn: auditor (1503); pensioner (1507); butler (1507–8); autumn reader (1510–11); marshal (1510–11); one of the governors (1511–12 and 1514–15); treasurer (1511 – elected but declined to serve); Lent reader (1514–15).

18
'The cyvyle Law of the Romaynys, the wych is now the comyn law almost of al Chrystyn natyonys'
Justinian, Emperor of Rome, *Institutiones*, etc, Strasbourg, Johann Grüninger, etc, 1491ff

Provenance From the library of Christopher Urswick (1448–1522), with contemporary blind-stamped leather binding.
Bibliography Hain, 1525*; *GKW*, 7622; Goff, J533; J. B. Oldham, *English blind-stamped Bindings*, Cambridge 1952, 31n., pl XXVII, nos. 419–22; Emden, *Cambridge*, 605–6, 685; id. *Oxford*, 1935–6.

The Dean and Chapter of York (York Minster Library, XV.A.14)

One of a composite set printed at various dates and bound as volumes containing the *Institutiones*, *Digest* (or *Pandects*), *Codex* and *Constitutiones novellae*, which together form the corpus of Roman law going under the name of Justinian, Emperor from 527 to 565. The *Corpus iuris civilis*, as it was later known, was one of the staples of a European legal education, the fundamental statement of the principles of jurisprudence as well as the basis of later Continental legal codes. It also had much influence on canon law. Any lay or ecclesiastical man of affairs and any royal servant such as Thomas More needed a familiarity with the contents of the *Corpus*, especially if the king's concerns took him into Europe.

This volume, like others in the set, bears the arms of Christopher Urswick (nos. 20, 41): argent on a bend sable three lozenges argent, on each a saltire gules.

19
Thomas More's 'Rueful Lamentation' on the Death of Queen Elizabeth, 1503
Manuscript on vellum, 16th century

Bibliography S. Ayscough, *A Catalogue of the MSS... in the British Museum*, 1782, f.101v; A. F. Pollard, *TLS*, XXI, 1932, 499; R. S. Sylvester, ed., *The History of King Richard III & Selections from the English Poems*, New Haven and London 1976, 119–22; F. B. Tromly, 'More's Transformation of didactic Lament', *Moreana*, LIII, 1977, 45–55.

The British Library Board (MS Sloane 1825, ff.88v–89v)

A Rueful Lamentation, More's first and perhaps his best English poem, was composed to commemorate the death of Queen Elizabeth of York, 'the Good', eldest daughter of Edward IV, wife of Henry VII and mother of Henry VIII. She died in childbirth on 11 February 1503. The poem is a dramatic soliloquy by the dead queen, bidding farewell to all her earthly belongings. The melancholy mood of the twelve Chaucerian stanzas is stressed by the refrain, 'For lo! now here I lie'; and all are called to 'take example' by her death and look to their own souls.

The *Lamentation* is here transcribed at the end of a fifteenth-century manuscript of the *De regimine principis* by Thomas Hoccleve (?1370–?1450).

20
Photograph: **St Augustine's 'City of God'**
Aurelii Augustini de Civitate Dei, Venice, Gabriele di Pietro, 1475

Provenance Christopher Urswick (1448–1522); College of Windsor; Matthew Parker, Archbishop of Canterbury (1504–75), by whom bequeathed to Corpus Christi College, Cambridge 1575.
Bibliography Hain, 2052; *GKW*, 2880; James, *Corpus Christi*, 1909, no. 346; Richard C. Marius, 'Thomas More and the early Church Fathers', *Traditio*, XXIV, 1968, 379–407.

Photograph by courtesy of Corpus Christi College, Cambridge (MS346)

The twenty-two books of the *City of God*, written between 413 and 426 by St Augustine, Bishop of Hippo (354–430), were More's preferred reading among the Fathers of the Church. He cites Augustine more frequently than any other Christian author. As a young man, perhaps about 1501, More had 'redde for a good space a publike lecture of St. Augustine, *de civitate dei*, in the Churche of St: Lawrens in the old Jury; wherunto there resorted Doctor Grosin [nos. 90, 91, 92], an excellent cunninge [ie learned] man, and all the chief learned of the City of London' (Roper).

The photograph shown here is taken from the copy of the incunable printed on vellum which was once owned and copiously annotated by Christopher Urswick (nos. 18, 41).

21
The Charterhouse of London
Plan of the London Charterhouse and its water supply
Unknown draughtsman, 15th century
Vellum, 50.8 × 300 (20 × 118)

Provenance Made for the House of the Salutation of the Virgin Mary (Charterhouse) in London and still in possession of Sutton's Hospital in Charterhouse.
Exhibition London Museum, *Chaucer's London*, 1972 (200).
Bibliography W. H. St John Hope, 'The London Charterhouse and its old Water Supply', *Archaeologia*, LVIII, i, 1902, 293–312; David Knowles and W. F. Grimes, *The Charterhouse in London: the Medieval Foundation in the Light of recent Discoveries*, 1954.

The Governors of Sutton's Hospital in the Charterhouse

The first house of the Carthusian Order in England was established in 1178–9, but there was no London Charterhouse until 1371. Water for its use had to be brought from the rising ground to the north and north-west, via an aqueduct. The aqueduct's flow is plotted on this map, which must have been made before the extensive building operations of the early sixteenth century and perhaps soon after 1431, when the aqueduct was installed. The annotations are in three hands, one of them later than the other two and referring to the cleansing of the system in 1511–12.

About 1500, the young Thomas More, uncertain whether his vocation lay for the monastic life but characteristically attracted by the special austerities of the Carthusians, 'gaue himselfe to devotion and prayer in the Charterhouse of London, religiously lyuinge there, without vowe, about iiijer yeares; Vntill he resorted to the house of one master Colte... having three daughters, whose honest conversation and vertuous educacion provoked him there specially to sett his affection' (Roper). Erasmus, in his letter to Hutten (no. 265), leaves it uncertain whether More was an inmate or not, inclining to the view that he lived nearby and shared only in the offices. The Inns of Court were no long walk away.

22
Thomas More, 'Life of John Picus'
Here is conteyned the Lyfe of Johan Picus Erle of Myrandula..., London, Wynkyn de Worde [*c*.1525]

Bibliography STC2, 19898; Gibson, 68; ed. J. M. Rigg, 1890; ed. W. E. Campbell, 1931; A. F. Bourdillon, *The Order of Minoresses in England* (British Society of Franciscan Studies, XII), 1926.

The British Library Board (276.c.27)

More's first work to be printed was dedicated to Joyeuce Lee or Leigh (sister of his friend Edward Lee), a Poor Clare. This dedication (New Year 1505) is More's first extant English letter (Rogers, 4). We know of his hesitation, as a student, between Holy Orders and Law (no. 21). When More had determined to marry, he 'propounded to himself as a pattern of life a singular layman, John Picus, Earl of Mirandula' (Cresacre More). It looks as if Colet first drew More's attention to the Italian humanist.

Giovanni Pico della Mirandola (1463–94) had studied at Italian and French universities, and finally settled in Florence where he was influenced by Ficino, Poliziano and Savonarola. Pico's name stood for the attempt to reconcile Plato and Aristotle with the Cabbala and with Christian doctrine as a foundation for faith and sanctity; he preferred the solitude of his study to court life.

From the Latin *Opera* More selected for his translation the gist of the life of Pico prefixed by his nephew Gianfrancesco. Leaving aside Pico's family history and earlier studies in 'obscure philosophy', More summarised his 900 Theses and selected an interpretation of Psalm 15, three letters and a prayer. Pico's appended Twelve Rules for Spiritual Warfare, Twelve Weapons, and Twelve Conditions of a Christian Lover More elaborated into his own version.

The *Lyfe of Picus* was first printed by More's brother-in-law, John Rastell, around 1510 (*STC2*, 19897.7). The exhibited edition used to be called pirated and dated to the same year, but is now attributed, as a line for line reset, to *c*.1525.

23
Giovanni Pico, Conte della Mirandola (1463–94)
By/in the manner of Niccolò Spinelli (Niccolò Fiorentino),
?1484–5
Bronze medal, diameter 8.5 (3⅜)

Bibliography Hill, *Corpus*, 998B, cf 1021, 1047, 1050; Hill-Pollard, 277, cf 288; E. Wind, *Pagan Mysteries in the Renaissance*, new edn. 1968, 36–52, 66–7; W. Deonna, 'Le groupe des trois Graces nues et sa descendance', *Revue archéologique*, XXXI, 1930, 274–332; G. B. Parks, 'Pico della Mirandola in Tudor Translation', *Philosophy and Humanism: Renaissance Essays in Honor of P. O. Kristeller*, ed. E. P. Mahoney, Leiden 1976, 352–69; W. Cappi, 'Iconografia di Pico della Mirandola', *Opera e pensiero di G. P. della M . . .*, Convegno internazionale, 1963, Florence 1965, 437–56.

The Trustees of the British Museum (Hill, 998B)

This medal apparently exists only in after-casts. The portrait on the obverse shows Pico, the 'Phoenix of the wits', with flowing locks and garment and a winged mask on the breast. The inscription reads: IOANNES PICVS MIRANDVLENSIS. The reverse shows the three Graces after the antique model, as on other medals by or in the manner of Niccolò Fiorentino. The reverse inscription reads PVLCRITVDO AMMOR VOLVPTAS (beauty, love, pleasure) and is perhaps derived from Marsilio Ficino (1433–99), the Florentine Neoplatonist, and his philosophy of love. Edgar Wind dates the medal's type 1484–5; Sir George Hill puts it within five years of Pico's death.

24
The 'Life' of Pico della Mirandola
Giovanni Pico, Conte della Mirandola (1463–94), *Opera Omnia*, including his *Vita* by his nephew Giovanni Francesco Pico della Mirandola (1469–1533), Venice, Bernardinus de Vitalibus, 1498

Bibliography Hain, 12992*; *BMC*, V, 548; Goff, P 634; G. B. Parks, 'Pico della Mirandola in Tudor Translation', in *Philosophy and Humanism: Renaissance Essays in Honor of P. O. Kristeller*, ed. E. P. Mahoney, Leiden 1976, 352–69; Charles B. Schmitt, *Gianfrancesco Pico della Mirandola (1469–1533) and his Critique of Aristotle*, The Hague 1967, p 195, no. 23 and p 203, nos. 1, 6.

The British Library Board (IB.24328)

Giovanni Francesco Pico della Mirandola wrote his Latin *Life* of his uncle expressly for his edition of the elder Pico's works published at Bologna in 1496. It is not clear from what edition Thomas More worked; it may well have been from this second printing or from a later edition, eg Strasbourg 1502, but he was certainly led astray by the reading 'uti manus' which he translated 'as it were in handes' instead of 'like a cart-horse'.

25
Sir Thomas Elyot's Translation of Pico and St Cyprian
A Swete and Devoute Sermon of Sayngt Ciprian of the Mortalities of Man and *The Rules of a Christen Life made by Picus Erle of Mirandula*, translated by Sir Thomas Elyot, London, Thomas Berthelet, 1534

Bibliography STC, 6157; cf STC2, p 236; Parks, loc. cit. (no. 24) no. 23; S. L. Lehmberg, *Sir Thomas Elyot, Tudor Humanist*, Austin, Texas 1960, 128–9; J. M. Major, *Sir Thomas Elyot and Tudor Humanism*, Lincoln, Nebraska 1964, 105–7.

The President and Court of Governors of Sion College

The two brief tracts of spiritual profit here translated and published by Sir Thomas Elyot (no. 279) were written by favourite authors of Thomas More's. St Cyprian, the 'holy doctour and martyr' who suffered in 258, was a Renaissance favourite; Erasmus edited him in 1521. Elyot's translation of this particular sermon was intended as consolation for his recently widowed step-sister. He reinforces St Cyprian with his prose version of the 'litel tretise, but wonderful fruitful, made by the vertuouse and noble prince John Picus Erle of Mirandula'. Elyot must have been familiar with More's verse translation of the same rules (no. 22).

23

III *Humanism and Royal Service*

Opting finally for life in the world, though maintaining throughout an austerity and frugality, More married Jane Colt in 1505 and for ten years was the busy, thriving father of a young family of three daughters and a son. He was also the rising City lawyer, passing through the *cursus honorum* of Lincoln's Inn, in demand as a negotiator (in extempore commercial Latin, if need be), acting as the City's delegate, becoming one of its under-sheriffs, the legal workhorses (1510), sitting for London in the Parliament of the same year (he had already been MP in 1504) and reaching the assured position of membership in Doctors' Commons in 1514.

Meanwhile, in 1511, Jane More died and Thomas quickly remarried to ensure the care of his children. His second wife, Alice, widow of John Middleton, mercer, he was later to describe as a model stepmother. The touching Latin verse epitaph that he wrote for Jane is evidence that his humanist interests were alive: he had written congratulatory epigrams for Henry VIII's coronation in 1509, as well as an English lament for Henry's mother some years earlier; in 1505–6 he and Erasmus translated Lucian together; he had visited the universities of Paris and Louvain in 1508; and he was now to write more Latin epigrams against Germanus Brixius (1512). He was also to engage strenuously, in favour of Erasmus's *Praise of Folly* (of which he was the dedicatee) and of Erasmus's project to edit and translate anew the New Testament, in controversy with Martin Dorp and others from 1515 onwards, and to admonish the University of Oxford for not giving sufficient status to Greek studies. His interest in humanist historiography and his power to foster an interpretation of history favourable to the Tudor dynasty are shown in the conception and writing of his *History of Richard III* at about this time.

In 1515, More had to leave family and official duties to go on embassy for the king to Flanders. His friend Cuthbert Tunstall was his companion on mission, and he found congenial company in Antwerp in the shape of Peter Gillis, the Chief Secretary. The garden of Gillis's house is the setting for the traveller's tale of the island that is nowhere – *Utopia*. The second book, with its satirical sketch of the ideal commonwealth, was written in the intervals of diplomatic business. Returning to London, More added the first book, with its criticism of English conditions and its extended meditation – the 'Dialogue of Counsel' – on whether the political life was a possible existence for the learned and virtuous man.

The problem he posed was no less a pressing personal one for having a respectable ancestry in Italian humanist debate. Was the true good to be pursued in remote and solitary study and pious exercise, or in active participation in government and affairs? He hankered still after the monastic life, he was later to tell his dearest child, Margaret Roper, but in vain, since he had a growing family to support. Should he then continue his valued work in the City, or should he allow himself to be drawn into the service of his king? To go on the 'Utopian' mission, Thomas More had to secure leave of absence from his City duties. On his return he turned to them again, consolidating the reputation he had already won as a just and conscientious officer, and playing a prominent part in minimising the danger from the riots of 'Evil May Day', 1517, as well as doing what he could to avert the royal anger. By August 1517 the matter was already decided: Thomas More was a member of the King's Council and launched on the career that was to bring him into contact with the centres and the men of power in Europe. He did not immediately resign his City functions. In 1522 he made the speech of welcome to the Emperor Charles V and to Henry VIII on behalf of the City. Nor did he, now or in the future, allow his talent for friendship to rust. On embassy and at home he managed to keep up, renew and initiate contacts with fellow humanists. Abroad, in 1520–1, he met old friends – Erasmus for the last time – and made new ones, such as Guillaume Budé of France, who had admired *Utopia*. At home, he welcomed Nicolaus Kratzer and later Joannes Ludovicus Vives.

In 1521, Thomas More was appointed Sub-Treasurer and knighted. He grew in influence as royal secretary, intermediary between Cardinal Wolsey and the king, was appointed Speaker of the Parliament of 1523, and High Steward of Oxford University in 1524.

26
Sir Thomas More (1477/8–1535)
(Frontispiece)
After Hans Holbein the Younger, 16th century
Oil on panel, 74.9 × 58.4 (29½ × 23)

Provenance 5th Duke of Bedford (1765–1805); Christie's 30 June 1827 (83); Nieuwenhuys; William II of Holland; by descent to Prinz zu Wied from whose family bt. Dr Peter Grčić; bt. NPG 1964.
Exhibition Erasmus, 1969 (66).
Bibliography Morison-Barker, no. 7; Strong, *Catalogue*, 228–9, pl 453.

National Portrait Gallery, London (4358)

No extant portrait of Thomas More can be identified certainly with the picture painted by Hans Holbein in London in 1527. There are several versions of the single half-length, differing only slightly in detail, but none has a history which can securely be documented earlier than 1827, when the 'Bedford'/NPG version was sold at Christie's. The portrait in the Frick Collection in New York is generally agreed to be the original from Holbein's hand, from which all others depend, but its provenance before 1858 can be reconstructed only by inference. X-rays taken in 1952 support the Frick portrait's claim to primacy: they show changes in the pose of the head. The 'Bedford'/NPG version is of sufficient quality to have been erroneously reproduced by Paul Ganz and by H. A. Schmid as the Frick painting in standard works on Holbein. The Prado owns a superb copy by Rubens.

The date MDXXVII appears just below the sill or table-top on which More rests his right forearm. The court official is shown at the age of almost fifty, royal servant by his collar of SS (no. 27), man of affairs from the paper in his right hand. His dress is plainer and less opulent than that of many of Holbein's other sitters, reflecting his more modest prosperity and position. This is something between a public and a private image. More is less dishevelled than we might expect from Erasmus's description (no. 265) of his carelessness in dress. His colouring seems darker than the brightness and clarity of complexion, the auburn hair and the blue-grey eyes also recorded by Erasmus.

27
Collar of SS
Unknown artist, 15th–16th century
Silver gilt, length 80.7 (31¾), width of links 1.3 (½)

Bibliography A. Hartshorne, 'Notes on collars of SS', *Archaeological Journal*, XXXIX, 1882, 376–83; A. P. Purey-Cust, *The Collar of SS, a History and a Conjecture*, Leeds 1910; Sir George Bonner, *The Gold Collar of SS and the Trial of the Pyx*, Cirencester 1943; A. H. Ormerod, 'The SS Collar', *The Catholic Lawyer*, II, 1956, 123–30; Morison-Barker, 86–8; W. N. Hargreaves-Mawdsley, *A History of Legal Dress in Europe until the End of the 18th Century*, Oxford 1963, 56–8.

Victoria and Albert Museum, London (1022–1926)

The collar of SS was a livery chain, signifying the allegiance or adherence of the wearer. Such collars began to be worn in the fourteenth century and were adopted by the houses of

27

York and of Lancaster: York used suns and roses, falcons and fetterlocks, Lancaster SS. Under the Yorkist kings, the collar of SS was out of favour, but Henry VII restored its use, adding the Tudor badges of a pair of portcullises for fastening and a pendant rose, as in the example worn by Thomas More in the Frick portrait and its descendants (no. 26). Perhaps the finest surviving Henrician specimen is that bequeathed to the City in 1544 by Sir John Alleyn and still worn by the Lord Mayor of London.

When More received his collar is not known; perhaps at his entry into royal service in 1517, or at his knighthood. Erasmus makes it a sign of his hatred of ostentation that he avoided wearing it whenever he could.

28
Photograph: **First Grant of a Royal Annuity to Thomas More, 1518**
1518 June 21, Westminster: grant of annuity of £100 for life, as from Michaelmas 1517

Bibliography LP, II, 4247; Routh, 92–3 and n. 3; G. R. Elton, 'Thomas More, Councillor', in R. S. Sylvester, ed., *St Thomas More: Action and Contemplation*, New Haven 1972, 89 and nn. 7, 8.

Photograph by courtesy of the Public Record Office, London (C.66/631.m.12)

After serving on a number of royal commissions at home (no. 105) and abroad (no. 48), More became a member of the King's Council by 26 August 1517, when he is mentioned as 'our councillor' in the commission for negotiating with the French at Calais (Rogers, 42; *LP*, II, 3634). Erasmus seems to have been kept ignorant of this, even after they met at Calais; yet the two combined to create the impression that More entered the royal service with reluctance. The present document establishes that 'for his good services' he was granted the usual councillor's pension of £100 for life from a much earlier date than his biographers admitted. He received his pension fairly regularly until Easter 1534 when he was imprisoned.

There is another copy of the grant among the Warrants for the Great Seal (PRO C.82/483).

29
Commission to Thomas Ruthall, Cuthbert Tunstall, Richard Pace and Thomas More to treat with the Emperor Charles V
Greenwich, 8 April 1520
Parchment

Bibliography LP, III, i, 732; H. J. Smit, *Bronnen tot de geschiedenis van de handel met Engeland...*, II, i, 1942, 363; Rymer, XIII, 718 (VI, 185); K. Lanz, *Actenstücke und Briefe*, 1857, 152–3; Rogers, 89; *Neue Briefe*, 89.

Haus-, Hof- und Staatsarchiv, Vienna (Allgemeine Urkundenreihe)

Original commission with the Great Seal appended; there exist some twenty official and unofficial copies. This is the royal command to More and others to treat with the commissioners of Charles V (no. 30) on the details of his visit to England, and to take up again the commercial problems to which More's first 'Utopian' mission to Flanders (1515; no. 48) had failed to find a solution. Agreement was reached on both counts and, before its conclusion, Henry commissioned More to attend at court to arrange for the reception of the Emperor at Canterbury.

30
Seals of Thomas More and Cuthbert Tunstall
Original of the English counterpart of the alliance with Charles V, dated London, 11 April 1520; signed by Ruthall, Tunstall, Pace and More
Parchment

Bibliography K. Lanz, *Actenstücke und Briefe zur Geschichte Kaiser Karl V* (Monumenta Habsburgica, pt II, vol I), Vienna 1857, 146–56, no. 43; *LP*, III, i, 740; *Neue Briefe*, 89; G. Demay, *Inventaire des sceaux de la Flandre*, 1873, I, 12, no. 67 (Tunstall), II, 2, no. 4868 (More); H. Meulon, 'Une intaille antique', *Moreana*, X, 1966, 6–10; J. B. Trapp, 'A double "mise au point"', ibid. XI, 1966, 50–1.

Archives du Nord, Lille (B.593/18128)

On 28 June 1519 Charles, King of Spain, was elected Emperor. In order to prepare his first visit to England, he sent particularly experienced diplomats in advance: Bernard de Mesa, Gerard de Plana, Phillipp Haneton and Johan de la Sauch. On 8 April 1520, Henry VIII commissioned Thomas Ruthall, Cuthbert Tunstall, Richard Pace and Thomas More to treat with them for an alliance and a mercantile agreement (no. 29). Only three days later, both treaties were concluded in London.

The document exhibited is the one signed by the English side on the foot of the addendum and across the tags: 'T.Dunolmensis' (Ruthall), Tunstall, Pace and More. Of the four seals appended, Ruthall's is now missing. Tunstall has an oval heraldic seal, with an escutcheon bearing three

30 *(enlarged)*

combs. The seal on Pace's tag is not his but, in all likelihood, that of one of the imperial commissioners. More's oval seal (diameter 20 mm) is in perfect condition. It is a Renaissance *rifacimento* after an antique coin, probably a gem-seal, with the legend round the edge T.VESPASIANVS AVGVSTVS and IVDEA CAPTA beneath the laurel-crowned bust of the Emperor. More used this as his private seal around 1519–25 (no. 190).

31 *(enlarged)*

31
Sir Thomas More's Seal as Sub-Treasurer of England
Unknown artist, *c*.1521
Silver, diameter 4 (1⅝)

Provenance Presented by Thomas More, SJ (1722–95), to the English College at St Omers 1755; presumably removed with the College to Bruges 1762, Liège 1773 and Stonyhurst 1794.
Exhibition Chelsea, 1929 (2b and cf 10).
Bibliography Bridgett, 455–8; John Gerard, *Stonyhurst College Centenary Record*, Belfast 1894, 247–8; British Museum, *Catalogue of Seals*, III, 1894, p 276, no. 11913.

The Trustees of Stonyhurst College

More became Sub-Treasurer in 1521 and remained in office until 1525, so this die must have been made during those years. It is circular, with a fleur-de-lis handle, and consists of an ornamental shield of arms, couché, quarterly first and fourth a chevron engrailed between three moor-cocks, for More; second and third, a chevron between three unicorns' heads erased, as many bezants. The crest, on a helmet, with ornamental mantling and wreath, is a Moor's head. Round the seal is the legend SIGILLVM . T. MORE . EQVITIS . AVRATI . SVBTHESAVRARII . ANGL. Beaded border. No contemporary impression is extant.

HUMANISM AND ROYAL SERVICE

32

**32
Richard Fox, Bishop of Winchester** (c.1448–1528)
Unknown artist, after Johannes Corvus, c.1575
Oil on panel, 43.8 × 35.6 (17¼ × 14)

Provenance Given to Corpus Christi College, Oxford, by John Hooker of Exeter 1579.
Exhibitions Oxford Historical Portraits, 1904 (12); Erasmus, 1969 (102).
Bibliography Emden, *Oxford*, II, 715–19; id. *Cambridge*, 239–41; G. R. M. Ward, *The Foundation Statutes of Corpus Christi College Oxford...*, 1843; P. S. and H. M. Allen, eds., *The Letters of Richard Fox*, Oxford 1929; J. K. McConica, *English Humanists and Reformation Politics under Henry VIII and Edward VI*, Oxford 1965, esp. 80–4; Mrs R. L. Poole, *Catalogue of Portraits in Oxford*, II, 1925, 263, no. 3; Erna Auerbach, *Tudor Artists*, 52–3, 141–2, 160–82; Strong, *Catalogue*, 124–5, pl 250; E. K. Waterhouse, *Painting in Britain 1530–1790*, 3rd edn. 1969, 3, 10.

The President and Fellows of Corpus Christi College, Oxford

Richard Fox, churchman, politician, diplomat and educator, became an adherent of Henry Tudor, Earl of Richmond. Made a member of the King's Council immediately after Bosworth Field, he was later Secretary of State and Lord Privy Seal, besides ambassador many times abroad until, with the rise of Wolsey, he relinquished public office in 1516. From 1487 he was successively Bishop of Exeter, of Bath and Wells and of Durham before being translated to Winchester in 1501.

Chancellor of Cambridge University 1498–1500, Fox supported his friend John Fisher in establishing St John's College, and was Master of Pembroke Hall, 1507–18. He set up grammar schools at Taunton in 1522 and Grantham in 1528. In Oxford, he founded Corpus Christi College in 1515–16 (nos. 91, 92, 93), but this attempt to establish a centre of clerical humanist education on up-to-date lines

met with the same sort of opposition that provoked More's letter of 1518 to the university (nos. 97, 98). According to Roper, Fox had some years before counselled More to be 'ruled by him' when More, 'a beardless boy', had incurred the royal wrath by securing a reduction in the sum granted to the king by the Parliament of 1504.

All extant portraits of Richard Fox are related to the original painting by Johannes Corvus of c.1518, now in Corpus Christi College. Corvus is almost certainly the Jan Rav who matriculated in the Painters' Guild in Bruges in 1512 and seems to have been continuously in England from about 1518 until his death in 1544. The later copy of the portrait shown here, also in Corpus Christi College, is inscribed: CLARVS WINTONIAE PRAESVL COGNOMINE FOXVS,/ QVI PIVS HOC OLIM NOBILE STRVXIT OPVS/TALIS ERAT FORMA TALIS DVA [sic] VIXIT AMICTV/QVALEM SPECTANTI PICTA TABELLA REFERT. Hanc repurgatam tabellam restituit Johannes Hooker Generosus Exoniensis 1579. (The famous Bishop of Winchester, Fox by name, the pious man who in former days built this work [ie College] was such in appearance while he lived and so dressed as this painted picture shows the spectator. John Hooker, gentleman, of Exeter, returned the picture, refurbished.) John Hooker (?1526–1601), the antiquary, was chamberlain of Exeter. The arms are Fox (a pelican in her piety) impaling the sees of Exeter (top left), Bath and Wells (top right), Durham (lower left) and Winchester (lower right). Another copy, painted by Sampson Strong in 1604, is also at Corpus Christi.

**33
Chalice and Paten, formerly the property of Richard Fox, Bishop of Winchester**
Unknown goldsmith, 1507
Gold, chalice: height 15.2 (6), diameter of bowl 9.8 (3⅞), diameter of foot 12.1 (4¾); paten: diameter 13.9 (5½)

Provenance Bequeathed to Corpus Christi College, Oxford, by Bishop Fox 1528.
Bibliography H. C. Moffat, *Old Oxford Plate*, 1906, 128–9, pl 62; E. Alfred Jones, *Old English Gold Plate*, 1907, XVII, 1–2, pl II; Charles Oman, *English Church Plate 597–1830*, 1957, 34, 45, 302, pls 18, 32.

The President and Fellows of Corpus Christi College, Oxford

The chalice from the chapel plate of Bishop Fox is among the finest surviving pieces of English medieval goldsmiths' work and, with the paten, the only extant example of English pre-Reformation gold plate. Both bear the London date letter for 1507, the maker's mark of a fleur-de-lis and a leopard's head crowned. The form of the chalice is simple, but the facets of the knop are enriched with crimson and green enamel. The six-lobed foot is engraved with a crucifix and figures of saints under canopies (Virgin and Child, St Jerome with his lion, St Augustine with an arrow, St Margaret with her dragon, St Mary Magdalen with her ointment jar). The paten is plain, with a cross and circle engraved on the rim. At the centre is engraved a vernicle (the image of Christ's face as believed to have been miraculously imprinted on the head-cloth of St Veronica, offered by her to Christ on the road to Calvary to wipe away the blood and sweat).

HUMANISM AND ROYAL SERVICE

Fox's bequest also included his pastoral staff (c.1490), a pair of altar basins (1493–1514), a standing salt and cover (fifteenth century) and probably a cup and cover (1515) and spoons (1506–16), all silver gilt and all also preserved at Corpus Christi.

34
Design for a Gold Cup
Hans Holbein the Younger, 1536–7
Point of the brush and black ink on paper, 37.5 × 14.3 ($14\frac{3}{4} \times 5\frac{5}{8}$)

Provenance William Beckford (1759–1844); bt. British Museum from Messrs Smith 1848.
Bibliography L. Binyon, *Catalogue of Drawings by British Artists...in the...British Museum*, II, 1900, no. 18; Ganz, *Handzeichnungen*, 207; *BM British Catalogue*, p 570, no. 186; and, on the Oxford drawing: Sir K. T. Parker, *Catalogue of Drawings in the Ashmolean Museum*, I, Oxford 1938, no. 299, pl LIX (with bibliog.); Schmid, *Holbein*, 404, 406, 407, 415–16; pls 105, 120; A. J. Collins, *Jewels and Plate of Queen Elizabeth I: the Inventory of 1594*, 1955, pp 65 n. 1, 168, 279, no. 47; F. G. Grossmann, *German Art 1400–1800, from Collections in Great Britain* (exbn. cat.), Manchester 1961, no. 155 (with bibliog.).

The Trustees of the British Museum (1848-11-25-9)

During his second stay in England (1532–43), Holbein made many designs for decorative art, large- and small-scale. Thomas More, his first English patron of the earlier visit, was now in eclipse. This drawing for a magnificent gold covered cup, perhaps intended as a wedding present from Henry to his third queen, Jane Seymour, is an earlier version of a still more elaborate design in the Ashmolean Museum, Oxford. The queen's motto, *Bound to obey and serve*, appears twice on the British Museum drawing and three times on the Oxford version. The initials H and I, for Henry and Jane, 'knitt together' with a love-knot, also appear. The cup was actually executed, but it was sent to the Netherlands by Charles I in 1625 to be pawned, and was melted down in 1629.

35
Henry VIII (1491–1547; reigned 1509–47)
Attributed to Lucas Horenbout, 1525
Body-colour on card in modern reproduction enamelled frame, 5 × 4.3 ($1\frac{15}{16} \times 1\frac{13}{16}$)

Provenance Magniac Collection; the Duke of Buccleuch, from whom bt. by Fitzwilliam Museum 1949.
Exhibitions Royal Academy, *British Portraits*, 1956–7 (604); Goldsmiths' Hall, London, *Treasures of Cambridge*, 1959 (326).
Bibliography A. B. Chamberlain, *Hans Holbein the Younger*, 1913, II, 233; Max J. Friedländer, 'Ein vlämischer Portrait-Maler in England', *Gentse Bijdragen*, IV, 1937, 18; C. Winter, 'The British School of Miniature Portrait Painters', *Proceedings of the British Academy*, XXXIV, 1948, p 7, pl 1A; T. H. Golding, *Aspects of Miniature Painting*, 1935, pp 63–5, fig 100; H. Paget, 'Gerard and Lucas Hornebolt in England', *Burlington Magazine*, CI, 1959, 396–402; Strong, *Catalogue*, pl 300.

Fitzwilliam Museum, Cambridge (PD 19–1949)

Lucas Horenbout (Hornebolte) first appears in the household accounts of Henry VIII in September 1525 and remained in

35

Henry's service until his death in 1544. In his early years in England he also worked for Wolsey. In 1534 he was given the title of King's Painter for life. This portrait of Henry, inscribed $\frac{HR}{VIII}$ $\frac{AN}{XXXV}$, with the monogram HK for Henry and Catherine of Aragon (no. 36), is usually attributed to Lucas. Henry is shown unbearded, as was then the fashion, in his thirty-fifth year, ie in 1525. The miniature was probably intended for presentation.

36
Catherine of Aragon (1485–1536)
Attributed to Lucas Horenbout, ?1525
Water-colour on vellum, stuck to card, diameter 3.9 ($1\frac{1}{2}$)

Provenance Bt. NPG from Leggatt Bros 1969.
Bibliography H. Paget, 'Gerard and Lucas Hornebolt in England', *Burlington Magazine*, CI, 1959, 400–1; G. Reynolds, 'Portrait Miniatures', *Connoisseur Period Guides, Tudor Period, 1500–1603*, 1956, 128, pl 69A.

National Portrait Gallery, London (4682)

This must be a companion-piece to a miniature of Henry VIII (no. 35); the inscription against the blue background reads: REGINA KATHERINA EIVS VXOR (Queen Catherine his wife). If it is by Lucas Horenbout (Hornebolte) it may have been made soon after his arrival in England in 1525. The queen wears a rich chain and her devotion is emphasised by the IHS monogram below.

37
Presentation Copy of Thomas More's Latin Epigrams to Henry VIII
Manuscript on vellum, 1509

Provenance Sir Robert Cotton (1571–1631); transferred to the nation with the Cottonian Library 1702; transferred to British Museum 1753.
Bibliography Thomas Smith, . . . *Bibliothecae Cottonianae Catalogus*, Oxford 1696, 128; [Joseph Planta], *Catalogue of the MSS in the Cottonian Library . . .*, 1802, 563–4; L. Bradner and C. A. Lynch, *The Latin Epigrams of Thomas More*, Chicago 1953, 16–24; Rogers, 6 (dedicatory letter).

The British Library Board (MS Cotton Titus D.IV, ff. 1–14v)

The five poems celebrating the coronation day of Henry VIII, the 'most glorious and blessed king of the British Isles', and Catherine of Aragon, his queen (23 June 1509), were presented in this manuscript to the young king, whom More had known from boyhood. The elegant Latin verses welcome the dawn of a new age and extol Henry's strength, his beauty, his nobility and his erudition, his virtuous ancestry and the union of the houses of Lancaster and York. The manuscript is decorated with the red and white roses symbolising the union, with the pomegranate of Aragon, the Westminster portcullis and other emblems. The poems were republished in the *Epigrammata* of 1518 and 1520 (nos. 40, 45).

38
A Bible for Henry VIII and Catherine of Aragon
New Testament, in Latin (Acts of the Apostles and Revelation only), Vulgate and Erasmus's translation
Peter Meghen, c. 1509
Manuscript on vellum

Bibliography Royal Commission on Historical Manuscripts, *Calendar of the MSS of the Marquess of Salisbury*, XIII, Addenda, 1915, no. 7; J. B. Trapp, 'Notes on MSS written by Peter Meghen', *Book Collector*, XXIV, 1975, 89; *The Cambridge History of the Bible*, III, *From the Reformation to the Present Day*, ed. S. L. Greenslade, Cambridge 1963, esp. 56–62, 79–81; W. Schwarz, *Principles and Problems of Biblical Translation*, Cambridge 1955, 92–166.

The Marquess of Salisbury (Hatfield House, Cecil Papers, MS 324)

Returning to England in the autumn of 1505, Erasmus began to make a new translation of the New Testament from the Greek. He was encouraged by John Colet (no. 11) for whom his translation, with the Vulgate text in parallel, was handsomely copied out by Peter Meghen in 1506 and 1509. Two of Colet's three volumes are now in the British Library (MS Royal I.E.V.) and the other in Cambridge University

38

Library (MS Dd. vii. 3). A later manuscript of the whole New Testament, also copied by Meghen, is now at Corpus Christi College, Oxford (MSS 13–14).

Colet's volumes do not contain the entire Testament: Acts and Revelation are missing. The present volume, comprising these two books, slightly larger and more imposing than Colet's, is decorated by an unknown Flemish artist in a richer and more accomplished manner. It must have been written for Henry VIII and Catherine of Aragon, whose linked initials appear on folio 4 on a background of green and white, the Tudor colours, with Tudor rose and portcullis. St Luke, traditionally the author of Acts, is shown writing.

The scribe, Peter Meghen, known as 'Monoculus', 'Unoculus', and 'Cocles', a one-eyed Brabantine from 's-Hertogenbosch (Bois-le-duc), acted as courier for Erasmus, Colet, William Warham (no. 206), Thomas More and Christopher Urswick (no. 41), as well as copyist for Colet, Urswick and Wolsey (no. 43), among others. He seems to have come to England in 1504 and was still active here in 1540.

39
New Testament, in Greek and Latin, edited and translated by Erasmus, 1516
Novum Instrumentum, diligenter ab Erasmo Roterodamo recognitum et emendatum..., Basel, Johann Froben, 1516

Bibliography See no. 38.

The British Library Board (675.h.10)

Some time after finishing his translation of the New Testament into Latin, Erasmus set to work in earnest on a new edition of the Greek text. In 1516 Johann Froben of Basel printed Erasmus's recension of the Greek with his Latin translation in parallel columns. Erasmus dedicated his work to Pope Leo X (no. 75). It is the first printed Greek Testament to be published. (The Alcalá version, though actually printed in 1514, was not released until 1522.) The Latin translation is a slightly subdued version of the translation Erasmus had left in manuscript for Colet (no. 38).

A second edition followed from the same press in 1519. This was entitled *Novum Testamentum*, and in it the daring retranslations (*congregatio* instead of *ecclesia* and *sermo* for the hallowed *verbum* at the beginning of St John's Gospel) are restored. Luther was to draw heavily upon this translation.

40
Thomas More's Epigram to Cardinal Wolsey on Erasmus's New Testament
Epigrammata clarissimi disertissimique viri Thomae Mori Britanni ad emendatum exemplar ipsius autoris excusa..., Basel, Johann Froben, 1520

Bibliography Gibson, 57; Adams, M1753; L. Bradner and C. A. Lynch, *Latin Epigrams of Thomas More*, Chicago 1953, no. 240.

Guildhall Library, London (Cock Colln. 1.5)

Froben, having published More's Latin epigrams in the same volume as *Utopia* twice in 1518 (no. 45), and received More's corrections of the second, November, edition, here omits three epigrams and adds eleven new ones. As a title-page border Froben re-uses Hans Holbein's 'Scaevola and Porsenna', which had been in use since 1516 and had served for the first edition of March 1518.

The epigram shown, entitled *Ad Reverendissimum &c. Thomam Cardinalem et Archiepiscopum Eboracensem in Librum Novi Testamenti ei ab Erasmo datum*, praises Wolsey as pre-eminent patron and fosterer of learning, whose virtues excel even his reputation. It is a dedicatory epigram by proxy, begging Wolsey's acceptance of Erasmus's *New Testament* (no. 39), published in 1516, and his benevolence.

41
A Miscellany of Sermons
St John Chrysostom, St Augustine of Hippo, Martin Luther, Girolamo Savonarola, *Sermons and Meditations*
Peter Meghen, c.1520
Manuscript on vellum

Provenance Christopher Urswick; William Rowe, 16th century.
Bibliography Emden, *Cambridge*, 605–6, 685; id. *Oxford*, 1935–6; McConica, op. cit. (no. 32) 70–2; J. B. Trapp, 'Notes on MSS written by Peter Meghen', *Book Collector*, XXIV, 1975, 80–96.

University College, Oxford (MS 40)

Christopher Urswick (1448–1522; nos. 18, 20), civil lawyer, canonist, diplomat, was eleven times Henry VII's envoy, his Grand Almoner from 1485, Dean of York 1488–94 and of Windsor 1495–1522. Later the friend and benefactor of Erasmus, who dedicated his translation of Lucian's *Gallus* to him, he was a prominent member of the London humanist circle to which Thomas More also belonged.

This miscellany of sermons, with Savonarola's Expositions of Psalms 31 and 51 (Vulgate 30 and 50), was written out by Peter Meghen for Urswick at an uncertain date, but perhaps about 1520. It was decorated by an unidentified artist. The leaves containing Luther's sermons on preparation for the Eucharist and on the Passion, though unimpeachably orthodox, have been excised.

Meghen transcribed a number of manuscripts for Urswick, Colet and others (nos. 38, 43, 188). The contents of this one epitomise the forward-looking pious interests of the 'London Reformers'.

42
Cardinal Thomas Wolsey (?1475–1530)
Unknown artist, 16th century
Oil on panel, 83.8 × 55.9 (33 × 22)

Provenance Sheldon family; recorded by George Vertue 1737; sold 3 September 1781 (38); W. Selby; perhaps picture sold H. Rodd 1824 (142); bt. NPG from Messrs Graves 1858.
Bibliography Strong, *Catalogue*, 335–6, pls 661–2; L. Campbell, 'The Authorship of the *Recueil d'Arras*', *JWCI*, XL, 1977, 301–13.

National Portrait Gallery, London (32)

Wolsey, or 'Wolfsee' as William Tyndale called him, is described by Sebastiano Giustinian, the Venetian ambassador, in 1519 as 'very handsome, learned, extremely eloquent, of vast ability and indefatigable'; and by Francesco Cornaro, likewise Venetian ambassador, in 1521, as 'hale, and of good presence, but proud and very choleric'.

Two types of Wolsey's likeness survive. One, showing him as he was about 1515–20, is preserved in the collection of portrait drawings by Jacques Le Boucq known as the *Recueil d'Arras*, perhaps put together in 1567. The extant painted portraits show him in profile, wearing cardinal's robes. In the Hampton Court painting of the Field of the Cloth of Gold (no. 67), Wolsey can be seen riding by the side of Henry VIII.

More's relations with Wolsey began early. The two must have known each other well before More first went on embassy for the king to Bruges and Antwerp in 1515 (no. 48). Thereafter, as More was drawn into royal service, they were constantly in contact, More coming to be a kind of secretary to Henry and intermediary between king and Council. They were both at the Field of the Cloth of Gold in 1520, and at the Parliament of 1523 (nos. 111, 112). More was involved, willy-nilly, in Wolsey's diplomatic manoeuvres first against France and then against Spain; he was consulted when the divorce was first mooted in 1527; he went with Wolsey to France in the same year (no. 195) and in Wolsey's stead in 1529 (no. 196), and in the same year opened the Reformation

42

43

Parliament, having taken the Great Seal (no. 197) in succession to Wolsey, with the obligatory sycophantic speech to Henry expressing the nation's gratitude for the removal of Wolsey, the 'scabbed wether', from the flock. Wolsey died early the next year.

43
Cardinal Wolsey's Epistolary
Peter Meghen; decorated by ? Gerard Horenbout, 1528
Manuscript on vellum

Provenance Perhaps made for Cardinal College, Oxford (Christ Church); first recorded at Christ Church by John Evelyn 12 July 1654.
Exhibitions Bodleian Library, Oxford, *Renaissance MSS*, 1948; Goldsmiths' Hall, London, *Treasures of Oxford*, 1953 (187); Royal Academy, *Flemish Art 1300–1700*, 1953–4 (623).
Bibliography G. W. Kitchin, *Catalogus codd. mss... Aedis Christi*, Oxford 1867, no. 101; E. Auerbach, *Tudor Artists*, 1954, 28, 42–5, 171; H. Paget, 'Gerard and Lucas Hornebolt in England', *Burlington Magazine*, CI, 1959, 400–1; J. B. Trapp, 'Notes on MSS written by P. Meghen', *Book Collector*, XXIV, 1975, 92.

The Governing Body of Christ Church, Oxford (MS 101)

This opulent manuscript was illuminated in 1528 and was perhaps, with its companion Lectionary (MS Magdalen College, Oxford, 223), intended for use in Wolsey's foundation, re-established by Henry VIII as Christ Church. The illumination has been attributed to Gerard Horenbout (Hornebolte), the Flemish artist active in England from 1526 or 1528 until 1531–2, whose son Lucas (nos. 35, 36) came to England in 1525 or earlier and died here in 1544. The scribe of each manuscript was Peter Meghen (nos. 38, 41, 188).

44
Thomas More's 'Utopia': First Edition, 1516
Libellus vere aureus nec minus salutaris quam festiuus de optimo reip. statu, deque noua Insula Vtopia authore clarissimo Thoma Moro... cura M. Petri Aegidii Antuerpensis..., [Louvain], Dirk Martens, [1516]

Bibliography Gibson, 1; Adams, M1755; H. Liebaers, *Exposition Thierry Martens c.1450–1534*, Brussels 1950, pp 7, 28, no. 70; *Tentoonstelling Dirk Martens 1473–1973*, Aalst 1973, pp 192–3, no. A273a; p 278, no. M136.

Guildhall Library, London

This is the first edition of the most famous of More's works, printed by Dirk Martens at Louvain. In September 1516 More committed the publication to Erasmus and asked him to obtain commendatory letters and verses by both scholars and men of affairs. In November, copy was in the printer's hands and by January 1517 the first copies were distributed. Written in Latin, the international language of the educated world, *Utopia* was an immediate success. By March 1517 the book was so well accepted everywhere that Erasmus and More talked of a new and revised edition.

45
Thomas More's 'Utopia': Third Edition, with Epigrammata, November 1518
De optimo reip. statu deque nova insula Vtopia Libellus vere aureus nec minus salutaris quam festiuus ... Epigrammata ... Thomae Mori ... Epigrammata Des. Erasmi Roterodami, Basel, Johann Froben, November 1518

Bibliography Gibson, 3; Adams, M1756.

Bodleian Library, Oxford (Wood 639)

There were two editions of *Utopia* from the press of Johann Froben in Basel during 1518, one in March and one in November. Five Latin editions appeared on the Continent within three years of the first publication in 1516. An attractive and corrected edition was printed in late 1517 by Gilles de Gourmont in Paris. Meanwhile, a new edition, with More's own corrections, was under way with Froben at Basel. It appears to be the last edition in which More had a direct hand.

Froben provided several title-page borders and woodcut illustrations by Ambrosius Holbein, the elder brother of Hans (nos. 51, 52). Hans Holbein contributed other borders.

46
Thomas More's 'Utopia': First German Translation, 1524
Von der wunderbarlichen Innsel Vtopia genant, das ander Buch durch ... Thomam Morum ... zu Latin gar kürtzlich beschriben vnd vssgelegt ..., Basel, Johann Bebel, 1524

Bibliography Gibson, 34; W. Bonacker, 'Der Basler Buchdrucker Johann Bebel', *Schweizerisches Gutenbergmuseum*, XI, 1943, 101–5.

Guildhall Library, London (Cock Colln. 1.5)

This first translation of the Latin *Utopia* into a vernacular, followed by an Italian (1548), a French (1550), an English (1551; no. 47), a Dutch (1553) and a Spanish (1637), was made by the learned law professor, councillor and later imperial chancellor for Alsace, Claudius Cantiuncula or Claude Chansonette (fl. 1530), and dedicated to the Basel Burgomaster Adalbert Meyer. More is referred to in the full title as knight (*Freiherr*) and Sub-Treasurer (*Schatzmeister*). Only the second book, with Hythlodaye's description of Utopia, is translated. The first book with its social criticism of contemporary England is omitted.

It was printed by Johann Bebel, alias Welschhaus, a printer from the canton of Valais, who had established himself at Basel around 1523, and was renowned for his editions of classical literature. The title-border was designed by Hans Holbein and resembles the 'Triton' border used for the November edition of 1518, as it had been for Pace's *De Fructu* of 1517 (no. 264), both printed by Froben.

47
Thomas More's 'Utopia': First English Translation, 1551
A fruteful and pleasaunt worke of the beste state of a publyque weale, and of the newe yle called Vtopia ..., London, Abraham Vele, 1551

Bibliography STC2 18094; Gibson, 25.

Guildhall Library, London

The social dream of the Utopian commonwealth was established on the European continent through five Latin editions before it was first published in English in 1551. Ralph Robinson, the translator, was a Lincolnshire man, educated at Corpus Christi College, Oxford; he later obtained the livery of the Goldsmiths' Company. His style as a translator shares the melodious charm of the English of the *Book of Common Prayer*. He dedicated his work to William Cecil (later Lord Burghley), though this does not seem to have been effective, for he died in poverty. Robinson's first edition was followed by a second in 1556, a third in 1597, and a fourth in 1624. It has often been reprinted.

48
The 'Utopian' Commission to Thomas More
Commission to Tunstall, Sampson, Spinelly, More and Clifford to treat with the commissioners of Charles of Castile, Duke of Burgundy [later Emperor Charles V], Westminster, 7 May 1515
Parchment

Bibliography LP, II, 422; Smit, op. cit. (no. 29) 215, no. 283; Rymer, XIII, 497 (VI, i, 97); Rogers, 10; Sir H. C. Maxwell-Lyte, *Historical Notes on the Use of the Great Seal of England*, 1926; E. Surtz, 'St Thomas More and his Utopian Embassy of 1515', *Catholic Historical Review*, XXXIX, 1953, 272–97.

Public Record Office, London (C.82/420)

This is the first of a number of royal commissions sending More abroad on diplomatic missions. The Burgundian Low Countries were the main trading partners of England, predominantly in wool. Arriving in mid May, the English side tried to secure a continuation of the *Intercursus Magnus* of 1495–6 and the *Intercursus Malus* of 1506, which had been favourable to them, whereas the Burgundians contested the validity of those two mercantile agreements. In July the negotiations were discontinued, so that More could go on to Antwerp (nos. 49, 50), meeting there Peter Gillis, (no. 54), and the fictitious Raphael Hythlodaeus (no. 51).

The head of the English delegation was More's friend Cuthbert Tunstall (nos. 55, 56); Richard Sampson (d.1554) then resided at Tournay to further Wolsey's interests there; Sir Thomas Spinelly (d.1522), a Florentine merchant, was employed by Henry on diplomatic missions; John Clifford acted as governor of the English merchants in Flanders.

More returned to England towards the end of October and long before a new treaty was signed at Brussels on 24 January 1516.

HUMANISM AND ROYAL SERVICE

49
View of Antwerp in Thomas More's Time
Unknown artist, 1515
Woodcut, 29.5 × 20 (12 × 8)

Bibliography NK, I, p 536, no. 1505; M. Funck, *Le livre belge à gravures*, Paris-Brussels 1925, 113 (ill. 45), 322; C. P. Burger, 'Lofzangen en prenten ter verheelijking van Keizer Maximiliaan', *Het Boek*, XVII, 1928, 23–48, and id., ibid. 145–6; A. J. J. Delen, *Iconografie van Antwerpen*, Brussels, 1930, no. 10, pl 4; Anne Rouzet, *Dictionnaire des imprimeurs, libraires et éditeurs des XVe et XVIe siècles dans les limites géographiques de la Belgique actuelle*, Nieuwkoop 1975, 70.

The British Library Board (C.38.h.14)

This view of Antwerp at the time of More's 'Utopian mission' in 1515 is taken from *Een corte verhalinge en bediedinghe alre en yegelike punten oft artikelen in desen loeflicken sanck bescreuen . . .* published in Antwerp by Jan de Gheet in 1515. The volume is a collection of woodcuts, verses and music, made in honour of the Emperor Maximilian I, collected by one Rutger Kynen of Nijmegen (de Novomagio) and sent to Johannes Neve of the same city. The music is the work of the brothers Benedictus and (?) Georgius de Opicijs or Opitiis. The woodcuts are apparently unique except for related smaller prints and initials in Antwerp books. They seem to have been commissioned for this book. The artist's name is not known. Only one other copy of the volume, a variant, is extant. The wood blocks were still in use in 1577.

50
Facsimile: **The Harbour at Antwerp**
Albrecht Dürer, 1520
Original pen drawing in the Albertina, Vienna

Bibliography Panofsky, 1408; Albrecht Dürer, *Tagebuch der Reise in die Niederlande*, ed. H. Rupprich, *Schriftlicher Nachlass*, I, Berlin 1956, 146–204; id. *Diary of his Journey to the Netherlands, 1520–1*, with intro. by J. A. Goris and G. Marlier, 1970.

Thomas More never saw Antwerp again after October 1515, but his friends Erasmus and Peter Gillis were both there five years later, when Albrecht Dürer arrived. Dürer spent nearly a year in the Low Countries. In Antwerp, then the wealthiest city in the Netherlands and a centre of culture and commerce, he admired the buildings and the richness of pageantry and festival, as well as 'the things brought to the King [Charles V] from the new golden land'. His fellow artists received him kindly, he visited Quentin Massys and, at Peter Gillis's house, he met Erasmus, whose portrait he was to draw and engrave.

51
Thomas More, Raphael Hythlodaeus, Peter Gillis and John Clement
Ambrosius Holbein, 1518
Woodcut, 6.2 × 10.5 (2½ × 4⅛)

Exhibition Basel, *Malerfamilie Holbein* (121).

The Trustees of the British Museum (1862–5–17–8)

Ambrosius Holbein (?1494–?1519) was the son of Hans Holbein the Elder (1460/5–?1524) and elder brother of Hans Holbein the Younger (1497/8–1543). Little is known of his life and work, but some of the woodcuts for the Basel edition of *Utopia*, the third, are usually ascribed to him.

The woodcut shows the bearded Raphael Hythlodaeus, the narrator of *Utopia*, telling his story to Peter Gillis and Thomas More in the garden of the house More was occupying during his stay in Antwerp. John Clemens (Clement) – 'my pupil-servant' as More calls him – is coming from the left to see to their comfort. All are fictitious portraits and the 'garden' a conventional landscape scene.

HUMANISM AND ROYAL SERVICE

52

52
The Island of Utopia
Ambrosius Holbein, 1518
Woodcut, 19 × 12 (7½ × 4⅝)

Exhibition Basel, *Malerfamilie Holbein* (120).

The Trustees of the British Museum (1862–5–17–6)

Holbein's woodcut of Utopia in the Basel edition of 1518, the third, is a sophisticated version of the crude cut prefixed to the first edition (Louvain, 1516) but missing from the second, Paris, edition of 1517. Raphael Hythlodaeus, below left, addresses a civilian while a soldier stands below right. Hythlodaeus points past his ship to the crescent-shaped island, with its town of Amaurotum (Shadow City, Dream Town) below the crest of the hill which runs down to the banks of the river Anydrus (Waterless). The river's source (*Fons Anydri*) and its mouth (*Ostium Anydri*) are likewise shown.

53
Desiderius Erasmus (?1469–1536)
Quentin Massys, 1517
Oil, transferred from panel to canvas, 59 × 46.5 (23¼ × 18⅜)

Provenance In Stroganoff Collection by 1807; given by Scherbatoff family, heirs of Count Gregory Stroganoff, to Galleria Nazionale, Rome 1912.
Exhibitions Rome, Galleria Borghese, *Mostra temporanea di insigni opere d'arte*, 1945; Florence, *Mostra d'arte fiamminga e olandese dei sec XV° e XVI°*, 1948 (18); Bruges, Venice, Rome, *I Fiamminghi e l'Italia*, 1951 (23/24); Rome, Palazzo Barberini, *Dipinti fiamminghi di collezioni romane*, 1966, p 29; *Erasmus*, 1969 (237).
Bibliography M. J. Friedländer, *Early Netherlandish Painting*, rev. edn. Leiden-Brussels 1971, pp 21–3, 64, nos. 36, 120, pl 40; K. G. Boon, *Q. Massys*, Amsterdam, n.d., 48f; A. Gerlo, *Erasme et ses portraitistes: Metsijs, Dürer, Holbein*, 2nd edn. Nieuwkoop 1969, 9–28; E. Panofsky, 'Erasmus and the visual Arts', *JWCI*, XXXII, 1969, 214; Margaret Mann Phillips, 'The Mystery of the Metsys Portrait', *Erasmus in English*, VII, 1975, 18–21; Allen, 584, 601, 616, 654, 681, 683–4, 688, 706; Rogers, 38, 40, 44–7, 52, 54.

Galleria Nazionale d'Arte Antica, Rome

In May 1517 Erasmus and Peter Gillis, in Antwerp, commissioned a diptych with both their portraits from Quentin Massys (1465/6–1530), the leading Antwerp painter of the day. It was to be sent to Thomas More as a memento, and More duly wrote from Calais on 7 October to acknowledge receipt and to thank each of his friends, adding verse epigrams on the diptych.

Erasmus must have chosen the pose of the scholar at his desk both to complement Peter Gillis's learned man-of-affairs on the other leaf and to declare affinity with St Jerome. Several sixteenth-century versions of the image are extant, the two most important being this Palazzo Barberini ('Corsini') portrait and that at Hampton Court. The Hampton Court version has not been cut down. The two leaves of the diptych were still together in the seventeenth century (Isaac Bullart, *Académie des sciences et des arts*, Amsterdam 1682, II, 391). They are here reunited for the first time since then.

The versions which have remained in England, as Mrs Margaret Mann Phillips has pointed out, still bear the inscriptions to which Thomas More's letter of thanks refers. The work Erasmus is writing, More notes, is his Paraphrase of the Epistle of St Paul to the Romans, the task on which he was actually engaged in 1517. In the Hampton Court picture, but not in the Corsini, the opening words of the Paraphrase are shown, in an imitation of Erasmus's script, on the right-hand page, with the key word of the Epistle, *Gratia*, grace on the left. More also speaks of inscriptions on the books on the shelves. In the Hampton Court picture the painted names MORIA, LOUKIANOS (in Greek), NOVUM TESTAMENTUM, and HIERONYMUS proclaim Erasmus's affinities. The *Praise of Folly's* title puns in Greek on More's name and the book was written in More's house; Lucian was an old favourite of both. In 1516, Erasmus had published his edition of the New Testament in Greek (no. 39) as well as his edition of St Jerome.

54
Peter Gillis (Petrus Aegidius) (1486–1533)
(Colour plate II, page 53)
Quentin Massys, 1517
Oil on panel, 73.75 × 55.25 (29 × 21¾)

Bibliography Friedländer, op. cit. (no. 53) pp 21–3, 64, no. 37, pl 41; A. Gerlo, loc. cit. (no. 53); E. Surtz, 'St Thomas More and his Utopian Embassy of 1515', *Catholic Historical Review*, XXXIX, 1953, 272–97; M. A. Nauwelaerts, *Nationaal Biografisch Woordenboek*, IV, 1970, 4–8; Allen, loc. cit. (no. 53); Rogers, loc. cit. (no. 53).

The Earl of Radnor

Peter Gillis (Giles, Aegidius) came of a distinguished Antwerp family and was made Chief Secretary *(Griffier)* of the city in 1510. His legal training was backed by humanist interests which won him the friendship of many of the learned men of the day – Jerome Busleyden (no. 57), Guillaume Budé (no. 68), Juan Luis Vives (nos. 185, 186), Martin Dorp (nos. 100, 101), as well as Erasmus and More. Gillis's house was a centre of intellectual life in Antwerp; More made its garden the setting for Hythlodaeus's tale of *Utopia* (no. 51). Gillis had frequently worked for the printer Dirk Martens before he helped to see *Utopia* through Martens's press in 1516. He had also published, with Martens, editions of Poliziano and Rudolf Agricola, as well as a treatise on Justinian's legal code (no. 18).

Thomas More and Gillis first met on More's 'Utopian' embassy in 1515. Erasmus had recommended More and Tunstall to Gillis and More's prefatory letter to Gillis, printed in *Utopia*, is a witness to the friendship that grew up.

When More wrote to thank Gillis and Erasmus for the diptych containing both their portraits that they had sent him, he remarked on the letter from himself that the painter had put into Gillis's hand and added a couple of epigrams in praise of friends, picture and painter. Massys shows Gillis with the symbols of his prosperity, his office and his learning: furred gown and covered cup; letter and sand-box; and books, including two by Erasmus. The portrait of Gillis exists in two versions. In this, the finer, some of the books are identified: (P)LATARCHVS VERSVS (ie Plutarch in Latin); SENECA; *Archontopaideia* (in Greek; ie Erasmus, *Institution of a Christian Prince*); SVETONIVS; (Q.) CVR(TIVS RVFVS); and, under Gillis's right forefinger, ANTIBARBARON (ie Erasmus, *Antibarbari*); the letter in Gillis's left hand is inscribed to him in an imitation of More's handwriting.

55
Cuthbert Tunstall (1474–1559)
Unknown artist, ?16th century
Oil on canvas, 90 × 76.2 (35⁷⁄₁₆ × 30)

Bibliography Emden, *Cambridge*, 597–8, 684; id. *Oxford*, 1913–15; C. Sturge, *Cuthbert Tunstal*, 1938, frontispiece, 398–9.

J. R. Chichester-Constable, Esq

Cuthbert Tunstall belonged to a Yorkshire family and was probably born illegitimate. Educated at Oxford and Cambridge, he studied at Padua, acquiring Greek and Hebrew as well as the doctorate of laws, and becoming the friend of Jerome Busleyden (no. 57). Returning to England in 1505,

55

he was in London in 1508, when he became a member of Doctors' Commons (no. 107).

He had humanist interests and humanist friends in common with More, and made his way in the Church. He and More advanced together into royal service, as fellow envoys. The year after More was made knight and Sub-Treasurer (1521), Tunstall became Bishop of London. They worked together to combat heresy (no. 140). They had been together on the 'Utopian' mission in 1515 (no. 48), both signed the treaty of 1520 with Charles V (no. 30) and they were together again at Cambrai in 1529 (no. 196). More's epitaph contains his ultimate praise of Tunstall: who so excelleth in learning, wit and virtue, that the whole world scant hath at this day any more learned, wiser or better'. In 1530 he was translated to Durham and was prominent in northern affairs. Deprived in 1553, he was reinstated under Mary and again deprived in 1559 by Elizabeth.

There are a number of portraits reputed to be of Tunstall; this type, in the possession of a descendant, has the best title to authenticity.

56
Cuthbert Tunstall's Arithmetic Book
Cuthbert Tunstall, *De arte supputandi libri quattuor*, London, Robert Pynson, 1522
Vellum

Bibliography STC2, 24319; McKerrow-Ferguson, 8; C. Sturge, *Cuthbert Tunstal*, 1938, 71–8.

Cambridge University Library (Sel. 3. 362)

De arte supputandi was Tunstall's farewell to secular learning, for five days after its publication he was Bishop of London and next year became Lord Privy Seal. He wrote it so that he and his friends could learn to make their own calculations and no longer be cheated by money-changers, and he dedicated it to Thomas More, recently knighted and made Sub-Treasurer of England (1521) because no one could more suitably receive such a dedication than one engaged in supervising the royal finances.

57
The Doctoral Diploma of Hieronymus (Jerome) Busleyden (c.1470–1517)
Diploma of the University of Padua, conferring the degree of *Doctor utriusque juris*, 8 February 1503
Vellum, 45.5 × 65 (17⁷⁄₈ × 25¹¹⁄₁₆)

Provenance Given by a resident of Fize-le-Marshal to Rt Rev B. Charpentier; bt. Professor H. de Vocht 1930; bequeathed by him to Universiteitsbibliotheek Leuven 1962.

Exhibition 500 *Jaar Universiteit Leuven*, 1976 (280).
Bibliography H. de Vocht, *Jerome de Busleyden, Founder of the Louvain Collegium Trilingue: his Life and Writings*, Turnhout 1950, 34–9, 125–9; J. Theys, *Nationaal Biografisch Woordenboek*, Brussels, II, 1964, 283–7.

Bibliotheek, Katholieke Universiteit Leuven (MS X.21)

Busleyden, churchman, lawyer, humanist, statesman, official and Maecenas, was one of Charles V's Great Council at Malines (Mechelen) and several times ambassador. About 1485 he began his university studies at Louvain and later read law at Orléans, where he met Erasmus. At Padua, where he graduated doctor of laws in 1503, he met Tunstall (no. 55). Busleyden came to England in 1509 as one of a mission to congratulate Henry VIII on his accession. Dying in 1517, he endowed the Collegium Trilingue at Louvain for the study of the three sacred languages, Greek, Latin and Hebrew. From More's letter to Erasmus (Allen, 388) we know that More met Busleyden during his mission to the Low Countries in 1515, and visited his mansion at Malines. More addressed three epigrams to Busleyden, congratulating him on his house and his collection of coins. More himself had a small collection of Roman coins. Busleyden's only printed piece is the letter addressed to More which is prefixed to the first edition of *Utopia*, but an elaborate manuscript of his works is in Brussels (Bibl. roy., MS 15676–7).

The initial I of Busleyden's diploma is formed of a mermaid framing a bust of St Jerome with her tail. Below are Busleyden's arms, supported by a male and a female satyr.

57A
Johann Froben (1460–1527)
Hans Holbein the Younger, *c*.1531
Oil and tempera on panel, diameter 9.5 (3¾)

Provenance ?Everard Jabach, d.1695; according to Strawberry Hill Sale Catalogue bt., with companion Melanchthon, by Horace Walpole at a sale of Sir William Hamilton's, 1761; Strawberry Hill Sale 17 May 1842 (44); George Tomline, Orwell Park, Ipswich 1854; George Pretyman, Orwell Park, until 1934; Christie's 1934.
Exhibition RA, *Holbein* (5).
Bibliography G. F. Waagen, *Treasures of Art in Great Britain*, III, 1854, 443; F. Grossmann, 'Holbein, Flemish Painting and Everhard Jabach', *Burlington Magazine*, XCIII, 1951, 23; Ganz, *Paintings*, no. 54; cf nos. 33, 60; A. Scharf, *Catalogue of the Collection of Sir Thomas Merton*, 1950, XXV; Basel, *Malerfamilie Holbein*, no. 185; J. Benzing, *Die Buchdrucker des 16. und 17. Jahrhunderts im deutschen Sprachgebiet*, Wiesbaden 1963, 30; Rogers, 67.

Merton Collection (Trustees of the late Lady Merton's Will Trust)

A native of Hammelburg in Franconia, Froben studied at the University of Basel. Becoming a citizen in 1490, he founded what was to be Basel's most famous printing house. In 1513, Erasmus came to Basel to live and work with Froben and to begin the great series of publications which Froben was to issue for him, including the *Novum Instrumentum* (no. 39). Erasmus also arranged that Froben should publish Thomas More's *Utopia* (no. 45) twice, with More's *Epigrammata*, in 1518; a separate edition of the *Epigrammata* followed in 1520 (no. 40). On 13 November 1518, Froben addressed More in a prefatory letter to Ulrich von Hutten's *Aula* (cf no. 123),

58

commiserating with him on the trials of a royal servant's life and remarking that his motive in publishing *Utopia* was to give the whole world, not Britain alone, a taste of More's wit. He asks to be commended to those other heroes of English learning Colet (nos. 11–14), Linacre (nos. 93–96), Grocyn (nos. 90, 91, 92), William Latimer, Tunstall (nos. 55, 56) and others.

This roundel was painted when Holbein was again at Basel (1528–32), after his first English visit (1526–8). It was perhaps a commission from Hieronymus Froben, Johann's son and Erasmus's godchild, intended as a pendant to the roundel of Erasmus also made by Holbein at about that time. In Basel, about 1522, Holbein had executed a half-length likeness of Froben, which is now at Hampton Court.

58
Willibald Pirckheimer (1470–1530)
Albrecht Dürer, 1524
Engraving, 18.2 × 11.4 (7 3/16 × 4½)

Bibliography Hollstein, 103; Panofsky, 213; *Willibald Pirckheimer, 1470–1970. Dokumente, Studien, Perspektiven anlässlich des 500. Geburtsjahres herausgegeben*, Nuremberg 1970.

The Trustees of the British Museum (1910–2–12–310)

Born into one of the oldest and richest families in Nuremberg, Pirckheimer added to a patrician upbringing the study of law and the humanities in the two fashionable universities of Padua and Pavia. Albrecht Dürer made a superb charcoal drawing of his best friend in 1503, and this magnificent engraving more than twenty years later. It is inscribed BILIBALDI. PIRKEYMHERI. EFFIGIES AETATIS SVAE ANNO LIII. VIVITVR INGENIO, CAETERA MORTIS ERVNT. M.D.XX.IV (A portrait of Willibald Pirckheimer at 53. We live in spirit; all else is mortal. 1524.)

Thomas More never met Pirckheimer, but his *Epigrammata*, Basel 1518 and 1520, bear a preface by Beatus Rhenanus recommending the poems to Pirckheimer.

59

60

59
Julius II (1443–1513; Pope 1503–13)
Copy after Raphael, 16th century
Red chalk, 36 × 25.3 (14⅛ × 10)

Exhibition Erasmus, 1969 (113).
Bibliography O. Fischel, *Raphael*, Berlin 1962, p 88, fig. 144;
O. Fischel, ed., *Raphaels Zeichnungen*, VI, 1948, no. 257; C. Gould, *Raphael's Portrait of Julius II: the Re-emergence of the Original*, 1970.

The Devonshire Collection, Chatsworth: The Trustees of the Chatsworth Settlement (50)

Giuliano della Rovere was raised to the cardinalate in 1471 and elected pope as Julius II in 1503. One of the greatest and most belligerent of Renaissance popes, he restored and enlarged the temporal power of the papacy, winning himself the nickname 'Il Terribile' and the denunciation of Erasmus in the *Praise of Folly* and the *Julius Exclusus*, in which St Peter refuses the dead pope admission to heaven. Julius raised Rome, by his patronage of Michelangelo, Raphael and Bramante, to a state of unparalleled magnificence.

Raphael drew Julius II near the end of the pope's life, about 1511. This copy after his drawing is inscribed 'Raffaelle da Urbino. Ritrato di Julio 2°,' in the hand of Padre Sebastiano Resta (1635–1714).

60
Maximilian I (1459–1519; Emperor 1508–19)
Hans Burgkmair, 1508
Woodcut, 32.4 × 22.7 (12¾ × 8¹⁵⁄₁₆)

Exhibition Stuttgart, *Hans Burgkmair, Das graphische Werk*, 1973, (22, cf 21).
Bibliography Hollstein, 323 (iv); T. Falk, *H. Burgkmair. Studien zum Leben und Werk des Augsburger Malers*, Munich 1968.

The Trustees of the British Museum (1895-1-22-377)

Maximilian I, 'the last of the knights', took the title of Emperor in 1508. This portrait commemorates the occasion by presenting him as the temporal protector of Christendom, mounted and fully armed, with peacock helmet-plume and baton against an architectural background bearing the arms of the Empire. In the same year, Burgkmair (1473–1531) made an equally splendid woodcut of the spiritual protector of Christendom, St George. Both woodcuts exist in various states, on blue and on brick-red paper, embellished by overprinting in silver and gold.

61
Grotesque Helmet, with Etched Decoration and Ram's Horns
Innsbruck, Konrad Seusenhofer, 1512–13
33 × 50 (13 × 19¾)

Provenance Part of gift from Emperor Maximilian I to Henry VIII 1514; Royal Armouries at Greenwich and Tower of London thereafter.
Exhibitions Innsbruck, Tiroler Landesmuseum, *Die Innsbrucker Plattnerkunst*, 1954 (87); Innsbruck, *Maximilian I*, 1959 (512).
Bibliography C. Blair, 'The Emperor Maximilian's Gift of Armour to King Henry VIII and the silvered and engraved Armour at the Tower of London', *Archaeologia*, XCIX, 1965, 1–52.

The Armouries, H.M. Tower of London (IV 22)

In 1511, Henry VIII, a great lover of tourneys and martial display, ordered two 'harnessys' for himself from the Innsbruck workshop of Konrad Seusenhofer. At the same time, the Emperor Maximilian I (no. 60) ordered armours from the same shop, one as a gift to Henry and another for the

61

Archduke Charles, later Charles V. This helmet, which may be intended as a grotesque portrait of Maximilian, formed part of the armour for Henry. The armour was ready for decoration in 1512 and the decoration paid for in 1513, but it did not reach England until May 1514, in the charge of Seusenhofer himself and Sir Richard Jerningham.

Maximilian's present was among the armour discarded before 1601 and sold in 1649–52. This helmet escaped the fate of the rest because it had, by 1638, become part of the hotch-potch known as the armour of Will Summers, fool to Henry VIII. Probably about the mid seventeenth century it was given a pair of latten spectacles and painted, to make it better fit its legend.

62
Helmet from Henry VIII's Silvered, Gilt and Engraved Armour
?Greenwich, c.1515
28.2 × 21.7 (11⅛ × 8½)

Provenance Royal Armouries at Greenwich and Tower of London from c.1515.
Bibliography C. Blair, loc. cit. (no. 61).

The Armouries, H.M. Tower of London (II 5)

This helmet was once believed to belong to an armour presented by the Emperor Maximilian to Henry on his marriage in 1509, and was later identified with the gift from the same to the same in 1514. It is now considered probable that the armour for man and horse of which it forms part was made after the arrival of Maximilian's gift in May 1514 and before 1519, probably in 1515, when Paul van Vrelant, the Flemish 'harness-gilder', was paid for work done. The armour itself was probably made at Greenwich by Milanese armourers in Henry's employ. It was intended primarily for parade, as is indicated by its engraved decoration: scenes from the lives of St Barbara and St George, Tudor roses (for Henry) and pomegranates (for Catherine of Aragon) on the bard (horse-armour), and by the applied initials H and K, with love-knots, round the edge of the base (skirt) of the suit itself.

63
Replica: **Charles V** (1500–58; Emperor 1519–56) as a Young Man
Circle of Conrad Meit, c.1517–18
Partial cast of polychrome terracotta bust, 52 × 63 (20½ × 25); original in Gruutehusemuseum, Bruges

Exhibitions (Original) Toledo, *Carlos V y su ambiente*, 1958 (261); Bruges, *Het Gulden Vlies*, 1962 (88); *Erasmus*, 1969 (226).
Bibliography C. Terlinden, *Charles Quint, Empereur des deux Mondes*, Brussels 1965, 129; G. Troescher, *Conrad Meit von Worms*, Freiburg i.B., 1927, 21–2; G. von der Osten and Horst Vey, *Painting and Sculpture in Germany and the Netherlands 1500–1600*, Harmondsworth 1969, 30–1, 238–40.

Victoria and Albert Museum, London

This bust shows Charles, grandson of Maximilian I, about the time he was elected to the Empire at the age of nineteen and a year or two before Thomas More first caught a glimpse of him in 1520. By the time he was elected emperor he was already ruler of Burgundy, the Netherlands, Spain and its American empire and the Kingdom of Naples, and he remained the most powerful man in Europe until his abdication in 1556 to enter the monastery of Yuste.

When Charles came to England in 1522, More appeared before him and Henry on their visit to the City, to speak formally and eloquently 'in the praise of the two princes, and of the peace and love between them'.

In the original of Conrad Meit's bust, Charles wears the collar of the Order of the Golden Fleece. Conrad Meit of Worms entered the service of Charles's aunt, Margaret of Austria, Regent of the Netherlands (no. 196), in 1514, and died in 1550.

64
The Emperor Charles V
Leone Leoni, 1555–6
Silver medal, diameter 6.9 (2¾)

Bibliography Armand, I, 164–5; cf Hill-Pollard, p 81.

The Trustees of the British Museum (Germ. M.21)

64

This medal's obverse shows the bust of Charles V in later life, laureate and cuirassed, with the badge of the Order of the Golden Fleece suspended from his neck. The legend reads .IMP.[erator] CAES.[ar] CAROLVS. V. AVG[ustus]. On the reverse, Hercules wields his club over two naked men (? the giants), with the Lernaean hydra to the right and a satyr seated under trees to the left. The legend runs: TV NE CEDE MALIS (Do not give way to evils). The same reverse is used on medals of Ferrante Gonzaga, Prince of Guastalla (1506–57), and others.

Leone Leoni, born near Como of an Aretine father, was Master of the mint in Milan for much of his working life. He was in the service of both Charles V and Philip II.

65
Francis I (1494–1547; reigned 1515–47)
Joos van Cleve, ?1530
Oil on panel, 83 × 58 (32¾ × 23)

Provenance Revoil Collection; Charles X of France.
Exhibition Erasmus, 1969 (257).

Musée national du Château de Fontainebleau

Francis I succeeded to the throne of France on the first day of 1515. Shortly afterwards he renewed the peace with England of the previous year, but soon began to eclipse and isolate Henry VIII with his victories in Italy and his alliances with Charles V and with Maximilian. On 2 October 1518, all Europe seemed united by the treaty of universal peace, to which Charles, Francis and Henry were signatories, but the peace was soon fragmented. Early in 1520, Francis proposed that he and Henry should meet face to face, at what became known as the Field of the Cloth of Gold (no. 67). Thomas More was present on the occasion, not much relishing its magnificence.

Later, More's contacts with Francis were few. He was on mission with Wolsey to France in 1527 (no. 195) and again in 1529 (no. 196), but there is no record of either man's opinion of the other.

This portrait is a version of that executed by the Flemish painter Joos van Cleve about 1530, when Francis was thirty-six or so. Van Cleve was master painter in Antwerp in 1511 and later travelled to the court of Francis, arriving in 1530.

66
Francis I, King of France
Benvenuto Cellini, ?1537–8
Bronze medal, diameter 4.1 (1⅝)

Exhibition Erasmus, 1969 (259).
Bibliography Armand, I, 147.3; E. Plon, *Benvenuto Cellini...*, 1883–4, pl XI.11; G. Habich, *Die Medaillen der italienischen Renaissance*, Stuttgart-Berlin 1922, pp 114–15, pl LXXVII, 2.

The Trustees of the British Museum (198A)

Cellini apparently made this medal for Francis I before he went to France and entered the king's employ as 'a man to be loved and cherished by everyone who knows him' (by his own account). The obverse shows a laureate head of Francis, who is holding a fleur-de-lis sceptre, with the inscription FRANCISCVS . I . FRANCORVM . REX round the rim. On the reverse is a mounted warrior chastising the naked figure of Fortune, whose attributes of ball and rudder lie at the horse's rear feet. The inscription reads: DEVICIT FORTVNAM VIRTVTE (He subdues Fortune by his virtue), and the medal is signed BENVENV [TVS] F[ECIT] in the exergue.

66

67

67
The Field of the Cloth of Gold
?Johannes Corvus, c.1520
Oil on canvas, 168.9 × 347.3 (66½ × 136)

Provenance Recorded in King's Privy Gallery at Greenwich at time of Charles I; sold to Captain John Stone and others 23 October 1651; recovered at the Restoration and placed in King's Privy Gallery at Whitehall Palace; thereafter at Windsor.
Exhibitions Royal Academy, *King's Pictures*, 1946–7 (506); *Erasmus*, 1969 (267).
Bibliography Millar, no. 25; S. Anglo, 'Le Camp du Drap d'Or', *Les Fêtes de la Renaissance*, II, 1960, 113–34; Joycelyne G. Russell, *The Field of the Cloth of Gold*, 1969.

Her Majesty the Queen (Hampton Court 520)

On 31 May 1520, Henry VIII, with Catherine of Aragon and a vast retinue, embarked from Dover for the meeting that had been arranged with Francis I. The embarkation is shown in a companion piece to the present picture, a carefree record of the week-long festivities at the Field of the Cloth of Gold itself, from 18 to 24 June. Henry is riding in state into Guisnes. Wolsey rides beside the king, and many other figures in the painted entourage are portraits. The dragon flying above Henry may represent the firework in sala- mander form (Francis's badge), released on 23 June. Behind are the king's golden dining tent and the sutlers' quarters; behind the dining tent, the meeting of Henry and Francis, now on foot; to the right, the tournament; in the right foreground, a banquet.

Thomas More met Guillaume Budé (no. 68) at the Field of the Cloth of Gold, and saw Erasmus for the last time. He went from it to settle disputes with the German Hansa (no. 69).

68
Guillaume Budé (1468–1540)
From André Thevet, *Les vrais pourtraits et vies des hommes illustres*, Paris, Veuve I. Kervert and G. Chaudière, 1584
Engraving, 37 × 22 (14½ × 8¾)

Bibliography G. Budé, exbn. at Bibliothèque nationale, Paris, 1968; R. Pfeiffer, *History of Classical Scholarship from 1300 to 1850*, Oxford 1976, 101–2; David O. McNeil, *G. Budé and Humanism in the Reign of Francis I*, Geneva 1975; P. Mellen, *Jean Clouet*, 1971, nos. 91, 145, pls 116–17; Rogers, 65, 66, 68, 80, 96, 97, 102, 154, 156.

University of London Library

Guillaume Budé was the first great French Renaissance classical scholar. His knowledge of the life and language of ancient Greece was encyclopaedic and his book on Roman coinage, *De asse* (1515), was greatly admired by Thomas More.

Budé contributed a prefatory letter to the second edition of *Utopia* (Paris, 1517), praising More and his book, though the two did not yet know each other personally. They began a correspondence in 1518 (the last extant letter is of 1527), and met at the Field of the Cloth of Gold in 1520 (no. 67). More made Budé a present of English hunting dogs, which Budé passed on to his friends.

The portrait type of Budé, of which this is a late version, was established from life by Jean Clouet about 1536. Thevet's book gave it wider currency.

69
Photograph: **Thomas More and the German Hansa, 1520**
'Recessus Brugensis anno 1520', a record of the negotiations between the Hansa delegates from Lübeck, Cologne, Hamburg, London (Steelyard), Stralsund and Danzig and the English commissioners at Bruges, 21 July to 12 August 1520

Bibliography D. Schäfer, ed., *Hanserecesse*, pt III, vol VII, Leipzig 1905, p 593; *Neue Briefe*, pp 27–31.

Photograph by courtesy of Historisches Archiv der Stadt, Cologne (Acta Anglicana, B.31, ff.312v–313r)

On 10 June 1520, Henry commissioned Knight, Husee, More and Hewester to treat with the delegates of the German Hansa on mercantile matters (Rogers, 94). After the Hansa merchants had been kept waiting for six weeks, the English delegates arrived at Bruges on 19 July. Negotiations dragged on for three weeks, and an adjournment was eventually agreed to just before the English departed on 12 August.

The pages exhibited are from the manuscript record kept by Jodocus Wilpurg von Erbach, one of the five orators of the Hanseatic town of Cologne. They witness More's role as a leading spokesman for the English side and illustrate his diplomacy, practised with 'soft words and impassive expression, in the English manner' – a reference to the final stage of the dispute, when More tells the Hansa that their credentials are insufficient, and an adjournment is desirable.

70
Henry VIII (1491–1547; reigned 1509–47)
(Colour plate III, page 72)
Hans Holbein the Younger, 1536
Oil and tempera on panel, 27.5 × 19.5 ($10\frac{3}{4} \times 7\frac{3}{4}$), probably reduced

Provenance Robert, Earl of Sunderland, by descent to Earls Spencer, until 1933–4.
Exhibitions National Gallery, London, 1957; ibid. *From Van Eyck to Tiepolo: An Exhibition of Pictures from the Thyssen-Bornemisza Collection*, 1961 (65); *Erasmus*, 1969 (157).
Bibliography Ganz, *Paintings*, no. 92, pl 135; R. Strong, *Holbein and Henry VIII*, 1967, 37; Strong, *Catalogue*, 157–8, pls 303–4.

Thyssen-Bornemisza Collection, Lugano (197)

This superb half-length is generally accepted as the only surviving representation of Henry VIII from Holbein's own hand, with the exception of the NPG cartoon (no. 71). In each, the king is shown threequarter face, bonneted, bearded and with hair cut close (no. 202), a chain round his neck, and his shirt having a high, stand-up collar (Strong, Type IV). The panel is our first record of Henry in his opulent majesty. It may be identical with one leaf of the diptych of Henry and Jane Seymour mentioned in the royal inventories of 1542 and 1547.

71
Henry VIII, with Henry VII
Hans Holbein the Younger, 1536–7
Black ink and water-colour washes on paper, mounted on canvas, 257.8 × 137.1 ($101\frac{1}{2} \times 54$)

Provenance Presumably as for Windsor Holbein drawings (nos. 9, 176–9, 182–4, 279); Lumley Inventory 1590; Lumley's widow 1609; Richard Lumley 1617; Earls of Scarborough; 2nd Duke of Devonshire by 1727; NPG 1957.
Exhibitions NPE, 1866 (134); Royal Academy, *Old Masters*, 1879 (231); BFAC, *Early English Portraiture*, 1909 (40).
Bibliography R. Strong, *Holbein and Henry VIII*, 1967; Strong, *Catalogue*, 153–4, 157–8, pls 305–6.

National Portrait Gallery, London (4027)

This is part of Holbein's original cartoon for the great wall-painting in the Privy Chamber of Whitehall Palace, finished in 1536–7 during his second stay in England. The wall-painting was destroyed by fire in 1698 and is now known in its entirety from two mid seventeenth-century small-scale copies by Remigius van Leemput (no. 72). The wall-painting was a commemoration of the Tudor dynasty and shows Henry VII and Henry VIII with their queens, Elizabeth of York (nos. 5, 19) and Jane Seymour, at their sides. It was commissioned shortly after Wolsey's palace, York Place, had been converted into Whitehall Palace at Henry's command. It was to dominate the room from above the royal chair and canopy of estate placed on the floor below and immediately in front of it. The painted architectural background was likewise intended to continue the architecture of the chamber itself and reinforce an impression of royalty in its proper abode.

Henry's regal image is related to that in the Thyssen-Bornemisza portrait (no. 70). The full-length figure of Henry VIII, legs astride, elbows out, chin jutting, commands both the foreground and the more gracefully posed figure of his father behind him, as well as the submissive queens on the other side of the altar. In the wall-painting as it was executed, the image of Henry VIII was still more dominant, turned full-face to stare down the spectator, the figure of monarchy triumphant, embodiment of the new myth of kingship.

Holbein's technique in this cartoon, as elsewhere, was to lay cut-out figures down on a background sheet. The head of Henry VIII is a separate cut-out from the body.

71

72
Henry VII, Elizabeth of York, Henry VIII and Jane Seymour
Remigius van Leemput, after Hans Holbein the Younger, 1667
Oil on canvas, 88.9 × 98.7 (35 × $38\frac{7}{8}$)

Provenance Copied for Charles II, apparently for £150, and at Whitehall Palace in reign of James II; thereafter at Kensington Palace.
Exhibitions RA, *Holbein*, 1950–1 (204); *Erasmus*, 1969 (159).
Bibliography Millar, no. 216; Strong, *Catalogue*, pl 306.

Her Majesty the Queen (Hampton Court 308)

Van Leemput's copy of the Whitehall fresco (no. 71) records the inscriptions:

SI IVVAT HEROVM CLARAS VIDISSE FIGVRAS,
  SPECTA HAS, MAIORES NVLLA TABELLA TVLIT.
CERTAMEN MAGNVM, LIS, QVAESTIO MAGNA PATERNE,
  FILIVS AN VINCAT.VICIT.VTERQVE QVIDEM.
ISTE SVOS HOSTES, PATRIAEQVE INCENDIA SAEPE
  SVSTVLIT, ET PACEM CIVIBVS VSQVE DEDIT.

FILIVS AD MAIORA QVIDEM PROGNATVS AB ARIS
  SVBMOVET INDIGNOS SUBSTITVITQVE PROBOS.
CERTAE VIRTVTI, PAPARVM AVDACIA CESSIT,
  HENRICO OCTAVO SCEPTRA GERENTE MANV
REDDITA RELIGIO EST, ISTO REGNANTE DEIQVE
  DOGMATA CEPERVNT ESSE IN HONORE SVO.

(If it pleases you to see the images of great heroes, look on these: no picture figures greater. Controversy and contention dispute whether father or son be supreme. Each was victorious indeed. The father many times endured the assaults of his enemies and the conflagration of his country, and brought peace everywhere to its citizens.
  The son, born to greater things, removed the unworthy from their altars and replaced them by upright men. The arrogance of the Popes put an end to proven virtue, but while Henry VIII held the sceptre true religion was restored and during his reign the decrees of God began to be honoured.)

The inscription on the lower half of the central plinth reads:
PROTOTYPVM IVSTAE MAGNITVDINIS IPSO OPERE TECTORIO/
FECIT HOLBENIVS IVBENTE HENRICO VIII./ ECTYPVM A REMIGIO
VAN LEEMPVT BREVIORI TABELLA/DESCRIBI VOLVIT CAROLVS II.
M.B.F.E.H.R./A°. DNI. MDCLXVII. (Holbein made the original, life size, in fresco, at the command of Henry VIII. Charles II willed that a copy be made on a reduced scale by Remigius van Leemput. In the year of Our Lord 1667.)

73
Henry VIII
Hans Schwarz, ?1524
Lead medal, diameter 6 ($2\frac{3}{8}$)

Bibliography Habich, I, i, p 44, no. 269, pl XXXV, 2; *Medallic Illustrations*, I, 1885, p 30, no. 14 and 1904, pl II, 4; A. Suhle, *Die deutsche Renaissance-Medaille*, Leipzig 1950, 13–28; Hill-Pollard, 110.

The Trustees of the British Museum (Med. Ill. I, 2, 4)

This uniface medal of Henry VIII shows the king bearded and bonneted. It is not certain when or where it was made.

There is a drawing for the portrait among those attributed to Schwarz in the Staatsbibliothek in Bamberg, with the inscription 'Wolffgang Rogendort'. The inscription round the medal's edge runs HENRICVS. VIII. DG. REX. ANGLI.[ae] FRANC.[iae] DOM.[inus] H.[iberniae]. There is no reverse on this example.

74
Design for a Fireplace for Henry VIII
Hans Holbein the Younger, 1540
Pen, with washes of grey, red and blue, on paper, 54 × 42.7 ($21\frac{1}{4}$ × $16\frac{3}{4}$)

Provenance Earl of Arundel (Inventory of 1655, no. 163); Jonathan Richardson, Snr; Thomas Hudson; sale 25 March 1779 (59); bt. Horace Walpole; Strawberry Hill Sale 17 May 1842 (64); bt. British Museum 1854.
Bibliography L. Binyon, *Catalogue of Drawings by British Artists... in the ...British Museum*, II, 1900, no. 16; Ganz, *Handzeichnungen*, 123; Schmid, *Holbein*, 343, 400, 401, 408, 409–10, 412, 419–20, 425; pl 141; Suppl., 38–9; *BM British Catalogue*, p 570, no. 188.

The Trustees of the British Museum (1854–7–8–1)

This superb example of the elaborate drafts for interior decoration produced by Holbein for Henry VIII was probably made for Bridewell Palace.
  The richly ornamented design is in two storeys, each bounded by two pairs of embellished columns, Doric below and Ionic above. The upper storey is divided into three compartments by herms and consists of two registers. In the three divisions of the upper register are, from left to right: Henry's initial H, with a fleur-de-lis badge below it; the royal arms, supported by lion and dragon, with the motto DEV ET MON DROIT; Henry's initials HR, with the portcullis badge below. Portcullis and fleur-de-lis are repeated on the

lintel. The lower register of the upper storey has, again from left to right: the figure of Charity, a combat of mounted men, and the figure of Justice. There are Tudor roses and Henry's initial supported by dragons, between the storeys. The lower storey has an open hearth with logs burning on firedogs at its centre; above this, in a semicircular lunette, is another combat of mounted men, with a central medallion of Esther and Ahasuerus. In the spandrels are smaller roundels with the heads of a lady and of a helmeted warrior. At the bases of the pairs of Doric pillars are blank tablets, for inscriptions.

The fireplace drawing is very possibly that mentioned by Henry Peacham in his *Compleat Gentleman*, 1622 (edn. Oxford 1906, 128).

75
Leo X (1475–1521; Pope 1513–21)
Giulio Romano, *c*.1515
Black chalk on grey paper, 48×29.3 ($18\frac{7}{8} \times 11\frac{1}{2}$)

Exhibitions Smithsonian Institution, Washington DC, *Old Master Drawings from the Devonshire Collection*, 1962–3 (69); *Erasmus*, 1969 (245); *500 Jaar Universiteit Leuven*, 1976 (58).
Bibliography F. Hartt, *Giulio Romano*, New Haven 1958, I, 51, 289, no. 39.

The Devonshire Collection, Chatsworth: The Trustees of the Chatsworth Settlement (38)

Giovanni de' Medici, second son of Lorenzo il Magnifico, was created cardinal in 1489 and elected pope in 1513, in succession to Julius II (no. 59). Like Julius he was a great patron of art and letters. During his pontificate it seemed that a new age favourable to humanism had dawned: Erasmus dedicated his *Novum Instrumentum* (no. 39) to Leo. The pope was soon in serious financial trouble and the sale of indulgences (no. 125) increased in consequence. In 1520, Leo excommunicated Luther, and in 1521, after receiving the *Assertio septem Sacramentorum* of Henry VIII (no. 117), conferred on Henry the title of Defender of the Faith.

This portrait drawing, labelled *Ritratto di Leone X°* in a later hand, is sometimes attributed to Sebastiano del Piombo.

76
Hadrian VI (1459–1523; Pope 1522–3)
Unknown Netherlandish medallist, *c*.1522
Lead medal, diameter 8.3 ($3\frac{1}{4}$)

Exhibitions Utrecht, *Paus Adrianus VI*, 1959 (94); *Erasmus*, 1969 (250–1).
Bibliography Hill-Pollard, 629.

The Trustees of the British Museum (485/34)

Hadrian VI, the teacher of Erasmus and of Charles V, was pope for a brief period between the pontificates of Leo X (no. 75) and Clement VII (nos. 200, 201). Wolsey had been a rival for election. Hadrian was renowned for his modesty, and instituted reforms in the Curia. Thomas More praises his *Quaestiones quodlibetales* in his letter to Dorp (nos. 100, 101).

Hadrian is shown in cope and tiara, between two shields bearing the papal arms and the arms of the city of Utrecht. The inscription reads: M[eester] ADRIAEN VAN GOD GHEKOREN PAVS VA[N] ROMEN TV TRECHT GEBOREN (Master Hadrian, born in Utrecht and chosen by God Pope of Rome).

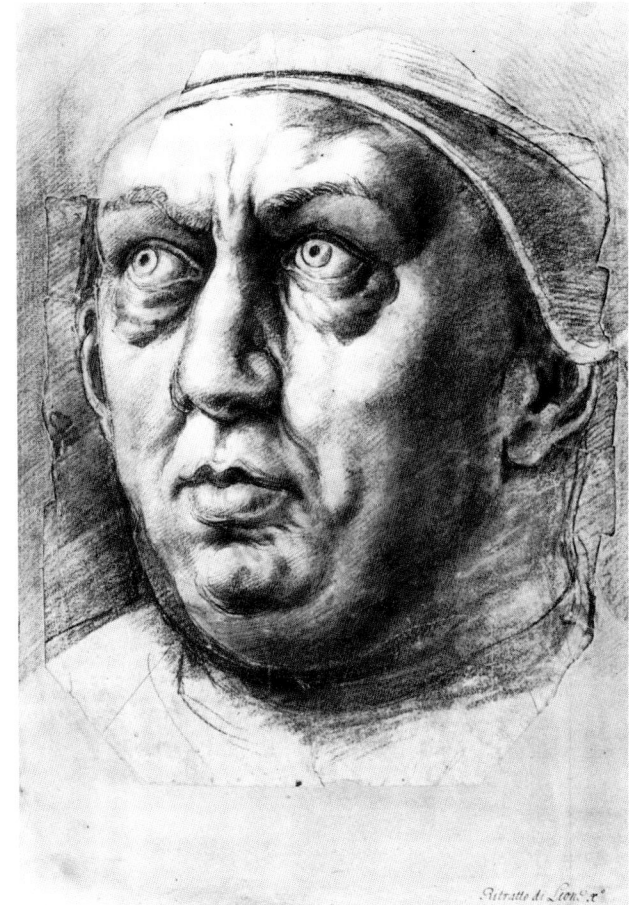

75

76

Books from Sir Thomas More's Library

Basel has Erasmus's library, Sélestat the books of Beatus Rhenanus, Corpus Christi College in Oxford the manuscripts of Grocyn (nos. 90, 91, 92), Cambridge a substantial gift of books from Tunstall (no. 56). Thomas More's books are nowhere preserved in quantity.

We know that More was a great lover of books and literature. Both his scholarly preoccupations and his humanist contacts must have contributed greatly to his library and when the demands of family and possessions made even his spacious Chelsea home too small, 'The New Building' erected in the garden included a gallery, a library and a chapel.

When, on 13 April 1534, More 'pulled the wicket after him' (Roper), he also left his books behind. Only a handful accompanied him to the Tower. One of them, the Yale *Hours* (no. 226), is exhibited here. On 12 June, they too were 'trussed up in a pack' (no. 212). By the Act of Attainder (no. 239) More suffered loss of all his goods: they were forfeit to the Crown.

The library was the world of the humanist; in destroying it More's enemies hoped to shatter the very centre of his existence. If they failed in that aim, they were successful in almost extinguishing More's library. Of his books, his manuscripts, his correspondence, next to nothing has survived. Of the six extant books known, or believed, to have been his, five are reunited for the first time in this exhibition.

77
Latin Grammatical Pieces
A Latin commonplace book
Vellum, chiefly second half of 14th century

Bibliography CMA, 1697, 135 (with full list of contents); SC, 2562.

Bodleian Library, Oxford (MS Bodl. 837)

This medley of classical authors, liturgical and legal texts, vocabulary, grammar and literature, suggests that it was a student's book for *grammatica*, the first and basic art of the *trivium*. The manuscript includes *Stans puer ad mensam*, Alexander of Hales's *Dictionarium difficilium vocabulorum* and his *Exoticon*, a Latin-English glossary beginning with the parts of the human body, a list of Latin proverbs in hexameters, etc. Thomas Baker, a fifteenth-century owner, was perhaps the Magdalen College chorister who was admitted in 1491 and died in 1493–4 (Emden, *Oxford*, 94). On folios 3r, 5r, 188v bis, we find the owner's mark 'Thomas Mor[e]' and 'T.M.'. Certain palaeographical similarities suggest that these signatures are the earliest extant examples of More's autograph.

78
Euclid, 'Elements', edited by Simon Grynaeus
Basel, Johann Herwagen, 1533

Provenance Presented to More by the editor, Symon Grynaeus, according to title-page inscription; presented to Thomas Clement by More; Emmanuel College, Cambridge; George Rennie; Ingram Bywater, Regius Professor of Greek at Oxford 1893–1908, who bequeathed it to the Bodleian Library.
Bibliography Adams, E980.

Bodleian Library, Oxford (Byw. C.3.3)

The copy of the Greek text of Euclid edited by Simon Grynaeus (1494/5–1541; no. 180) was presented to More ('clarissimo heroi ... patrono') by Grynaeus in continuing gratitude for the extraordinary favour shown by the chancellor to the Protestant scholar during his visit to England in 1531. The Thomas Clement to whom More gave it was a younger son of John Clement (no. 51), More's pupil-servant, to whom Grynaeus dedicated his edition of Proclus *De motu* (1531). John Clement married Margaret Gigs, More's foster-daughter (no. 184), in 1526. The gift must have been made to Thomas when he was no more than a baby. Like his father John, Thomas Clement grew to be a fine Greek scholar. He died at Louvain in 1595.

79
St Anselm of Canterbury, 'Opera et Epistolae'
Manuscript on vellum, first half of 12th century

Provenance John Theyer (1597–1673), who describes it as having belonged to Lord Chancellor Thomas More; Theyer's collection of 336 MSS (in 1678 in the hands of Robert Scott) acquired by Frederick Thynne for the Royal Library at St James's, 1678 sale (125), valued at £1.
Bibliography CMA, II, 6519, 149 (among MSS of Charles Theyer); Sir G. F. Warner and J. P. Gilson, *Catalogue of Western MSS in the Old Royal and King's Collections*, 1921, I, 122–3; *S. Anselmi Opera*, PL, CLIX, 587, 702; ed. F. S. Schmitt, Edinburgh 1946–61.

The British Library Board (MS Royal 5.F.IX, ff.57–196)

Theyer's description of the volume as More's applies only to its last four components, ie *De Concordia prescientie et predestinationis et gratie Dei cum libero arbitrio*, *De processione Spiritus Sancti*, *De fide Trinitatis et de incarnatione Verbi*, and excerpts from letters. If we accept it, the volume is testimony to More's interest in systematic theological studies. The *Concordia* deals with the problem of reconciling God's predestination with men's free will, a subject which More was to take up again, when he wrote his *Confutation of Tyndale's Answer* (no. 148).

St Anselm may well have contributed to More's view of the use of human reason for the critical scrutiny of questions of faith, as well as the use of dialogue in the field of apology and

Colour plate II *Peter Gillis* by Quentin Massys (no. 54)

controversy. The *Confutation* refers repeatedly to Anselm.

St Anselm was born at Aosta *c*.1033/4, and died, probably at Canterbury, in 1109. He was a monk of Bec (Normandy), and later abbot (1078), and succeeded Lanfranc as Archbishop of Canterbury in 1093. He was canonised in 1163.

80
Chronicles and Prophecies
Manuscript on vellum, 14th century

Bibliography H. J. Todd, *Catalogue of the Archiepiscopal MSS at Lambeth Palace*, 1812, 67; M. R. James and Claude Jenkins, *Descriptive Catalogue of the MSS in the Library of Lambeth Palace*, Cambridge 1932, 725–7.

His Grace the Lord Archbishop of Canterbury and the Trustees of Lambeth Palace Library (MS 527)

This collection of chronicles and prophecies concerning England seems to have been put together and written out in the fourteenth century. The opening chronicle goes as far as the reign of Edward I. It belongs to the group of manuscripts at Lambeth which includes codices collected by two successive Archbishops, Richard Bancroft (1604–10) and George Abbot (1611–33). On the last page (f. 68v) is the inscription 'Ex dono amicissimi mei Thomas More generosi et honestissimi viri Daniel Gray (?)'. This may refer to Thomas More II (nos. 1, 170, 272).

81
Photograph: **Thomas More's Merry Jest**
A mery gest how a sergeaunt wolde lerne to be a frere, London, Julian Notary, [1516]

Bibliography STC2, 18091; Gibson, 69.

Photograph by courtesy of Henry E. Huntington Library and Art Gallery, San Marino, California

This is the first of 'these fowre thinges... Mayster Thomas More wrote in his youth for his pastime', as Rastell introduces them in his 'great volume'. A. W. Reed suggested that these verses might have been composed for the Serjeants' Feast of 13 November 1503, John More being newly elected one of the serjeants-at-law.

Upon the death of a thrifty man a young good-for-nothing inherits a small fortune – which he spends easily enough, borrows more and seeks refuge with friends. Eventually, a serjeant is sent to arrest him. In order to get access he disguises himself as an Augustinian friar visiting the sick. He is overpowered by the women of the house and contemptuously thrown down the stairs. The moral: the cobbler should stick to his last. T. E. Bridgett did not find 'much merriment in this piece', and Chambers calls it 'a boisterous piece of knockabout fun'.

82
Thomas More's Verses for the Book of Fortune
The Boke of the fayre Gentylwoman, that no man shulde put his truste, or confydence in..., London, Robert Wyer, [*c*.1540]

Bibliography STC2 18078.5; Gibson, 47; H. R. Plomer, *Robert Wyer*, 1897, no. 19; H. Schulte Herbrüggen, 'Sir Thomas More's Fortuna-Verse', *Lebende Antike. Symposion für Rudolf Sühnel*, Berlin 1967, 155–72.

His Grace the Lord Archbishop of Canterbury and the Trustees of Lambeth Palace Library

More's verses to the *Boke of Lady Fortune* exist in two printed versions of which the present is the earlier, the other being Rastell's incomplete text in *EW*. The small octavo format is characteristic of Robert Wyer's (fl. 1527–56) production. Since it carries the 'Suffolk colophon' it must be later than February 1536. There is also a manuscript version of the verses, as they appear in Rastell's edition, in Richard Hill's *Boke of dyveris tales and balettes and dyveris Reconynges*, a commonplace book (MS Balliol College, Oxford, 354; ed. Roman Dyboski, *EETS*, ES, 101, 1908).

More's verses were apparently written about 1503. According to Rastell, More intended them as a preface 'to be printed in the begynning of that boke' [of Fortune]. This was perhaps the highly popular fortune-telling book, the *Libro delle sorti* by Lorenzo Spirito (Gualtieri) of Perugia. More than fifty different editions are extant in Western European languages.

83
Thomas More's and Erasmus's translations of Lucian
Luciani viri quam disertissimi complura opuscula longe festiuissima ab Erasmo Roterodamo et Thoma Moro interpretibus optimis in latinarum linguam traducta..., [Paris], Jodocus Badius Ascensius, 1506

Bibliography Gibson, 78; Adams, L1621; Craig R. Thompson, ed., *CW*, III, 1, 1974, esp. lv–lvii.

Cambridge University Library

Ever since their meeting during Erasmus's first visit to England (1498–9) Erasmus and More had been close friends. When Erasmus returned to Britain in 1506, he was More's guest in his new house, The Old Barge, in Bucklersbury. There they decided to share in the Latin translation of the *Dialogues* of Lucian of Samosata (fl. A.D. *c*.120–95), brilliant, witty satires. It is characteristic of More, the young lawyer, that he chose them for his rhetorical exercises in translation. He selected for himself *Cynicus*, *Menippus* or *Necromantia*, *Philopseudes* and *Tyrannicida*, to the last of which both scholars wrote a *declamatio* in reply. They were first published in this slim volume, with a dedicatory letter (Rogers, 5) from More to Thomas Ruthall. Erasmus dedicated his translations to Richard Whitford, with a letter in which he also praises More as 'the sweetest of all my friends'.

84
Thomas More's and Erasmus's translations of Lucian
Luciani Erasmo interprete dialogi & alia emuncta...Quaedam etiam a T. Moro latina factae, Paris, Jodocus Badius Ascensius, 1514

Bibliography Gibson, 79; Adams, L1622.

Universitätsbibliothek Basel

This is the second printed edition of More's and Erasmus's translations from Lucian. These two were followed, in rapid succession, by at least fourteen other editions in the sixteenth century (eight during More's lifetime), printed in Italy, Switzerland, the Low Countries, France and Germany, signalling the immense popularity they enjoyed. In England there appeared only one in 1530, prepared by John Rastell, in which he prints More's Latin version of the *Menippus* and an English translation side by side (Gibson, 395; *STC2*, 16895). This copy was once the property of Erasmus.

85
Erasmus's 'Praise of Folly'
Moriae encomium. Erasmi Roterodami declamatio, Paris, Gilles de Gourmont, 1511

Bibliography Bibliotheca Belgica, 838; Allen, 222.

The British Library Board (C.57.i.46)

Erasmus's most famous work was conceived as he journeyed over the Alps from Italy in 1509, and written in Thomas More's house, The Old Barge, in Bucklersbury, while Erasmus, laid low by an attack of kidney stone, waited for his books to arrive. He did not publish the *Folly* until 1511; it was issued by the same printer who later published the second edition of More's *Utopia* in 1517. Fifty editions appeared in Erasmus's lifetime.

In a prefatory letter, Erasmus dedicated the work to More in token of the pleasure he had derived from friendship with such a man. The pun on More's name and the Greek word for folly, *moria*, had given him the idea for the book. Though More is himself remote from folly, he enjoys witty frolics of this kind, for he is a sort of laughing philosopher, a man for all seasons (no. 266).

86
Facsimile: **Erasmus's 'Praise of Folly'**, with marginal drawings by Hans Holbein the Younger and others
Erasmi Roterodami Morias encomion, i.e. Stultitiae laus..., Basel, Johann Froben, 1515

Bibliography Erasmi Roterodami Encomium Moriae i.e. Stultitiae Laus: Lob der Torheit: Basler Ausgabe von 1515, mit den Randzeichnungen von Hans Holbein d.J. ..., hrsg. Heinrich Alfred Schmid, Basel 1931; Allen, 861; F. Saxl, 'Holbein's Illustrations for the *Praise of Folly* by Erasmus', *Burlington Magazine*, LXXXIII, 1943, 275–9.

At about the turn of the year 1515–16, Hans Holbein the Younger (1497/8–1543) and others decorated the margins of a copy of the *Praise of Folly*, with the commentary of Gerardus Listrius, in the edition published by Froben in Basel, 1515, with drawings illustrating the text. According to one of many manuscript notes by the book's owner, Oswald Myconius (Geisshüsler, 1488–1552) of Lucerne, the drawings were made in ten days, to divert Erasmus; Myconius also tells a story of Erasmus's comment on his own portrait in one of the drawings. Myconius was a follower of Zwingli (no. 137) in Zürich and moved to Basel after the death of Oecolampadius (nos. 138, 139) in 1531. From Oswald Myconius the book seems to have passed to Jakob Myconius, a physician of Mulhouse, and later to a certain Daniel Wieland, before becoming the property, by 1586, of Basilius Amerbach, and passing in 1662, with the sale of the Amerbach Collection, to the City of Basel, in whose possession it remains.

87
Desiderius Erasmus (?1469–1536)
Quentin Massys, ?1519
Lead medal, diameter 10.5 (4⅛)

Exhibitions Bibliothèque royale, Brussels, *Médailleurs et numismates de la Renaissance dans les Pays-Bas*, 1959 (19, 20); *Erasmus*, 1969 (269–71).
Bibliography Habich, 47a; Hill-Pollard, 629a; A. Gerlo, *Erasme et ses portraitistes*, 2nd edn. Nieuwkoop 1969, 18–27; E. Wind, 'Aenigma Termini', *JWI*, I, 1937–8, 66–9; E. Panofsky, 'Erasmus and the visual Arts', *JWCI*, XXXII, 1969, 214–19; Rogers, 47.

Victoria and Albert Museum, London (4613-1858)

It is not known exactly when Massys (1465/6–1530) made this medallic portrait of Erasmus, but it was probably after he had made his painted portrait (no. 53). The head of Erasmus on the obverse is labelled ER. RO., and round the edge run inscriptions in Greek: TĒN KREITTŌ TA SYGGRAMMATA DEIXEI (His writings give a better picture), and in Latin: IMAGO AD VIVAM EFFIGIEM EXPRESSA (His portrait taken from the life). The Greek is precisely the same as, the Latin an abbreviated version of, the captions of Dürer's engraving of 1526 (no. 88). On the reverse of a few examples of the medal is the image of the god Terminus, the personal device of

87

Erasmus from 1509 until his death. It is carved on his tombstone in Basel Cathedral. The motto CONCEDO NVLLI (I yield to none) refers to the ancient legend that Terminus was the only god who refused to give up his home on the Capitol at Rome to make way for Jupiter. Legends are added round the rim, again in Greek: HORA TELOS MAKROU BIOU (Look to your end, however long your life) and in Latin: MORS VLTIMA LINEA RERVM (Death is the final boundary of things) – Horace, *Epp.*, I, 16, 79.

88
Desiderius Erasmus
Albrecht Dürer, 1526
Engraving, 24.9×19.3 ($9\frac{15}{16} \times 7\frac{5}{8}$)

Bibliography Hollstein, 105; Panofsky, 214; A. Gerlo, op. cit. (no. 87) 9–28; E. Panofsky, 'Erasmus and the visual Arts', *JWCI*, XXXII, 1969, 220–7.

The Trustees of the British Museum (C.37 vol 4)

The Greek on this portrait is the same as the Greek on the medal by Massys (no. 87); the Latin is to the same effect, but longer by the names of artist and sitter. Dürer made two drawings of Erasmus in 1520 during his stay in the Low Countries. Only the second survives, in the Louvre. Erasmus hoped that Dürer might work his drawing up into a painting or engraving, but was disappointed in the likeness achieved when Dürer finally did so in 1526.

Like the panel portraits by Massys (no. 53), which Dürer probably saw, and Holbein (in the Louvre), Dürer's engraving shows Erasmus pen in hand, surrounded by his books. It may be that Massys's medal and this engraving were sent to More as more up-to-date likenesses than the panel, the two men not having seen each other since 1521.

88

89
Desiderius Erasmus with a Term
Hans Holbein the Younger, 1535
Woodcut, 28.4×15 ($11\frac{3}{16} \times 6$)

Bibliography Hans Koegler, 'Hans Holbein d.J. Holzschnitt-Bildnisse von Erasmus und Luther', *Jahresbericht der Öffentlichen Kunstsammlungen in Basel*, N.F. XVII, 1920, 35–47; Gerlo, op. cit. (no. 87) 45–67.

The Trustees of the British Museum (1864-7-14-79)

Erasmus is shown in old age, a year from death, his right hand resting on the head of his personal emblem, Terminus (no. 87), within an architectural framework, which gives the composition the title 'Erasmus Roterodamus in ein ghüs' (Erasmus of Rotterdam in a setting) by which it is described in Basilius Amerbach's catalogue of his print collection about 1580. The inscriptions run: ER. ROT.; TERMINVS; *Pallas Apellaeam nuper mirata tabellam,/Hanc ait, aeternum Bibliotheca colat./Daedaleam monstrat Musis* HOLBEINNIVS *artem,/Et summi ingenii Magnus Erasmus opes* (Pallas, marvelling at this picture to rival Apelles, says that a library must preserve it forever. Holbein shows his Daedalian art to the Muses, and the great Erasmus the power of his supreme intellect). Later states of the woodcut bear the distich: *Corporis effigiem si quis non uidit Erasmi,/Hanc scite ad uiuum picta tabella dabit* (If you never saw Erasmus in the flesh, know that the painted picture will give him to the life).

90
The Books of William Grocyn
Lists of William Grocyn's books by Thomas Linacre, Thomas Lupset and another
Manuscript on paper, 1519–20

Bibliography Emden, *Oxford*, 428–30, 827–30, 1147–9; Montagu Burrows, 'Linacre's Catalogue of Grocyn's Books, followed by a Memoir of Grocyn', *Collectanea*, Oxford Historical Society, 2nd series, XVI, 1890, 317–80; P. S. Allen and H. W. Garrod, *Merton Muniments*, Oxford Historical Society, 1928, 47.

The Warden and Fellows of Merton College, Oxford (Records, 1046, 4252c, i–iv)

William Grocyn (*c*.1446–1519) was educated at Winchester College and at New College, Oxford, becoming Reader in Divinity at Magdalen College in 1483. He studied in Italy 1488–91 and returned to become Oxford's chief instructor in Greek. It is possible that Thomas More began to learn Greek from him in Oxford but more likely that he was Grocyn's pupil later, in London, about 1500. Grocyn came to London to be rector of St Lawrence Jewry, where More was to lecture on St Augustine (no. 20), in 1496. In a letter of 1504, More calls Grocyn one of the guides of his life (no. 11). Grocyn died at Maidstone in 1519.

Grocyn owned a considerable library, which was listed for transport to Oxford, and dispersal by gift, soon after his death, by Thomas Linacre (nos. 91, 93–6) and Thomas Lupset (nos. 191, 192). Linacre was the executor of Grocyn's will.

91
William Grocyn's Manuscript of Theophylact
Enarrationes in quattuor Evangelistas
Manuscript on vellum, late 12th century

Provenance William Grocyn (?1446–1519); before 1519 to Thomas Linacre (c.1460–1524); ? at whose death to John Claymond (?1468–1537); bequeathed by him to Corpus Christi College, Oxford.
Bibliography H. O. Coxe, *Catalogus codd. MSS qui in collegiis aulisque Oxoniensibus hodie adservantur*, II, Oxford 1852, 8–9; G. Barber, in *Essays on the Life and Work of Thomas Linacre*, ed. F. Maddison, M. Pelling and C. Webster, Oxford 1977, 335.

The President and Fellows of Corpus Christi College, Oxford (MS 30; F.3.7)

According to its inscriptions, this volume was bought by Linacre from Grocyn at the price Grocyn had paid (f.4); another manuscript note (f.5) asks the reader to pray for the soul of John Claymond (no. 93) first President of Corpus Christi College, who has given the manuscript to its library. At the front of the volume have been bound some leaves in Greek uncial script, probably of the ninth century, and two evangelist portraits, perhaps of the thirteenth.

Theophylact was a Byzantine exegete who became archbishop among the Bulgarians about 1078, and wrote commentaries on almost the whole New Testament as well as on some of the Old. He was something of a favourite among the humanists. Erasmus, to his later embarrassment, for some time believed him to be an author named Vulgarius.

92
William Grocyn's Manuscript of Chrysostom
In S. Matthiae Evangelium homiliae XC
Manuscript on vellum, 1499

Provenance Probably written for William Grocyn; John Claymond, by whom bequeathed to Corpus Christi College, Oxford.
Bibliography Coxe, op. cit. (no. 91) 5–6; R. Weiss, *Humanism in England during the Fifteenth Century*, 3rd edn. Oxford 1967, 147–8, 173–4.

The President and Fellows of Corpus Christi College, Oxford (MS 23)

The sermons on St Matthew's Gospel by St John Chrysostom (c.347–407), Bishop of Constantinople, were among the most popular of all sacred writings in Greek during the Reformation.

This manuscript is one of a pair containing all ninety homilies, written at Reading by the Greek scribe John Serbopoulos of Constantinople, perhaps for Grocyn, in 1499–1500. Serbopoulos was in England by 1484 and may have lived in Oxford before moving to St Mary's Abbey in Reading in 1489. His presence, and that of other scribes, illustrates the growing taste for Greek studies in England at the end of the fifteenth century. The manuscript bears Grocyn's name and the injunction to pray for the soul of the donor, John Claymond.

93
Letter from Thomas Linacre to John Claymond
Manuscript on paper, ?1516

Bibliography R. Weiss, 'Notes on Thomas Linacre', *Miscellanea Giovanni Mercati*, Vatican City 1957, IV, 373–80; C. B. Schmitt in *Essays on the Life and Work of Thomas Linacre*, ed. F. Maddison, M. Pelling and C. Webster, Oxford 1977, 71, n.1.

The President and Fellows of Corpus Christi College, Oxford (MS 318, f.135)

John Claymond (c.1468–1537) was educated at Magdalen College, where he was President 1504–17 before becoming first President of his friend Richard Fox's (no. 32) new foundation of Corpus Christi College – an appointment of which Erasmus approved.

Linacre here reports, in an elegant italic script, on a joint pupil whom he is sending back to Claymond not much more learned though more fit to be taught. He exhorts Claymond to continued efforts, especially in Greek studies, reinforcing this with a precept from Plutarch, in Greek.

94
Aristotle's 'Meteorologica'
Venice, Aldus Manutius, 1497

Bibliography Emden, *Oxford*, 1147–9; R. Weiss, *Humanism in England during the Fifteenth Century*, 3rd edn. Oxford 1967, 153–9; *Essays on the Life and Work of Thomas Linacre*, ed. F. Maddison, M. Pelling and C. Webster, Oxford 1977.

The Warden and Fellows of All Souls College, Oxford

In his prefatory letter to this second volume of the *editio princeps* of the Greek text of Aristotle (Venice, 1495–8), the scholar-printer Aldus Manutius singles out Thomas Linacre for praise. Linacre seems to have been a member of the so-called Aldine Academy by 1498.

Born about 1460, Linacre was at Oxford by 1481 and Fellow of All Souls in 1484. In Italy from 1487, he studied Greek for two years in Florence. In 1496 he graduated in medicine at Padua, and by August 1499 was back in London. He got to know Erasmus and was entrusted with the education of the young Prince Arthur.

Thomas More had studied Galen with Linacre and with Grocyn at the turn of the century, according to Erasmus. He also heard Linacre lecture on Aristotle's *Meteorologica*, a work he greatly admired, as he tells Martin Dorp in his letter to him (nos. 100, 101).

95
Galen's 'De temperamentis'
Edited and translated by Thomas Linacre, Cambridge, John Siberch, 1521
Vellum, blind-stamped leather binding

Provenance ? Presented to Henry VIII and by him to Cuthbert Tunstall (1474–1559).
Bibliography Emden, *Oxford*, 1147–9; STC, 11536; McKerrow-Ferguson, 10; Richard J. Durling, 'A chronological Census of Renaissance Editions of Galen', *JWCI*, XXIV, 1961, 230–305; O. Treptow, *John Siberch: Johann Lair von Siegburg*, Cambridge 1970, 55; G. Barber, 'Thomas Linacre: a bibliographical Survey of his Works', *Essays on the Life and Work of Thomas Linacre*, ed. F. Maddison, M. Pelling and C. Webster, Oxford 1977, 299–300.

Bodleian Library, Oxford (Arch. A. e. 71)

The Greek physician Galen of Pergamon (d. A.D. 199–200) was still the greatest medical authority of the Renaissance. Linacre, who edited and translated several of his works into Latin, was England's most famous physician in his day as well as one of her best Greek scholars. He was appointed physician to Henry VIII in 1509 and became first President of the Royal College of Physicians in 1523.

John Siberch, the printer of this book, worked in Cambridge and was the first to use Greek type in England. Linacre dedicated the work to Pope Leo X (no. 75), recalling that they had shared Greek lessons in Florence. The binding of this copy bears the same panel stamps as some of the eleven surviving presentation copies of Henry VIII's *Assertio septem Sacramentorum*, 1521 (no. 117). Henry may have presented it to Cuthbert Tunstall (no. 55).

Thomas More told Martin Dorp (nos. 100, 101) that he ranked Galen above Aristotle in medical matters. In the *Dialogue of Comfort* (nos. 221, 222), Anthony tells how a young girl brought her Greek to bear to identify in Galen a 'fitt' of fever which had baffled the doctors. Harpsfield (no. 272) applies the story to More himself, and makes Margaret Gigs (no. 184) the girl.

96
A Grammar Book by Thomas Linacre
Progymnasmata grammatices vulgaria, London, John Rastell, [*c*.1512–15]

Provenance Richard Heber (1773–1833); Thomas Grenville (1755–1846), by whom bequeathed to British Museum.
Bibliography STC2, 15365; Barber, op. cit. (no. 95) 292–5; D.F.S. Thomson, 'Linacre's Latin Grammars', in *Essays on the Life and Work of Thomas Linacre*, Oxford 1977, 24-35.

The British Library Board (G.7569)

This work is in English, despite its Latin title, and is traditionally a later form of the book asked for by John Colet as a simple Latin grammar for St Paul's School. Linacre's original work was rejected by Colet as too complicated. Linacre published two more grammar books, *Rudimenta grammatices* (1523) and *De emendata structura latini sermonis* (1524). The *Progymnasmata*, printed at a date which has not satisfactorily been fixed, have prefatory verses by Linacre himself, by Thomas More and by William Lily (no. 15).

97
Thomas More's letter to the University of Oxford, 1518
Manuscript on paper, late 16th century

Provenance Robert Doue (Dewe) of All Souls (fl.1574); Peter Thompson of Bermondsey (18th century); Thomas Rodd, bookseller(s) (Sr. 1763–1822, Jr. 1796–1849); bookplate of John Trotter Brockett (1788–1842); bt. 1862.
Bibliography SC, 28841; T. S. K. Scott-Craig, 'T. More's 1518 Letter to the University of Oxford', *Renaissance News*, I, 1948, 17–24 (with English translation); Rogers, 60; SL, 19.

Bodleian Library, Oxford (MS Top. Oxon. e. 5, pp. 292-302).

A letter of 22 April 1519 from Erasmus (Allen, 948) tells how a barbarous preacher at Oxford had publicly attacked the study of Greek. The king, whose court was then at Abingdon, heard of it from Pace and More, and gave orders to encourage such studies at the university. More, recently appointed member of the Council, wrote to 'the Most Reverend Fathers, the Vice-Chancellor, Proctors and Faculty of the University of Oxford' the present letter, which embodies humanist aspirations for education (cf nos. 100, 101).

The original letter is not extant. The exhibited copy was written in a neat humanistic hand about 1580.

98
Thomas More's letter to the University of Oxford, 1518
Epistola Thomae Mori ad Academiam Oxoniensem..., Oxford, John Lichfield, 1633

Bibliography STC2, 18087; Gibson, 59; Rogers, 60; SL, 19.

The British Library Board (1608/5936)

Extracts from this letter were given in Stapleton's *Tres Thomae* (1588; no. 273), but it was not until the more lenient days of Charles I and Henrietta Maria that the complete letter was printed for the first time.

99
Photograph: Oxford University asks Sir Thomas More to be its High Steward
From *Letter Book of the University of Oxford: Registrum FF, sive Libri Epistolarum Regnum et Magnatum ad Academiam Oxon. una cum Responsis ab A.D. 1508 ad annum 1597*
Paper, 16th century

Provenance Acquired by Bodleian Library *c*.1603–5.
Bibliography SC, 2949; Rogers, 132, 133.

Photograph by courtesy of the Bodleian Library, Oxford (MS Bodl. 282, ff. 67v–68r)

Within a month of the death of Sir Thomas Lovell, Oxford University, on 24 June 1524, wrote to More asking him to become its new High Steward. The *Registrum FF*, the official letter book of the university for 1508–97, shows on the left (no. 127) the university's invitation to More (Rogers, 132) and opposite (no. 128) a copy of More's letter (Rogers, 133), dated from London *vii calend. Augusti* (= 26 July), in which he accepts the office of 'the complete handling of your business affairs and law suits', declaring 'I promise you may expect from More, who is and will always be yours wholeheartedly, all that you would desire, either as a group from a most devoted patron and friend, or individually, from a very dear comrade or brother.' Later in the letter book are letters thanking More for his help in individual cases or in defending rights and privileges.

100
Thomas More's Letter to Martin Dorp
Thomae Mori apologia pro Moria Erasmi ad Mart. Dorpium, Bruges, 21 October [1515]
Manuscript on paper, 1515

Bibliography Catalogus Codicum Manuscriptorum Bibliothecae Regiae, part III, vol IV, 1744, 484; Rogers, 15; SL, 4; Sr M. Scholastica Cooper, 'More and the Letter to Martin Dorp', *Moreana*, VI, 1965, 37–44.

Bibliothèque Nationale, Paris: Cabinet des Manuscrits (MS lat. 8703)

Erasmus's *Moriae Encomium* appeared in 1511 (no. 85). Traditionalist theologians at Louvain smelled unorthodoxy and an implied attack on their learning. They prevailed upon their young colleague, Martin van Dorp (1485–1525) to enter into controversy about the *Moria* and about Erasmus's project for a printed Greek New Testament. Erasmus and More wrote long and detailed replies but suppressed their publication. Erasmus's is no longer extant, but More's has survived in two manuscripts (Paris and Sélestat) and a transcript (Bodleian Library), and was first printed in More's *Lucubrationes*, Basel 1563 (no. 261).

More draws a distinction between truly learned theologians and *retardataire* opponents of the humanist maxim 'ad fontes'. Taking his arguments from reason and textual scholarship, he stresses that many revisions of Holy Scripture must be made by sound scholars before a 'perfect' Latin text can be established. Superstition and her daughter ignorance, not scholarship, he tells Dorp, are the enemies of religion.

More had the rare pleasure of seeing his learned antagonist converted. In a public lecture in the *Collegium Trilingue* at Louvain he admitted his error, but was later a backslider.

101
Thomas More's Letter to Martin Dorp
Thomae Mori ... Dissertatio epistolica, de aliquot sui temporis Theologastrorum ineptiis ... ad Martinum Dorpium, Leiden, Ex Officina Elzeviriana, 1625

Bibliography Gibson, 55; see no. 100.

Guildhall Library, London (Cock Colln. 1.1)

Thomas More's *Letter to Dorp* of 1515 was not published separately until 1625.

102
Thomas More's Letter to a Monk
Epistolae aliqvot ervditorvm, nunquam antehac excusae, multis nominibus dignae quae legantur a bonis omnibus, quo magis liqueat, quanta sit insignis cuiusdam sycophantae virulentia, [Basel, Johann Froben, 1520]

Bibliography NK, 765; Gibson, 153; *LP*, III, 567; Rogers, 83; *SL*, 26; David Knowles, *Religious Orders in England*, III, Cambridge 1959, 469; Emden, *Oxford*, 132, s.v. Batmanson.

Bodleian Library, Oxford (Allen e.46)

Another of More's pamphlet-letters (nos. 100, 101, 133), also written in defence of Erasmus, is addressed to an unnamed monk, now identified as John Batmanson, later prior of the London Charterhouse. He had been employed by Edward Lee in attacking Erasmus and wrote a letter to More warning him against the dangers to his soul from his friendship with the Dutch scholar. More defends Erasmus's translation of the New Testament as a truly religious attempt at discovering the exact meaning of the Scriptures. True piety lies not in mere observance but in the practice of the Christian virtues.

103
Germanus Brixius against Thomas More
Antimorus, Lutetiae (Paris), C. Resch, ex officina P. Vidoue, 1519

Bibliography Adams, B2870; L. Bradner and C. A. Lynch, eds., *The Latin Epigrams of Thomas More*, Chicago 1953, XXIX–XXXI, 170–2, 176, 178–9, 193, 250–2; Hoyt H. Hudson, *The Epigram in the English Renaissance*, Princeton, N.J. 1942, 49–52.

Guildhall Library, London (Cock Colln. 1.4)

On 10 August 1512, the English fleet surprised a French fleet off Brest and, the English *Regent* grappling the French *Cordelière*, both were destroyed by the explosion of the *Cordelière's* magazine. Germanus Brixius wrote a Latin poem on the occasion in praise of the French, to which More retorted in a series of epigrams. Despite their author's hesitation, Erasmus allowed them to appear in More's printed *Epigrammata*, 1518 (no. 40). Brixius replied with his *Antimorus*, charging More not only with the humanist crime of errors in Latin metre and grammatical solecisms, but also with having denigrated Henry VII, earlier in his career.

Germanus Brixius (Germain de Brie), born in Auxerre, learned Greek at Padua and became Secretary to Anne de Bretagne in 1512. He died in 1538.

104
Thomas More replies to Brixius
Thomae Mori Epistola ad Germanum Brixium: qui ... Morus in libellum eius quo contumeliosis mendacijs incesserat ..., London, Richard Pynson, 1520

Bibliography Gibson, 60; *STC2*, 18088; Rogers, 86; McKerrow-Ferguson, 7.

Cambridge University Library

More's reply to Brixius's *Antimorus* of 1520 echoes his complaint to Erasmus (Allen, 1087) about Brixius's 'drunken abuse'. Erasmus implored both More not to impair his reputation by answering in kind (Allen, 1093) and Brixius not to attack so eminent a scholar. Before More received Erasmus's letter, Pynson had printed the *Epistola ad Brixium* which the author did his best to suppress, though a handful of copies had already been sold. In it he resorts to sarcasm: if his feet are not sound, nor is Brixius's head, and if his metres are barbarous, so are his opponent's manners. More later silently corrected his solecisms.

105
Photograph: Thomas More's First Royal Commission, 1509
Commission to John More, Thomas Jakes and Thomas More, to take inquisitions, in Middlesex, as to the possessions, heir, etc, of William Viscount Beaumont, deceased, Westminster, 5 July 1509

Bibliography LP, I, 266 = 2nd edn. 132 (26).

Photograph by courtesy of the Public Record Office, London (C.66/611, P.2, m.1.d.)

Only ten weeks after Henry VIII's accession to the throne, John More and his son 'young More' (Thomas) were joined on a royal judicial commission, with Thomas Jakes, to enquire into the possessions of William Viscount Beaumont, who had died, without issue, on 19 December 1507, the viscountcy then becoming extinct and the barony falling into abeyance. By the commission thirty-seven commissioners were directed in eleven counties and in the city of York to hold an *Inquisitio post mortem*.

This, the first of a long series of royal commissions to More, seems to have escaped the notice of More's biographers; it was to be followed by at least thirty-five others.

106
Thomas More as Interpreter for the Mercers' Company, 1509
Acts of Court of the Mercers' Company 1453–1527, ff. 174v–175r, *c.*1527
Manuscript on paper

Provenance Mercers' Hall (transcribed *c.*1527).
Bibliography Letitia Lyell, ed., *Acts of Court of the Mercers' Company, 1453–1527*, Cambridge 1936, 330–5.

The Worshipful Company of Mercers, London

The first book of the Acts of Court of the Mercers' Company is a transcript made by William Newbold (no. 13), former servant to John Colet and later Clerk to the Company. The Mercers and Merchants Adventurers dealt almost entirely in cloth, chiefly with the Low Countries. There had been difficulties for some time about the position of the English merchants in the Netherlands, even after the *Intercursus magnus* of 1496, and the Merchants Adventurers withdrew themselves from Antwerp, refusing to establish a staple in any one place. In 1508, Margaret of Austria (no. 196) wrote to the company on behalf of Antwerp, urging them to return, and this letter was followed by a visit to London from Jacob de Vocht, Pensionary of Antwerp. At a General Court on 6 September 1509, de Vocht offered the company, in Latin, any street in the city which they fancied as headquarters, and Thomas More interpreted him to the assembly. Discussion continued and the negotiations were finally successful. The Adventurers re-established their staple at Antwerp and More was rewarded.

107
Thomas More admitted to Doctors' Commons
Register of Doctors' Commons, London
Manuscript on vellum, 1514

Bibliography H. J. Todd, *A Catalogue of the Archiepiscopal Library at Lambeth Palace*, 1812, 242; Hodgson's, April 1861 (withdrawn); E. W. Bradbrook, 'On an Unrecorded Event in the Life of Sir Thomas More', *Transactions of the Royal Society of Literature*, 2nd series, XII, 1882, 160–72; P. W. Chandler, 'Doctors' Commons', *London Topographical Record*, XV, 1931, 38f.

His Grace the Lord Archbishop of Canterbury and the Trustees of Lambeth Palace Library (MS S.R. 136, f. 18v)

Doctors' Commons was thus called from the community of board (and sometimes lodging) of their members in a small house (later the Queens' Head Tavern) in Paternoster Row. It was a self-governing society of practitioners of canon and civil law, whose members practised in the ecclesiastical courts and in the court of admiralty, taking cognizance of cases of arbitration involving international law. The society soon attracted both church dignitaries and distinguished laymen who, upon payment of a nominal yearly sum, might enter their names in the register and thus enjoy collegiate privileges (as 'contributors'). Doctors' Commons was dissolved after 1857.

This is the original register of the college treasurer, given in 1511 by Robert Spenser, containing the statutes, constitutions and decrees of the Court of Arches, together with minutes. It was signed by each member in order of admission. Against 'Thomas Morus Laicus etc.' we have, in More's own hand: 'Ego T. Morus 3° die decembris Anno a Christo nato 1514to admissus sum in hanc societatem et polliceor me soluturum in annos singulos s.6. d.8.'

Other members mentioned in the register include John Colet (no. 11), Polydore Vergil, William Grocyn (nos. 90, 91, 92), Andreas Ammonius and Nicholas Harpsfield (no. 272), More's biographer.

108
'Evil May Day', 1517
From Edward Halle, *The Vnion of the two noble and illustre famelies of Lancastre & Yorke*, London, Richard Grafton, 1548

Bibliography STC, 12721; Thomas More, *The History of King Richard III*, CW, II, xvii, xx–xxix.

The British Library Board (C.122.h.4)

One of Thomas More's most notable doings in the City of London concerned the anti-foreigner riots of Evil May Day, 1 May 1517. As an under-sheriff since 1510, More was one of those responsible for the maintenance of law and order, when the attempt to enforce a May Eve curfew caused a mob to form. They broke open gaols, released prisoners and rampaged about. More interposed himself, addressed them and 'almost brought them to a stay', but stones were thrown and again they got out of hand. Order was restored without loss of alien life and the rioters were packed off to prison. Thirteen were later executed. On 12 May, More and others went to sue for the king's pardon and More was on the commission which looked into the causes of the riot: he was subsequently to say that all was begun by the 'ungracious invention' of two young lads, apprentices in Cheapside. The *Play of Sir Thomas More* (no. 275) shows him quelling the riot and obtaining pardon for the offenders by his own unaided eloquence.

109
Thomas More's 'History of Richard III' in Latin
Historia Richardi Regis Angliae eius nominis tertii . . .
Manuscript on paper, first half of 16th century

Exhibition Chelsea, 1929 (12).
Bibliography W. H. Black, *Catalogue of the Arundel MSS in the College of Arms*, 1829, 69; *CMA*, no. 5546. 121; R. S. Sylvester, ed., *CW*, II, 1963; Pamela Tudor-Craig, *Richard III*, NPG 1973; Alison Hanham, *Richard III and the Historians*, Oxford 1975.

The College of Arms, London (MS Arundel 43)

Thomas More's *History of Richard III* exists in two versions, Latin and English, neither of them printed in More's lifetime. Neither is a translation of the other. They independently tell the same unfinished story, the Latin text ending somewhat before the English, so that it omits the murder of the Princes and Richard's death at Bosworth and finishes abruptly in the middle of the sentence introducing Buckingham's speech at Baynard's Castle. The English text, the first to be published, appeared in a corrupt form in the continuation of Hardyng's *Chronicle* (no. 110) in 1543 and later in Halle (no. 108). This manuscript is the first of the Latin versions, from which were derived the other extant manuscripts, as well as the no longer extant revised version.

Nineteenth-century doubts as to More's authorship of the *Richard III* have been disposed of by Bridgett, Chambers and Sylvester. The work is famous for its skilful incorporation of dramatic dialogue. Shakespeare profited not only from this but also from More's portrayal of Richard as the cruel and wicked tyrant, warped in body and mind, an image highly agreeable to the House of Tudor's view of the king it had supplanted. More's *History of Richard III* is an early landmark in English biography.

110
Thomas More's 'History of Richard III', in English
The chronicle of Jhon Hardyng, from the firste begynnyng of England . . ., London, Richard Grafton, 1543

Bibliography STC, 12767; as for no. 109; A. F. Pollard, 'The Making of Sir Thomas More's *Richard III*', *Historical Essays in Honour of James Tait*, Manchester 1933, 223–38.

The British Library Board (C.30.e.9, ff. lxxvii^v–cvii^v)

John Hardyng (1378–?1465), who had become interested in the chronicles of Trogus Pompeius at Rome, later wrote a verse chronicle of England. From manuscripts no longer extant, Richard Grafton (d. 1572) printed two different editions of Hardyng's *Chronicle* in 1543, adding a prose continuation down to his own days 'out of the most credible and authentic writers'. It was here that More's unfinished English *History of Richard III* was first published. Grafton did not mention More's name as author; Henry VIII was still on the throne.

111
Thomas More at the Opening of Parliament, 1523
Unknown artist, *c.*1723
Engraving, 28.6 × 19.5 (11¼ × 7¾)

Bibliography R. Fiddes, *Life of Wolsey*, 1724, 302; id. *Collections*, 1726, 108–14; J. E. Neale, 'The Commons' Privilege of Free Speech in Parliament', *Tudor Studies presented to A. F. Pollard*, ed. R. W. Seton-Watson 1924, 257–86; repr. *Historical Studies of the English Parliament*, II, *1399–1603*, ed. E. B. Fryde and E. Miller, Cambridge 1970, 157–8; A. F. Pollard, *The Evolution of Parliament*, 2nd edn., 1926, 380–3; R. J. B. Walker, *A Catalogue of Paintings, Drawings, Sculptures and Engravings in the Palace of Westminster*, pt VI, 1965.

The Speaker of the House of Commons (G5)

Henry's war with France, declared in 1522, was expensive. Failing to make ends meet by a forced loan, Henry summoned the only Parliament that assembled during the supremacy of Wolsey. It met on 15 April at Blackfriars.

In this picture of its opening, the king is enthroned in solitary eminence on a dais, with three earls before him holding sword, baton and cap of maintenance. Garter King of Arms is to the right, before a group of eldest sons of peers. Cuthbert Tunstall, Bishop of London (no. 55), stands left to deliver his oration, with the Archbishops of York (Wolsey) and Canterbury (Warham) to his side. The bishops flank the floor of the House to the left with the abbots behind them extending onto the cross-bench; the lords temporal are to the right. The barons begin on the cross-bench and continue along the side behind the two dukes and the earls. To the other side of the throne are councillors. In the centre of the floor the judges, including Sir John More (no. 9), sit on woolsacks, the clerks behind them. In the foreground at the bar stand the Commons with their Speaker, Sir Thomas More, in their midst.

This engraving was made for Richard Fiddes's *Life of Wolsey* from a drawing provided by John Anstis, Garter King of Arms to George I. The drawing was made from the painting on vellum in the Wriothesley Roll, now in the Royal Library, Windsor Castle, executed to the order of the Garter King of Arms to Henry VIII, Sir Thomas Wriothesley (d. 1534).

112
Photograph: **Sir Thomas More as Speaker of the House of Commons, 1523**
Parliament Roll, 14 & 15 H.VIII, m.1, 1523

Bibliography LP, III, ii, 2956 (1); as for no. 111.
Photograph by courtesy of the Public Record Office, London (C.65/137)

Called upon 'to elect them a Speaker, or their Common Mouth', the Commons of the Parliament of 1523 (no. 111) elected Sir Thomas More, Sub-Treasurer, and presented him to the king in the Parliament Chamber three days later, 18 April 1523. Having 'disabled' (attempted to excuse on grounds of lack of ability) himself and been reassured, More requested the Speaker's privilege of referring to the Commons in case of mistaking their instructions. Further, he solicited royal indulgence for unintentional offence. More's subsequent plea for the Commons to be allowed to speak their mind, without fear of reprisals, has been called 'the first recorded plea for freedom of speech in Parliament' (J. E. Neale).

On 29 April Wolsey demanded a subsidy which the Commons thought excessive, but More pressed the demand and finally got the matter through. On 24 August 1523, Wolsey wrote to Henry asking for £100 over the customary Speaker's fee of £100 for More (no. 120), and two days later More acknowledges the king's agreement to this.

113

IV *Sir Thomas More and the Defence of the Church*

i *Luther and the Continental Reformers*

In 1517, the year that Thomas More entered royal service, Martin Luther advanced his 95 Theses. His views began to make their way into England, and Henry VIII commenced a rebuttal of the Lutheran propositions, but abandoned it. In 1521, in response to Luther's further attack on the sacramental system of the Church and on its practice of granting indulgences for money, Henry – aided by More as a 'sorter out and placer of the principal matters therein contained' – published his rejoinder, the *Assertio septem Sacramentorum*, winning for himself the title of Defender of the Faith. Solemn sermons had already been preached against the contagion of heresy, and Lutheran books publicly burned. Sir Thomas More, in the years that followed, was active in attempts to suppress the circulation of Lutheran opinions in England, as he was later to be in the suppression and refutation of English translations of the Bible and heretical tracts. He was always deeply conscious of the threat to the unity of the Church and the peace of the realm represented by dissent. In 1523, More published pseudonymously his *Responsio ad Lutherum*, a counterblast to Luther's reply to Henry. He was once again to engage in religious controversy in Latin, with his *Letter to Bugenhagen* (1526), before he abandoned such activities on the European stage. Throughout, he was in touch with Luther's Catholic antagonists, Thomas Murner, Johannes Cochlaeus, Hieronymus Emser and Johann Eck.

113
Martin Luther (1483–1546)
Lucas Cranach the Elder, 1525
Oil on panel, 40 × 26.6 ($15\frac{3}{4} \times 10\frac{1}{2}$)

Provenance Duke of Newcastle; by descent to Earl of Lincoln; Christie's 1 April 1939 (12); Agnew; H. A. Buttery 1939; F. P. M. Schiller, bequeathed to Bristol City Art Gallery 1946.
Exhibitions Nottingham Castle, 1879 and 1938; Manchester City Art Gallery, *German Art 1400–1800 from Collections in Great Britain*, 1961 (82); Royal Academy, *Primitives to Picasso*, 1962 (37); London, Wildenstein, *Pictures from Bristol*, 1969 (4).
Bibliography Max J. Friedländer and J. Rosenberg, *Die Gemälde von Lucas Cranach*, Berlin 1932, pls 159–60; M. Levey and Christopher White, *Burlington Magazine*, CIII, 1961, 487; *Erasmus*, 1969, nos. 401–2; *Catalogue of Oil Paintings in the City Art Gallery, Bristol*, 1970 (1972), p 146; Koepplin-Falk, pp 295–6, nos. 177–81.

City of Bristol Museum and Art Gallery (K 1650)

This panel represents a second image of Luther established, like that of the engravings of 1520 (no. 114), by the elder Cranach. Several replicas exist. Most are dated or datable 1526 and some are accompanied by a companion portrait of Katharina von Bora, the Cistercian nun whom Luther married in 1525.
The present splendid panel may be the earliest extant of the approximately life-sized versions of this image: it is signed with Cranach's winged dragon device, and cleaning in 1939 revealed the date 1525 beneath that of 1526 on the overpainted background. Small roundel double portraits of Luther and Katharina, dating from 1525, are also extant (eg that in the Öffentliche Kunstsammlungen, Basel). Later likenesses of Luther are based on new designs.

114
Martin Luther as an Augustinian Friar
Lucas Cranach the Elder, 1520
Engraving, two states mounted together: 11 × 9.7 ($4\frac{3}{8} \times 3\frac{7}{16}$); 14.8 × 11.8 ($5\frac{7}{16} \times 4\frac{3}{4}$)

Exhibitions Berlin, *Von der Freiheit eines Christenmenschen*, 1967 (3); Coburg, *Martin Luther*, 1967 (2); *Erasmus*, 1969 (318).
Bibliography Bartsch, VII, 278, 5; Hollstein, K6 and 7; Koepplin-Falk, 35–6.

The Trustees of the British Museum (1854-11-13-32; 1837-6-16-363)

Luther, like Erasmus, was a professed member of the order of Augustinian Hermits; he entered their house at Erfurt in 1505. He did not finally discard the habit he is wearing in this portrait until 1524, though he had been excommunicated in 1521.
Cranach's portrait of his friend, made when Luther was thirty-seven and at the height of his activity against the Roman Church, is the first extant rendering of Luther's features. Another version shows him wearing his doctor's bonnet (Hollstein, 8), and Cranach later made several painted versions (no. 113). This one is signed with Cranach's dragon monogram and carries the legend: AETHERNA IPSE SVAE MENTIS SIMULACHRA LUTHERUS/EXPRIMIT AT VVLTVS CERA LVCAE OCCIDVOS/M.D.X.X. (Luther himself gives expression to the immortal images of his mind; Lucas's picture [lit.: wax] to his mortal countenance 1520). In the second of these two engravings, on which the woodcut of Hans Baldung Grien (no. 115) is based, Cranach has set his subject in a niche, included his left hand and given him a book to emphasise his devotion and learning.

115
Martin Luther and the Holy Ghost
Hans Baldung Grien, 1521
Woodcut, 15.4 × 11.5 (6 × 4½)

Exhibitions Karlsruhe, *Hans Baldung Grien*, 1959 (XXXVII); Berlin, *Von der Freiheit eines Christenmenschen*, 1967 (4); Coburg, *Martin Luther*, 1967 (5); *Erasmus*, 1969 (320).
Bibliography Bartsch, VIII, 313, 39; Hollstein, 270; lit. cited in Karlsruhe exbn. cat., op. cit. above.

The Trustees of the British Museum (1871-8-12-1423)

This woodcut first appeared in *Acta et res gestae Dr Martini Luther*, Strasbourg, Johann Schott, 1521, and was later used in several other books. The image of Luther goes back to that established by Lucas Cranach the Elder in 1520 (no. 114) in which he wears the tonsure and the habit of an Augustinian friar. In Baldung Grien's variant, the halo and the dove of the Holy Ghost over his head proclaim Luther the new Evangelist or Doctor of the Church, holding the Scriptures (he was to publish his first German version of the New Testament in September 1522).

116
Martin Luther's 'Babylonian Captivity of the Church'
De captivitate Babylonica ecclesiae praeludium, Strasbourg, Johann Schott, 1520

Bibliography J. Benzing, *Lutherbibliographie*, Baden-Baden 1966, nos. 704–17; *Martin Luthers Werke*, VI, Weimar 1883, 484–573; Thomas More, *Responsio ad Lutherum*, CW, V, 717–31.

The British Library Board (697.h.21)

On 6 October 1520, at Wittenberg, Martin Luther published a shattering attack on the sacramental system of the Church of Rome. *The Babylonian Captivity of the Church* was the second of three celebrated brief tracts published in that year, which together represent a comprehensive indictment of Rome and a call for breaking with her. The *Babylonian Captivity* attacked the Church's denial to the laity of communion in both kinds and its doctrines of transubstantiation and of the mass as sacrifice. The seven sacraments hallowed by the Church were to be reduced to three: baptism, penance and the Eucharist.

The papal bull *Exsurge Domine* of 1520 condemned forty-one of Luther's Theses: Luther burnt it publicly, was excommunicated on 3 January 1521 and refused to recant at the Diet of Worms later in that year. *The Babylonian Captivity* had five editions (this is the third) in its original Latin during 1520, and the same year saw five printings of the translation into German made by Thomas Murner (no. 120). It was probably already available in England when Cuthbert Tunstall wrote to Wolsey that it should be kept out of the country at all costs; it was early recognised by Erasmus as representing an irrevocable break with Rome. Luther's books were publicly burned in Cambridge early in 1521 and again, at Henry VIII's orders, in London on 12 May 1521, following the precedent of Louvain, Liège and Cologne the previous year. John Fisher preached on the occasion (no. 122).

117
Henry VIII, Defender of the Faith
Assertio septem Sacramentorum adversus Martin. Lutherum, aedita ab invictissimo Angliae & Franciae rege, & domino Hyberniae Henrico eius nominis octavo
Manuscript on vellum, 1521

Bibliography N. Vian, 'La Presentazione e gli esemplari Vaticani della *Assertio septem sacramentorum* di Enrico VIII', *Collectanea Vaticana in honorem Anselmi M. Card. Albareda*, Città del Vaticano 1962, II, 355–75; E. Gordon Duff, 'The *Assertio Septem Sacramentorum*', *The Library*, N.S. IX, 1908, 1–16; E. Doernberg, *Henry VIII and Luther*, 1961; J. J. Scarisbrick, *Henry VIII*, 1968.

Biblioteca Apostolica Vaticana (MS Vat. Lat. 3731)

Henry VIII had early taken an interest in religious affairs. As a younger son, he had been intended and educated for an ecclesiastical career. Later, he and Wolsey badgered the pope for a title to emulate the King of Spain's 'Most Catholic', the King of France's 'Most Christian' or the Emperor's 'Protector of the Holy See'. About the same time, Luther's 95 Theses stimulated Henry to begin a reply early in 1518. The matter rested for three years. By April 1521 Henry had received Luther's *Babylonian Captivity* and was soon engaged 'in scribendo contra Lutherum', as Pace informed Wolsey. The cardinal was seen with a copy of the king's book in his hands when, on 12 May at Paul's Cross, he declared Luther a heretic. More later recalled that he found in that book 'the prymatie of that [Holy] see shold be bygone by the institution of God' and he moved the king 'either to leve owt that point, or ellys to towche it more slenderly', but

Henry 'wold in no wise eny thing minishe' (Rogers, 199).
In May Henry indicated to Leo X his intention of dedicating
his book to him. A manuscript, luxuriously bound in cloth of
gold, is the presentation copy for the pope here exhibited,
with Latin verses chosen by Wolsey and, as he requested, 'to
be written in the book of your own [ie Henry's] hand':
  Anglorum rex Henricus, Leo decime, mittit
  Hoc opus et fidei testem et amicitie,
with the subscription of your name to remain *in archivis
ecclesie ad perpetuam et immortalem vestre magestatis
gloriam, laudem et memoriam*' (*LP*, III, i, ccccxxi f).

The pope praised the book 'supra sidera' and arrangements
were made for the formal presentation in private consistory
on Wednesday 2 October 1521. Later that same month the
pope bestowed the title of *Fidei Defensor* on Henry VIII.

Ever since the book's publication, its attribution to Henry
has been questioned. We have, apart from secondary
evidence, Henry's own word for his authorship in an open
letter to Luther in 1526: 'Now, however much you may
pretend to believe that the book published by me is not mine,
but forged in my name by cunning sophists, yet many far
more worthy of credence than your "trustworthy witnesses",
know it to be mine; and I myself acknowledge it'. There can
be no doubt that the book was Henry's in part and that he
was assisted in the task by others.

118
Sir Thomas More's Reply to Luther, 1523
Ervditissimi viri Ferdinandi Baravelli opus..., London,
[Richard Pynson], 1523

Provenance Richard Sparchford, Tunstall's chaplain; Dr M. J.
Routh (1755–1854) by whom bequeathed to Durham University.

*Durham University Library: from the Collection of M. J. Routh,
1755–1854*

As a retort to Henry's *Assertio*, Luther published, in 1522,
his scurrilous *Contra Henricum Regem Angliae*. It was
impossible for the English Defender of the Faith to embroil
himself in open controversy with a heretic and the task of
replying on the king's behalf fell on John Fisher (no. 121)
and Thomas More. Since More was already knight and
Sub-Treasurer of England (no. 31), his retort was published pseudonymously and without the printer's name (he
was, in fact, Richard Pynson of London, the king's printer).
The work replies to Luther in kind. Writing unwillingly, at
command, in defence of Church and King, More was deeply
offended by Luther's excessive abuse and vulgar raillery, and
he apologises for the vigour and foulness of his own language
in retort, the staple of Reformation controversy.

The book exists in two versions. The earlier purports to
have been written in Spain by one Ferdinandus Baravellus.
Only one copy is extant. From the absence of contemporary
evidence it may be assumed that it was never widely released,
or even that it was suppressed. Later that same year the
unissued sheets were mostly re-used. The present copy has a
contemporary blind-stamped panel binding by John Reynes,
stationer, of London.

119
Sir Thomas More's Reply to Luther, 1523

Provenance Johann Eck (1486–1543) by gift of the author; Landshut
University; Bayerische Staatsbibliothek.
Bibliography (both items): *STC*2, 18088.5, 18089; Gibson, 62–3;
Neue Briefe, p 53; McKerrow-Ferguson, 11; ed. John M. Headley
as *Responsio ad Lutherum*, *CW*, V, 1969.

Bayerische Staatsbibliothek, Munich (4o Theol. 4401 = Cim.58)

The second, 'Rosseus', version of More's answer was actually
released. Re-using title-border and sheets from the preceding
'Baravellus' version, its signature H is considerably expanded
by additional material. The copy exhibited has the ownership
inscription: *Codex iste donodatus est michi Johanni Eckio, ab
illius autore in Anglia, dum videndi cupidus in Insulam
traiecissem 1525 Augusto* (This book was given to me, John
Eck, by its author in England, where, longing to see him, I
went over to the island in August of 1525). Eck must have
known the true author, since he wrote 'Thomas More' in the
margin of the title-page against Guilielmus Rosseus; Fisher
once mentioned 'the book of Master More against Luther',
and Tyndale, too, may have known of it.

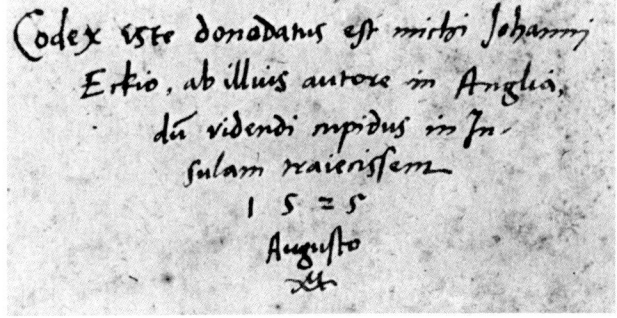

120
Sir Thomas More to Cardinal Wolsey (*Back cover*)
More, acting as the king's secretary, instructs the lord
chancellor of the royal pleasure in military, foreign and
domestic affairs
Easthampstead, 26 August [1523]

Bibliography LP, III, ii, 3270; *SP*, I, 125, no. LXX; Joseph
Delcourt, *Essai sur la langue de Sir Thomas More*, 1914, app. I, 326,
no. VI; Rogers, 115.

The British Library Board (MS Titus B.I., ff. 329r–332v)

For some years More, as member of the King's Council, had
followed the court, and for at least a year had acted as king's
secretary, writing royal letters and despatching royal instructions to the Lord Chancellor, Cardinal Wolsey. This letter is
one of a series from More to Wolsey between 1522 and 1528.
It deals with Thomas Murner, the German Franciscan, who
translated Henry's *Assertio* into German and wrote against
Luther in the king's defence. He had been persuaded by 'a
simple person', to come to England. The king desires to have
him paid a reward of £100 towards his return to Germany,
'for he is one of the chief stays against the faction of Luther in
that parties'. The letter is probably autograph.

121
John Fisher's Refutation of Martin Luther
Assertionis Lutheranae Confutatio per Reverendum Patrem Ioannem Roffensem Episcopum..., Antwerp, Michael Hillen, 1523

Bibliography Adams, F 513; E. Surtz, *The Works and Days of John Fisher*, Cambridge, Mass. 1967, 309ff; Emden, *Cambridge*, 229–30.

The Master and Fellows of St John's College, Cambridge

Fisher's confutation was the first published answer to Luther's attack on Henry VIII's *Assertio* (no. 117), preceding More's *Responsio* by almost a full year. Fisher is praised in a preliminary poem as 'Christ's bruiser' *(pugil)*, and forty-one articles are attacked. Amongst them are Lutheran theses like 'Sacraments give no grace', 'faith alone suffices', 'heretics are not to be burned', and there are chapters on the primacy of the pope and on free will.

122
John Fisher's Sermon against Luther
Contio quam Anglice habuit Reverendus Pater Ioannes Roffensis Episcopus... versa in Latinum per Richardum Paceum, Cambridge, John Siberch, 1521 [1522]

Provenance Bequeathed by Thomas Barlow (1607–91), Bishop of Lincoln.
Bibliography STC, 10898; E. Surtz, *Works and Days of John Fisher*, Cambridge, Mass. 1967, 302ff; Carl S. Meyer, 'Henry VIII burns Luther's Books, 12 May 1521', *Journal of Ecclesiastical History*, IX, 1958, 173–87.

Bodleian Library, Oxford (A 15.11. Linc.)

John Fisher was a celebrated preacher. Following the condemnation of Luther's teachings by Leo X, Wolsey, as Papal Legate, ordered a public burning of heretical books at Paul's Cross on 12 May 1521. On this occasion Fisher preached a sermon against Luther in the presence of other dignitaries, ambassadors and many people. Printed at once and several times reprinted, it was translated into Latin by the king's first secretary, Richard Pace, to ensure currency among foreigners at home and on the Continent. Dr Nicholas Wilson, Fisher's friend – later confined to the Tower at the same time as More and Fisher – wrote a prefatory letter. Fisher's sermon consists chiefly of four 'Instructions' on the primacy of the pope, the efficacy of works, the validity of tradition and the refutation of divers arguments of Luther's.

123
Ulrich von Hutten (1488–1523)
From J. J. Boissard, *Icones diversorum hominum illustrium*, Frankfurt a.M., 1645
Engraving, 14×10.5 ($5\frac{1}{2} \times 4\frac{1}{8}$)

Bibliography Hajo Holborn, *Ulrich von Hutten*, rev. edn. Göttingen 1968 (rev. English trans. New York 1965).

National Portrait Gallery, London

The best brief sketch of Thomas More is Erasmus's letter of 1519 to Ulrich von Hutten – ironically enough, since Erasmus was to quarrel bitterly with Hutten within a few years, and Hutten's own career exemplifies the instability, stridency, heresy and violence which More found so repugnant in his opponents.

The eldest son of a family of Franciscan free knights, Hutten fled in 1505 from the convent in which he had been placed and led a wandering scholar's life. He was involved in the satirical *Epistolae obscurorum virorum* (1515), which Thomas More enjoyed, and he was admired by Erasmus and by Budé (no. 68). In 1517 he was crowned poet laureate by Maximilian I.

Hutten made overtures to Luther and plunged into controversy with the Catholic party, urged a German crusade against the Turk and pressed for the advancement of the knightly order *(Ritterstand)* as the agent in the regeneration of the Empire, via the reformed religion. After the collapse of his hopes he fled, finally to Zwingli (no. 137), and died in 1523 of the syphilis he had earlier contracted.

Hutten admired More's epigrams and wished to know more of the author of *Utopia* – hence Erasmus's letter. All portraits of him go back to the woodcut by Hans Baldung Grien, on which this later engraving is based. Hutten is shown as champion in arts and arms.

124
Christ, the True Light
Hans Holbein the Younger, c.1524
Woodcut by Hans Lützelburger, 8.3×27.2 ($3\frac{1}{4} \times 10\frac{3}{4}$)

Exhibitions Basel, *Holbein*, 1960 (407); Berlin, *Von der Freiheit eines Christenmenschen*, 1967 (143); *Erasmus*, 1969 (447)
Bibliography F. Saxl, 'Holbein and the Reformation', in id. *Lectures*, 1957, 277–85.

The Trustees of the British Museum (1895-1-22-839)

This pictorial statement of reforming-evangelical doctrine by Holbein is usually dated about 1524, but may be earlier. Christ shows the true pure light of the Gospels, signified by the flame of the candle in its candlestick adorned with the symbols of the four Evangelists, to the poor, the humble, the meek and the pious, the peasant with his flail bringing up the rear. To the right, the churchmen, bishops, monks, friars, doctors of law and divinity, vainglorious of dignity and erudition, turn away from simple truth. Led by their mentor Aristotle, the prince of their scholastic philosophy, they grope in darkness towards the pit into which Plato has already fallen.

125
The Traffic in Indulgences
Hans Holbein the Younger, c.1524
Woodcut by Hans Lützelburger, 8×27 ($3\frac{1}{8} \times 10\frac{5}{8}$)

Exhibitions Basel, *Holbein*, 1960 (408); *Erasmus*, 1969 (446).
Bibliography Saxl, loc. cit. (no. 124).

Fitzwilliam Museum, Cambridge

This woodcut, probably designed by Holbein about the same time as no. 124, made its first appearance in a calendar by Johann Copp, before 1527. To the left, the new faith: King David and King Manasseh kneel and stand respectively, in attitudes of repentance, giving the example of direct

THE DEFENCE OF THE CHURCH

125

acknowledgement of sins to God in public to 'Offen Synder' (Open, ie Avowed, Sinner) standing humbly in full view. God the Father pardons them with open arms. To the right, the old faith: the pope (identified as Leo X, 1513–21, or Clement VII, 1523–34, by the Medici coat of arms above and to the side of him), surrounded by cardinals, priests and religious, gives an indulgence to a kneeling religious. Below his dais, men and women sue for absolution. Those with money obtain it, the poor and maimed do not. To the right, a boy and a young girl make their confessions and have payment prescribed as a penance.

126
'Passional Christi und Antichristi'
Woodcuts by Lucas Cranach the Elder (1472–1553) and workshop, [Wittenberg, J. Grunenberg, 1521]
$16.8 \times 12.2 \ (6\frac{5}{8} \times 4\frac{13}{16})$

Bibliography Hollstein, 66a–z; Koepplin-Falk, nos. 218–20; Benzing, 1015–24; Martin Luther, *Werke, WA*, IX, 1893, 685ff; F. Saxl, in *Lectures*, 1957, 264–6.

The Trustees of the British Museum (158. d. 67)

The *Passional Christi und Antichristi* is one of the most striking examples of the anti-papal pictorial propaganda issued by the German reformers. A century earlier, in Bohemia, the pope had been characterised as Antichrist, for which the ideas of John Wiclif were ultimately responsible. Luther encouraged Lucas Cranach to publish a series of twenty-six woodcuts, arranged in thirteen antithetical pairs, with accompanying texts, which would contrast Christ's example with that of his vicegerent upon earth. The *Passional* first appeared, in German, after the Diet of Worms, probably in May 1521; further editions of the German and a Latin translation followed in the same year. All were published without author's or printer's name, date or place of publication; Melanchthon (nos. 134, 135), the jurist Johann Schwertfeger and Luther (nos. 113, 114, 115) all probably had a hand in the text.

127
A Counterblast from the Catholic Side
Johannes Cochlaeus, *Septiceps Lutherus, ubique sibi, suis scriptis, contrarius*, Leipzig, Valentin Schumann, 1529

Bibliography Adams, C2287; M. Spahn, *Johannes Cochlaeus*, 1898; More, *Responsio ad Lutherum*, ed. Headley, *CW*, V, 1969, esp. 826–9.

Edinburgh University Library

Johann Dobneck (c.1479–1552), called Cochlaeus, was a peasant's son who became professor in Cologne and was later attached to the court of George of Saxony. He was a member of the orthodox party in the Reformation struggle and, besides being instrumental in interrupting the progress of William Tyndale's New Testament towards print, at Cologne in 1525, published many anti-Lutheran books and pamphlets. The title-page of his *Seven-Headed Luther* is a retort to the reformers' portrayal of the Catholic Church as the Beast of Revelation (no. 142).

Cochlaeus was More's correspondent from 1527, and his major informant on the progress of heresy in Germany. He later published a defence of More and Fisher against Richard Sampson (Leipzig 1536).

128
An admiring Dedication to Sir Thomas More
M. Aurelii Cassiodori Senatoris Chronicon, in J. Sichardus, ed., *Chronicon Divinum*, Basel, Henricus Petrus, 1529

Bibliography Adams, E1075.

The British Library Board (584.i.i)

This edition of Cassiodorus's *Chronicle* was dedicated to Thomas More, as Chancellor of the Duchy of Lancaster, on 11 November 1528, by Johannes Cochlaeus (no. 127). The letter dedicatory compares More to the Roman aristocrat Cassiodorus (c.485–c.580), who renounced politics after a distinguished career to become a Benedictine monk: both are rich in learning and honour, both have defended true religion.

129
Dr Johann Eck dedicates his Handbook to Sir Thomas More
Johann Eck, *Enchiridion Locorum Communium adversus Lutheranos... Novissime recognitum...*, Cologne, [Peter Quentel], 1526

Provenance J. Fr. Van de Velde, Vienna 1803.
Bibliography J. Eck, *Enchiridion*, 3rd edn. Landshut 1526; *Neue Briefe*, 142A; T. Wiedemann, *Dr J. Eck*, Regensburg 1865, no. XLIV; P. Fraenkel, 'Johann Eck und Sir Thomas More 1525–1526', in R. Bäumer, ed., *Von Konstanz nach Trient. Beiträge zur Geschichte der Kirche von den Reformkonzilien bis zum Tridentinum. Festgabe für August Franzen*, Munich etc 1972, 481–95.

The British Library Board (C.28.a.9)

Eck, along with Emser, Murner (no. 120) and Cochlaeus (nos. 127, 128), stepped in on Henry's side in the pamphlet battle with Luther. In England he presented to Henry, in August 1525, his handbook of orthodox Catholic doctrine, refuting the main Protestant objections. Long afterwards he remembered the hospitality of Fisher, Polydore Vergil and More, who had presented him with a copy of his *Responsio* (no. 119). This explains the dedicatory inscription by Eck in this copy of the second edition of his *Enchiridion*, sent on after his return to Ingolstadt early in 1526. It has been suggested that this was Eck's own author's copy. The letter to More mentions Eck's abortive attempts to have the 'Rosseus' *Responsio* (no. 119) published in Germany also.

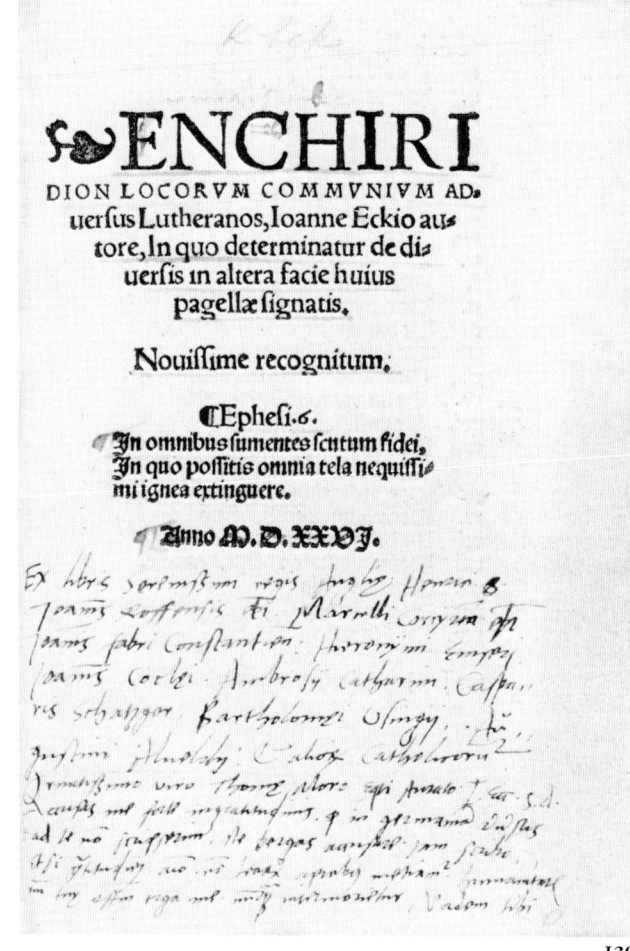
129

130
Johann Eck (1486–1543)
Unknown medallist, 1529
Silver medal, diameter 4.8 (1¾)

Exhibition Erasmus, 1969 (316).
Bibliography Habich, I, 1, 889, pl CIX,2; Thomas More, *CW*, V, 825–6.

Staatliche Münzsammlung, Munich

On the obverse of this medal Eck wears doctor's robes and bonnet. The inscription reads: ICON. IOAN. ECKII. THEOL. PROTHON. ET. INQVISITOR. (The portrait of Johann Eck, theologian, protonotary and inquisitor). The message is reinforced on the reverse, with its legend SOLI. DEO. GLORIA. M.D.XXVIII. (Glory to God alone, 1529). A prelate's hat, with tassels, signifies the Church's authority, and the device on the shield stands for the cornerstone (*Eckstein*) of the Church as well as being a pun on Eck's name. The year after this medal was struck, Eck was to lead the Catholic attack on the Protestant Augsburg Confession.

130 (*enlarged*)

THE DEFENCE OF THE CHURCH

131

131
Johann Bugenhagen (1485–1558)
Lucas Cranach the Younger, *c.*1559
Woodcut, 14.1 × 10.7 (5⅝ × 4¼)

Bibliography Hollstein, 26b; Koepplin-Falk, no. 641, cf no. 552; H. Bethe, 'Die Bildnisse Bugenhagens', *Monatsblatt der Gesellschaft für pommersche Geschichte*, XLIX, 1935, 116–23; LII, 1938, 13–15; O. Thulin, *Cranachaltäre der Reformation*, 1955, pls 6, 23, 26, 98, 110; H. W. Janson, 'The Putto with the Death's Head', *Art Bulletin*, XIX, 1937, 423–49; repr. *16 Studies*, New York 1973.

The Trustees of the British Museum (1870-10-8-1110)

Johann Bugenhagen (Johannes Pomeranus) was born in Wollin, Pomerania. He was at first opposed to Luther but after the publication of the *Babylonian Captivity of the Church* (no. 116) came to Wittenberg as an ardent sympathiser and later became Luther's confessor.

This woodcut is probably memorial. Made by the younger Cranach about 1559, on the model of one of his father's portraits of Bugenhagen, it is signed with the Cranach dragon device and was perhaps intended as a pendant to portraits of Luther and Melanchthon (no. 134). Its inscription reads: 'A faithful likeness of the venerable Master Johann Bugenhagen of Pomerania, Doctor of Sacred Letters and Pastor of the Christian congregation of Wittenberg etc.', and the verses below: 'If anyone wants to know what manner of man was our beloved Dr Johann Bugenhagen, whose portrait he sees here before him, where he taught, what he did, how old he was when he departed hence, I advise him to read what is epitomized on this sheet'. The *memento mori* below, the putto with the death's head and hour-glass and the warning *Hodie mihi, cras tibi* (What I am today, you will be tomorrow), is common in German sixteenth-century iconography.

132
Bugenhagen's 'Letter to the English' and Cochlaeus's Retort
Johannis Pomerani Epistola ad Anglos. Responsio Iohannis Cochlaei, [?Cologne], 1526

Bibliography RGG3, s.v. Bugenhagen; Adams, B3161; G. Geisenhof, *Bibliotheca Bugenhagiana*, Leipzig 1908, no. 189, cf nos. 181–8.

Cambridge University Library

Bugenhagen was one of the great propagandists for the ideas of the Wittenberg Reformers, and was prominent in establishing the Lutheran church in half a dozen German towns as well as Denmark. In 1525 he addressed a letter to men of goodwill in England, rejoicing in the spread of evangelical belief there and advancing the Lutheran teaching on free will, monastic vows, satisfaction, the Eucharist and prayer to the saints. The work was several times issued in Latin, once in this form, with a point by point refutation by Cochlaeus (no. 127), in German, and later in English.

133
Sir Thomas More's Letter to Bugenhagen, 1525
Thomae Mori ... Epistola, in qua ... respondit Literis Ioannis Pomerani ..., Louvain, John Fowler, 1568

Bibliography Gibson, 61; Rogers, 143.

Glasgow University Library

More's long letter to Bugenhagen was not included in the Latin collected works of 1563 and 1565–6 (nos. 261, 262). The first edition was produced by John Fowler (Fouler), an Elizabethan exile in the Low Countries, who married Alice, daughter of John Harris, More's former secretary, by Dorothy Colley, Margaret Roper's maid, all fellow exiles. Fowler took his text from More's autograph of more than forty years before. Though the letter was written for publication, following up the *Responsio ad Lutherum* (nos. 118, 119), More, for reasons unknown, did not issue it in his lifetime. It takes up two major issues: free will and the political consequences of Lutheranism. For the first, More follows Erasmus's *De libero arbitrio*; for the second, he can claim to have been right to express fear of 'tumult, slaughter and rapine' in the devastation of the German Peasants' War.

134
Philipp Melanchthon (1497–1560)
Albrecht Dürer, 1526
Engraving, 17.7 × 12.7 (7 × 5)

Bibliography RGG3, s.v. Melanchthon; Panofsky, 212, p 238; Hollstein, 104.

University College London

Philipp Schwarzerdt, 'Praeceptor Germaniae', Graecised his name to Melanchthon in token of allegiance to Greek studies, of which he became Professor at Wittenberg in 1520. Here he fell under Luther's sway and acted as his adviser and moderating influence. While Luther was in the Wartburg

134

(1521), he was the leader of the Reformation movement. His *Loci communes* of 1521 were an influential statement of reformed doctrine and the Augsburg Confession of 1530 was chiefly his work. Thomas More mentions Melanchthon little in his controversial works, but derides him for taking a Greek name in earnest (something he had accepted for himself, in jest) and reserves great scorn for his 'gaye, golden dystynccion' between different types of faith.

Melanchthon likened the style of his friend Dürer to the grand style of rhetoric and this profile head contrasts with the younger Cranach's woodcut of more than thirty years later. The inscription VIVENTIS POTVIT DVRERIVS ORA PHILIPPI/ MENTEM NON POTVIT PINGERE DOCTA MANVS (The skilled hand of Dürer could portray the features of Philipp as he was in life, but could not show his intellect) is, like that on the portrait of Erasmus of the same year (no. 88), self-deprecatory, but the Melanchthon is much the more successful image.

135
Philipp Melanchthon
Lucas Cranach the Younger, 1560
Woodcut, two states mounted together, 27.5 × 21.3 ($10\frac{13}{16} \times 8\frac{1}{2}$)

Bibliography Dodgson II, nos. 31, 31a; Hollstein, 48c, 48f; Koepplin-Falk, no. 650; W. L. Strauss, *German Single-Leaf Woodcut 1550–1600*, New York 1975, I, 150.

The Trustees of the British Museum (*1871-12-9-793*; *1875-7-10-538*)

Lucas Cranach was trained in his father's workshop, which he took over in 1553. His portrait of Melanchthon was made in the year of Melanchthon's death. It is perhaps a companion piece to portraits of Bugenhagen (no. 131) and Luther by the same artist and is signed with the Cranach dragon device.

136
Otto Brunfels (*c*.1488–1534)
Hans Baldung Grien, 1525
Woodcut, 19 × 12 ($7\frac{1}{2} \times 4\frac{3}{4}$)

Exhibitions Karlsruhe, *Hans Baldung Grien*, 1959 (46); Berlin, *Von der Freiheit eines Christenmenschen*, 1967 (164); *Erasmus*, 1969 (430).
Bibliography Hollstein, 267; *Dictionary of Scientific Biography*, ed. C. C. Gillispie, II, 1970, 535–8.

The British Library Board (*C.66.g.7(1)*)

Otto (Otho) Brunfels, educated at the University of Mainz, was professed Carthusian at Strasbourg some time after 1510, and fled from his monastery before 1521, with the help of Ulrich von Hutten (no. 123). He was for some time a schoolmaster at Strasbourg, before being appointed physician to the city of Bern in 1533. Brunfels wrote and translated prolifically on astrological, medical, pharmacological and botanical, as well as pedagogical and Lutheran-theological matters. For More, who refers to him as Otho or (Dan) Otho the Monk, Brunfels is the type of the religious whom lechery has led to desert his order, in this case the Carthusian, for which More had a special veneration (nos. 21, 252). More takes no issue with Brunfels on theological grounds, reproaching him only for his apostasy and his marriage (1524).

Hans Baldung Grien's is the only extant portrait of Brunfels: it is the frontispiece to Brunfels's *Annotationes in Quattuor Evangelia*, Strasbourg, 1525.

137
Huldrych (Ulrich) Zwingli (1481–1531)
Hans Asper, 1531
Oil on parchment, mounted on panel, monogrammed and dated, 35 × 24.5 ($13\frac{3}{4} \times 9\frac{5}{8}$)

Provenance Baron Fr. von Sulzer-Wart; in 1868 to Kunstmuseum Winterthur.
Exhibition Erasmus, 1969 (435; cf 436–8).
Bibliography P. Boesch, 'Der Zürcher Apelles', *Zwingliana. Beiträge zur Geschichte Zwinglis, der Reformation und des Protestantismus in der Schweiz*, IX, 1949, 16–28; id. 'Die Bildnisse von Huldrich Zwingli', *Toggenburgerblätter für Heimatkunde*, XIII, 1950, 1–2; G. R. Potter, *Zwingli*, Cambridge 1977, and Historical Association Pamphlet.

Kunstmuseum Winterthur

Zwingli, the leader of the Reformation in Zürich, ordained priest in 1506, a fervent admirer of Erasmus, taught himself Greek and some Hebrew in order to study the Scriptures better. Minister at Zürich in 1518, he attacked the Catholic doctrines of purgatory, the invocation of saints, clerical celibacy, fasting, and the institutions of monasticism. In 1524 he married. His most radical and famous doctrine was the denial of every form of the carnal presence of Christ in the Eucharist. Zwingli fought with the Zürich Protestants at Kappel (11 October 1531) against the Catholics of the Forest

137

138 *(enlarged)*

Cantons and was killed there. His name is never mentioned without obloquy in More's works of religious controversy.

Hans Asper (1499–1571), the outstanding portraitist of Zürich, began his career under the influence of Holbein. He was a strong sympathiser with the Reformation and this is a commemorative picture, the earliest extant portrait by Asper. It is inscribed OCCVBVIT ANNO AETATIS XLVII. 1531 (He died in his 47th year, 1531), and is related to the medallic portrait made in 1531 by Hans Jakob Stampfer (1505/6–79) of Zürich. A version, probably later, is in the National Gallery of Scotland, Edinburgh. In 1550, Asper painted, for the Englishman Christopher Hales, a series of five memorial portraits of the Zürich reformers Zwingli, Pelikan, Bibliander, Bullinger and Gwalther.

138
Johannes Oecolampadius (1482–1531)
Hans Jakob Stampfer, signed and dated *H.S., 1531*
Silver medal, diameter 3.7 (1½)

Exhibition Erasmus, 1969 (432).
Bibliography Habich, I, i, 849, pl CVI, 2; E. Staehelin, *Das theologische Lebenswerk Johannes Oekolampads*, Zürich 1939; E. Gordon Rupp, 'Oecolampadius: the Reformer as Scholar', in his *Patterns of Reformation*, 1969, 3–48.

Staatliche Münzsammlung, Munich

Johann Huszgen, the reformer of Basel, was born at Weinsberg in the Palatinate and later Graecised his name to Oecolampadius. More mocked him for it. Oecolampadius's sympathies for a time lay with Luther, but he entered a monastery in 1520, only to leave it in 1522, return to Basel, play a major part in securing that city's allegiance to Protestantism, marry and publicly defend the Eucharistic doctrine of Zwingli (no. 137). Oecolampadius is not handled at length in Thomas More's controversial works, but is given as an example 'of many vertuouse chyldren of god, that haue fallen from that estate & becomen by synne the chyldren of the deuyll'.

This medal shows the bust of Oecolampadius wearing a cap, with the inscription EIKON D[omini] IOANNIS OECOLAMPADII T[ie died] ANNO AET[atis] 49 (The image of Johannes Oecolampadius who died in the forty-ninth year of his age), with the date 1531. The inscription on the reverse, in a wreath, is an elegiac couplet reading DVM VIXI IN DOMINI FVLSI FAX SPLENDIDA TEMPLO/ET NOMEN CVM RE GRATIA DIVA DEDIT: HS (While I lived I shone, a blazing light in the temple of the Lord [cf no. 139], and divine grace gave me a name answering to my achievements. Hans Stampfer). This memorial medal of Oecolampadius is a companion piece to the memorial medal of Zwingli by the same artist.

139
Johannes Oecolampadius
Hans Asper, *c*.1545
Oil on panel, signed *H.A.*, 61 × 51.5 (24 × 20)

Exhibition Erasmus, 1969 (431).
Bibliography P. Boesch, 'Der Zürcher Apelles', *Zwingliana. Beiträge zur Geschichte Zwinglis, der Reformation und des Protestantismus in der Schweiz*, IX, 1949, 16–26, 28–30; E. Staehelin and E. Gordon Rupp, op. cit. (no. 138).

Kunstmuseum Basel

The portraits of Oecolampadius and Zwingli (no. 137) by Hans Asper of Zürich (1499–1571) are posthumous, and probably based on the memorial medals of the two men by Hans Jakob Stampfer (no. 138). The present portrait is not identical with that commissioned from Asper in Zürich in 1550, by Christopher Hales, which was one of a series of likenesses of Swiss reformers painted by Asper for the young English Protestant. Oecolampadius is shown wearing cap and gown, a large volume, probably of the Scriptures, in his left hand and his right hand outstretched, as if expounding. The inscription reads: JOAN. OECOLAMPADIVS. IN DOMINI QVONDAM FVLSI LVX SPLENDIDA TEMPLO/CVM TALI VVLTV CONSPICIENDIS ERAM/SI VELVTI VVLTVS POTVISSENT PECTORA PINGI/STAREM DOCTRINAE CVM PIETATE TYPVS (Johannes Oecolampadius. Once I shone, a blazing light in the temple of the Lord [cf no. 138] and presented this appearance to those who looked upon me. If the spirit could be painted in the same way as the features, I would stand as the embodiment of learning and piety).

Colour plate III *Henry VIII* by Hans Holbein the Younger (no. 70)

THE DEFENCE OF THE CHURCH

ii *The English Reformers*

Thomas More's last work of religious controversy in Latin was his letter to Bugenhagen of 1526 (no. 133). During the 1520s Lutheranism had been making its way in England, adding its subversive influence to the still doctrinally active and socially disturbing effects of native Lollardy. The chief matters at issue were the nature and number of the sacraments, and especially the nature of the Eucharist, the relative status of faith and works as the way to salvation, the authority of the Church as against that of Scripture and the legitimacy of vernacular translations of the Bible.

In 1528 More was commissioned by his friend and bishop, Cuthbert Tunstall, to write refutations of the heretical works which were surreptitiously being distributed in England. In the next five years he wrote nearly a million words in English in defence of the Church's doctrine and its clergy. His chief antagonists were the Protestant exiles William Tyndale, Robert Barnes, John Frith and George Joye, the lawyer Simon Fish and, probably, the jurist Christopher St German. By the time he was writing against St German, the question of the Supremacy was looming large and there was a more definite political slant to the attack on the Church.

140
Photograph: **Licence granted by Cuthbert Tunstall to Sir Thomas More**
From the Register of Cuthbert Tunstall, Bishop of London, folio 138

Bibliography Rogers, 160; *CW*, VIII, 1137–8.

Photograph by courtesy of Guildhall Library, London

On 7 March 1527–8 Cuthbert Tunstall, Thomas More's bishop, disturbed at the growing dissemination of heresy in England, addressed a letter to his 'dearest friend and brother'. Hard upon the infestation of Germany, Tunstall writes, a flock of the sons of iniquity have been detected in the act of importing into England printed books in the vernacular setting forth the ancient and damnable heresies of Wiclif and of Luther. All must rally to the cause, defend the Church in writing and put the truth out of peril. Thomas More, the rival of Demosthenes in eloquence and ever the Church's advocate, must use his leisure hours (how could he employ them better?) to compose books that will help the ordinary person to see these heresies for what they are. Henry VIII's *Assertio septem Sacramentorum* (no. 117) has shown the way. More must do likewise in English. So that he may not fight blindfold, Tunstall is sending him some of these mad trifles in English and some of the works of Luther from which they draw their misshapen opinions. These he is licensed to read and retain for his purpose, the accomplishment of which will bring him an immortal name and eternal glory in heaven.

The original of this letter is no longer extant; we have it only in the file copy made for the register of the Bishop of London.

141
Royal Proclamation against Heresy
Before 6 March 1530
Paper, 49.5 × 30.5 (19½ × 12)

Bibliography STC, 7772, cf 7775–6; *LP*, V, 311; Wilkins, *Concilia*, III, 738, cf 740; P. L. Hughes and J. F. Larkin, eds., *Tudor Royal Proclamations*, I, New Haven 1964, no. 122, pp 181–6, cf no. 129, pp 193–7; Thomas More, *Confutation*, *CW*, VIII, 1463, 1528–9.

The Society of Antiquaries of London

This proclamation was issued while Thomas More was Lord Chancellor, to enforce the statutes against heresy in the realm made in the early fifteenth century. It reminds its readers of Henry's capacity as 'Defensor of the Faith', forbids his subjects to 'preach, teach, or inform anything openly or privily, compile or wryte any book, or hold, exercise or keep any assembles or scoles ... contrary to the catholyke fayth', charges them not to aid heretics and to deliver up heretical books to their bishops within fifteen days.

At this point the unique printed version shown here ends. It must have continued on another sheet, the contents of which can be reconstructed from the *Publick Instrument* drawn up by an ecclesiastical commission, which included Thomas More, in May 1530. This listed 253 heretical and erroneous opinions and was followed, on 22 June, by a further proclamation prohibiting the import and distribution of Tyndale's New Testament and many other named books.

The Bible and its Translation

In 1520, Martin Luther asserted that Scripture, the only true guide to life and so the ultimate recourse of every Christian, had been corrupted by its papal interpreters to serve their own purposes. He undertook to translate the New Testament into the vernacular, so that it should be available to all.

The Church's Bible had for more than a thousand years been the Latin translation made by St Jerome (c.342–420), the Vulgate, accessible only to the learned. By Luther's time, the Vulgate text had come under attack both from the humanists, who wished to go back to the original Greek of the New Testament, and from those who wished to go a step further and bring the Gospel message to all, in their native language.

Erasmus belonged to both parties. He made great efforts to establish the Greek text of the New Testament and to render it accurately in Latin (nos. 38, 39). He also wrote that he wished that all good wives should read St Paul, that the Scriptures should be translated into all languages, that the farmer at his plough, the weaver at his loom, the traveller on his journey, should recite them to themselves.

In Thomas More's England, unauthorised translation of the Bible, or even the possession of unauthorised translations, was a punishable offence. Lollard versions had been in circulation for over a century. The new English translations made by William Tyndale and printed in Germany and Antwerp from 1525 to 1535 were smuggled in and clandestinely distributed. An English translation of the whole Bible did not exist until 1535, and it was not until 1539 that the 'Great Bible', a version authorised by Henry VIII, was set up in every church in England.

More was not opposed to vernacular translations of Scripture as such. He objected to translations that relied on the single, individual judgement of one or two men, not approved by the Church. He held to the Vulgate and the interpretations of the 'old, holy doctors' of the Church, which combined to give a body of doctrine common to and accepted by all Christendom. He was active in the campaign to suppress unauthorised translations.

142
Martin Luther's New Testament, 1522
Das Newe Testament Deutzsch, Wittenberg, M. Lotther the Younger, 1522

Bibliography Cambridge History of the Bible, III, 167–212; W. Schwarz, *Principles and Problems of Biblical Translation*, Cambridge 1955, 94–109; Koepplin-Falk, nos. 221–30.

British and Foreign Bible Society, London

In Luther's day an older version of the New Testament, in German, made about 1350, was in circulation. It was unacceptable to Luther because its language was obscure and because it had been made from the Latin, not the Greek. Helped by his friend Melanchthon (nos. 134, 135), Luther completed a first draft of his translation in two and a half months and published it in September 1522, whence the nickname 'September Testament'. A second version followed in three months ('December Testament'). Luther's complete German Bible was published in 1534. Luther based himself on Erasmus and the Vulgate, and his version had much influence on William Tyndale's, and so on English Bible translation throughout the century.

Both Testaments of 1522 have a series of twenty-one woodcuts by Lucas Cranach the Elder (1472–1553) and his workshop illustrating Revelation, in which the Beast and the Whore of Babylon are identified with the Roman Church. In the earlier version they wear the papal tiara; in the later this is altered to a crown.

143
William Tyndale's Revised New Testament, 1534
The newe Testament, dylygently corrected and compared with the Greke by Willyam Tindale, Antwerp, Marten de Keyser, 1534
Vellum

Bibliography STC, 2826; NK, 2487; A. S. Herbert, *Historical Catalogue of Printed Editions of the English Bible 1525–1961*, 1968, no. 13; J. F. Mozley, *William Tyndale*, 1937, 268–93; *Cambridge History of the Bible*, III, 141–9.

The British Library Board (C.23.a.8,8*)

The Bible versions made by the Lollard followers of John Wiclif (c.1350–84) were used hardly at all by William Tyndale in making his translation. When he came to London in 1523 to begin his attempt, he must have known Erasmus's work and at least of the existence of Luther's. In spring 1524 he set off for Germany and in Wittenberg met the apostate friar William Roye, who became his collaborator in a version strongly influenced by Luther. In autumn 1525 the printing of their English New Testament at Cologne was interrupted on the initiative of Cochlaeus (nos. 127, 128) and the two fled to Worms with some of the sheets. At Worms, the first complete English printed New Testament was issued. By May 1528, Tyndale was in Antwerp, whence he issued polemical tracts and, in 1534, his revised New Testament. A final version, again revised, came out in 1535. In 1534 George Joye (nos. 157–60) had published, without consultation, his own revision of Tyndale.

The woodcuts which illustrate Revelation in Tyndale's revised Testament are anonymously executed, crudely printed smaller imitations of Cranach's compositions.

The copy of Tyndale's New Testament shown here is printed on vellum and belonged to Anne Boleyn.

144
Coverdale's Bible
Biblia, The Bible that is, the holy Scripture of the Olde and New Testament, faithfully and truly translated out of Douche and Latyn in to Englishe, ? Zürich, ? Christoph Froschauer; ? Cologne or Marburg, ? E. Cervicornus (Hirschhorn) or J. Soter (Heil), 1535

Bibliography STC, 2063; McKerrow-Ferguson, 31; A. S. Herbert, *Historical Catalogue of Printed Editions of the English Bible 1525–1961*, 1968, no. 18; J. F. Mozley, *Coverdale and his Bibles*, 1953; Campbell Dodgson, 'Woodcuts designed by Holbein for English Printers', *Walpole Society*, XXVII, 1938, 1–4; *Cambridge History of the Bible*, III, 147–53.

The British Library Board (G.12208)

This is the first complete Bible in English. Tyndale had translated some Old Testament books as well as the New Testament, and Joye had made some Old Testament versions also. The translator of the 1535 version was Miles Coverdale, a Cambridge man who had helped Robert Barnes (nos. 151, 152) in 1526, had adopted Lutheranism and was later to be Cromwell's friend. At Antwerp he began to translate, using Luther's 'Douche' (German) and the Vulgate, with reference to two other Latin versions and to Tyndale. This English Bible was also printed abroad and, despite the implications of royal support embodied in its woodcut title-page and its dedication to the king, was not authorised by Henry. Coverdale's translation was succeeded in 1537 by 'Matthew's Bible', issued with 'the King's most gracyous lycence': it is a composite of Coverdale and Tyndale, edited by one John Rogers.

Holbein's woodcut border for the original issue had legends set in type in English, only the names of the biblical books being in Latin. The border is composed of four blocks: the Fall of Man at the top left balanced by the Resurrection at top right, with the risen Christ trampling on Sin, Death and Devil. The left upright panel contrasts the Law (Moses on Sinai, Esdras reading the Law to the Jews), with the Gospel on the right (Christ sending the Apostles into the world and

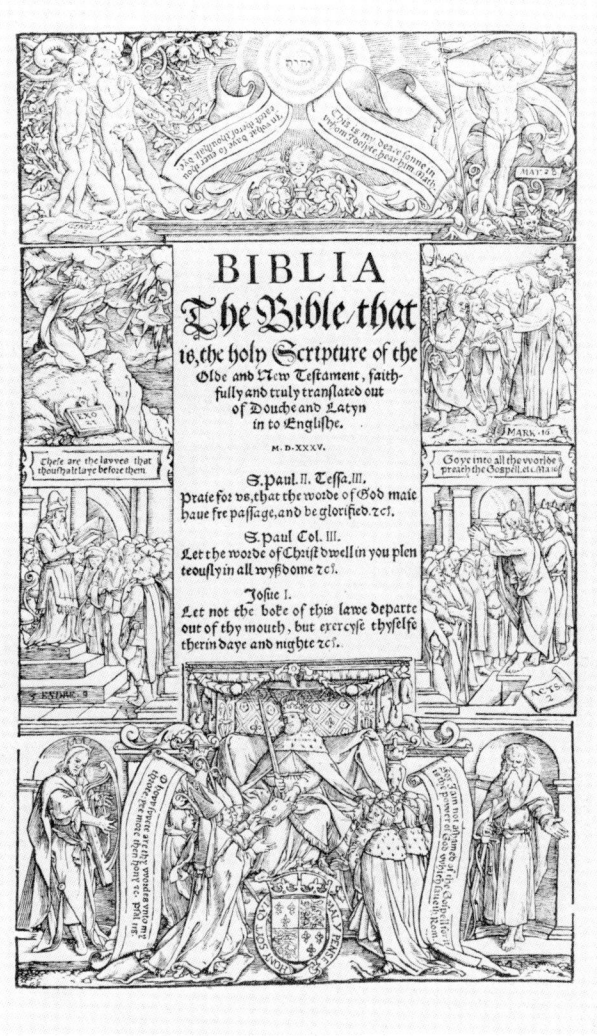

Peter and the others, tongues of fire on their heads, preaching to the Jews after Pentecost). The lowest compartment shows the king of England enthroned, sword in hand, delivering the Word to the lords spiritual, the lords temporal attending. David and St Paul, in niches, represent the Old and the New Testaments.

Sir Thomas More's Controversy with William Tyndale

William Tyndale (?1494–1536), alias Hutchens, was the most formidable of Thomas More's English antagonists in matters of religion. Self-exiled to Germany in 1524, and coming strongly under Luther's influence, he removed to Antwerp in 1528 and remained there, probably without interruption, for the rest of his life. From Antwerp he began, in 1528, to issue a series of polemical works in English, several of them, like the works of other English reformers, under the false imprint 'Marlborowe in the lande of Hesse', ie Marburg. The printer's name was given as Hans Luft. The name, which means 'air', was apt, though Johann Luft was a real printer who issued many Lutheran books from Wittenberg. Tyndale's first book, known as the *Parable of the Wicked Mammon*, was a statement of the Lutheran doctrine 'that fayth the mother of all good workes iustifieth us'; like all his books, as More was to point out, it was an exposition of 'the worst heresies picked out of Luther's books'. *Mammon* was followed by a series of tracts, to some of which More replied, in pursuance of the duty laid on him by Tunstall (no. 140).

145
Tyndale's 'Obedience of a Christian Man'
William Tyndale, *The obedience of a Christen man and how Christen rulers ought to governe...*, [Antwerp, Johannes Hoochstraten, 1528]

Bibliography STC2, 24446; *CW*, VIII, 1135–1364; A. Hume, ibid. 1065–8, 1071 no. 7, cf 1090, no. 41; Emden, *Oxford 1540*, 567–9; J. F. Mozley, *William Tyndale*, 1937, esp. 134–44.

The John Rylands University Library of Manchester

This is Tyndale's second book in the 'Marburg' series, published on 2 October 1528. Its title promises the reader 'eyes to perceaue the crafty conveyance of all iugglers', ie interpreters of the Scriptures to serve their own ends, and is a defence of the reformers against the accusation of fomenting rebellion, with a fervent plea for the Scriptures in English. 'The emperor and kings are nothing nowadayes but even hangmen unto the pope and bishops', and kings must assert the authority that they have directly from God. More called the book 'a holy book of disobedience, whereby we were taught to disobey Christes holy catholic church'. According to John Foxe, Anne Boleyn gave it to Henry, who thought it 'a book for me and all kings to read'. It was included in the proclamation against heretical books of 22 June 1530 (no. 141).

146
Dialogue Concerning Heresies
Sir Thomas More, *A dyaloge... wherin be treatyd dyuers maters...*, London, John Rastell, 1529

Bibliography STC2, 18083, cf 18084; Gibson, 53–4; W. E. Campbell, ed., with intro. and notes by A. W. Reed, *Thomas More's Dialogue against Tyndale*, 1927; *CW*, VIII, 1184–7.

Guildhall Library, London (Cock Colln. 1.5)

More's massive reply to Tyndale was rapidly put together, the first edition being published in June 1529 and followed by a second in May 1531. It is in the form of a debate between a messenger 'of very merry wit' and 'of nature nothing tong-tayed' and More himself, on – to quote the title – 'the veneration & worshyp of ymagys & relyques, prayng to sayntys, & goyng on pylgrymage. with many othere thynges touchyng the pestylent sect of Luther and Tyndale, by the tone bygone in Saxony, and by the tother laboryd to be brought in to England'. Issue is especially taken with Tyndale's New Testament (no. 143), for its tendentious translations.

The *Dialogue on Heresies*, as it is usually known, covers the whole range of the Church's defence against Protestant attack. More insists especially on the rage and railing manner of his opponents and voices his fear of civil disorder if their doctrines prevail.

147
Tyndale's Answer
William Tyndale, *An answere vnto Sir Thomas Mores dialoge...*, [Antwerp, Symon Cock or Martinus de Keyser, 1531]

Bibliography STC2, 24437; A. Hume, in *CW*, VIII, 1165–8, 1081, no. 25; J. F. Mozley, *William Tyndale*, 1937, 191–7, 218–23.

The British Library Board (C.37.a.26)

Tyndale, in Antwerp, had his answer ready in January 1531, but did not publish it until July. He defines the nature of the true church and defends his translation of the New Testament, and 'answereth particularlye vnto everye chaptre' of More's *Dialogue*.

148
Sir Thomas More's Confutation
Sir Thomas More, *The Confutacyon of Tyndales answere...*, London, William Rastell, 1532–3

Bibliography STC2, 18079–80; McKerrow-Ferguson, 20; Gibson, 48–9; ed. L. A. Schuster, R. C. Marius, J. P. Lusardi and R. J. Schoeck as *CW*, VIII, 1973.

Guildhall Library, London (Cock Colln. 1.6);
Cambridge University Library

Tyndale's *Answer* drew a refutation of about five times its length (the proportion is usual with More), in two instalments. The first three books were written while More was Chancellor – the only polemical work he composed in office – and came out early in 1532. The second part was written and published during the year which followed More's resignation of the chancellorship; it came out early in 1533, before the publication of the *Apology* about Easter (no. 165). Unfinished at more than 560 pages, it devotes an eighth book to the refutation of Barnes (nos. 151, 152). In *EW* a fragmentary ninth book was added.

149
The Execution of William Tyndale, October 1536
Unknown artist, in John Foxe, *Actes and Monuments of the English Church*, 1563
Woodcut, 12.7 × 17.5 (5 × 6¾)

Bibliography Strong, *Catalogue*, 313–14; J. F. Mozley, *William Tyndale*, 1937, 294–342.

The Trustees of the British Museum (English History File, Henry VIII)

No authentic portrait of Tyndale is extant. A false type, based on the portrait of John Knox in the French translation of Theodore Beza's *Icones* (*Vrais Pourtraicts*, Geneva 1581), was established by the early seventeenth century. There are variants of an oil painting based on this in Hertford College, Oxford, in the British and Foreign Bible Society and in the NPG.

In 1530 Thomas Cromwell (no. 209) made overtures to Tyndale in Antwerp. Tyndale was naturally wary of returning to England while More was Chancellor, but undertook to return and never to write again if Henry would 'grant only a bare text of the scripture to be put forth among his people'. At the end of 1531, Henry instructed his ambassador to demand Tyndale's delivery from the imperial authorities, but Tyndale evaded capture. He was finally betrayed to the Emperor's officers and remained in prison in the castle of Vilvorde, just north of Brussels, for nearly sixteen months. Early in October 1536 he was executed, 'crying thus at the stake with a fervent zeal and a loud voice: Lord, open the king of England's eyes' (Foxe).

150
Barlowe's Satire on the Clergy
Jerome Barlowe, *Rede me and be nott wrothe...*, Strasbourg, Johann Schott, 1528

Bibliography STC2, 21427; A. Hume in *CW*, VIII, 1070, no. 5.

Bodleian Library, Oxford (Tanner 59)

Jerome Barlowe, like his and Tyndale's collaborator William Roye, was an apostate Observant Franciscan of Greenwich, who left England in 1527. His satirical tract attacking the ecclesiastical establishment is written in rhyme royal, with a title in rhyming couplets. More described it as 'a foolish raylyng boke against the clergy', but never paid it the compliment of refutation, partly because Wolsey, who is attacked in it, had managed to prevent its entering England in any quantity. In its own time, the tract was known as *The Burying of the Mass*.

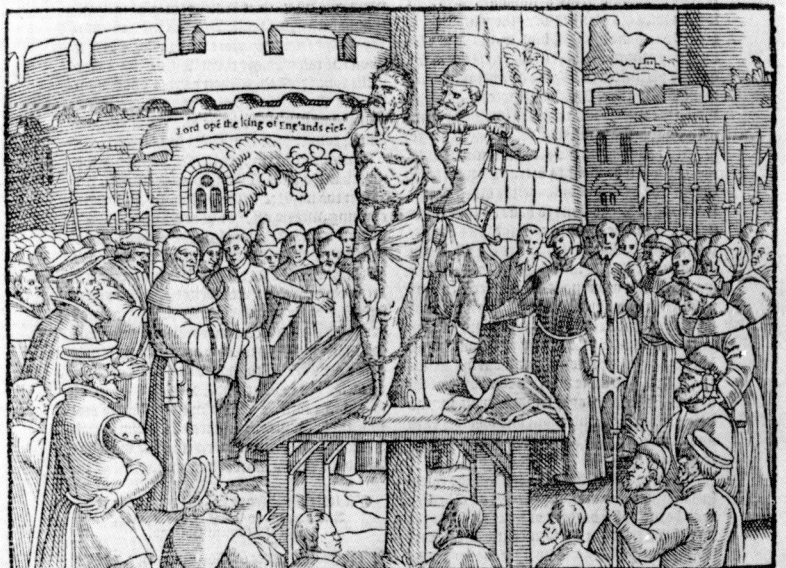

149

Sir Thomas More's Controversy with Robert Barnes

Robert Barnes (?1495–1540) began his adventurous career as an Augustinian novice in Cambridge, perhaps as early as 1505. He later became prior of his house, lectured in Cambridge and joined the group of Lutheran sympathisers who met at the tavern of the White Horse ('Little Germany'). On Christmas Eve 1525 he preached in St Edward's against abuses in the Church and was examined by Wolsey and others, abjured his heresy and did penance. In 1528 he fled to Antwerp and was later at Wittenberg, where he obtained a letter from Luther favouring the royal divorce, which he brought to England under safe conduct in 1531. For some years he was in favour with Henry and shuttled back and forth to Germany, but the fall of Anne Boleyn made the climate less favourable for him. He was active on Cromwell's behalf until the victory of Stephen Gardiner's (no. 206) conservative party in 1540. He was burned in Smithfield as a heretic on 30 July, two days after Cromwell's execution.

151
Barnes's Supplication
Robert Barnes, *A supplicatyon... vnto... kinge henrye the eyght*, [Antwerp, Symon Cock or Martinus de Keyser, 1531]

Bibliography STC, 1470; W. D. J. Cargill-Thompson, 'The sixteenth-century editions of *A Supplication*... by Robert Barnes, D. D.: a Footnote to the History of the Royal Supremacy', *Transactions of the Cambridge Bibliographical Society*, III, 1960, 133–42; *CW*, VIII, 1035–62, 1365–1416; A. Hume, ibid. 1082, no. 27.

Cambridge University Library

Barnes's *Supplication* was first published at Antwerp in 1531, with a second edition in London, 1534. Both contain an account of the articles on which Barnes had been examined in 1526, the second being 'What is holy church and who be therof and whereby men may know her'. More answered this at length in Book VIII of the *Confutation* of Tyndale (no. 148), and Barnes added a retort in the second edition of his *Supplication*.

152
The Burning of Robert Barnes, Thomas Garrard and William Jerome
Unknown artist, in John Foxe, *Actes and Monuments of the English Church*, 1563
Woodcut, 12.7 × 17.5 (5 × 6¾)

Bibliography CW, VIII, 1365–1416.

The Trustees of the British Museum (English History File, Henry VIII)

Robert Barnes, William Jerome and Thomas Garrard were all well-known members of the reforming party, when appointed in 1540 to preach a series of Lenten sermons at Paul's Cross. Barnes's sermon attacked Bishop Gardiner (no. 206) for his condemnation of the doctrine of justification by faith, Gardiner complained to Henry and Henry summoned Barnes. Barnes, Garrard and Barlowe were each ordered to preach a recantation sermon. Each began his sermon with the required abrogation, but withdrew it before the end. On 30 July the three suffered the cruel death of heretics, while three others were put to death as papists and traitors.

Sir Thomas More's Controversy with John Frith and George Joye

More's controversy with John Frith (1503–33) and George Joye (?1495–1553) chiefly concerned the Eucharist, though his answers to Frith involve the doctrine of purgatory as well. It seems that he also involved his son John in the eucharistic controversy (no. 156). Frith was one of Wolsey's young men, brought from Cambridge in 1525 to the newly-founded Cardinal College in Oxford. He became a disciple of Luther and Tyndale, a spreader of 'Lutronous opinions' and fled to Marburg in 1528. After 1531 he came increasingly under the influence of Zwingli (no. 137) and Oecolampadius (nos. 138, 139). He returned to England in July 1532, three months after More's resignation, and was imprisoned in October. In prison he wrote five works. Frith was burned in Smithfield on 4 July 1533.

George Joye (Jaye, Gee, Geach), a Bedfordshire priest and Fellow of Peterhouse, escaped to the Continent in 1527. He translated a number of Old Testament books and reworked Tyndale's New Testament (no. 143), to Tyndale's fury. Probably in 1529, he produced the first English primer, now lost, but followed by a second edition in 1530 (no. 160). Joye almost certainly wrote *The Souper of the Lorde*, to which More replied, and continued to publish after More's death. He returned to England in late 1535, left again between 1541 and 1546 and returned under Edward VI.

There was much disagreement among the English reformers about the Eucharist, and More made capital of this.

153
Frith's Attack
John Frith, *A pistle to the Christen reader. The Revelation of Antichrist. Antithesis wherin are compared to geder Christes actes and oure holye father the Popes*, [Antwerp, Johannes Hoochstraten], 1529

Bibliography STC, 11394; NK, 3044; *CW*, VIII, 1065–7, 1073, no. 11, 1467–8; William A. Clebsch, *England's earliest Protestants*, New Haven 1964, 78–136.

The British Library Board (C.37.b.53)

This is another work in the 'Marburg' series, printed in Antwerp for dissemination in England and issued pseudonymously under the name Richard Brightewell. It was Frith's first published work and is a translation of Luther's *Offinbarung des Endchrists...*, Wittenberg 1524 (cf his *De Antichristo*, 1521), an account of the surrender of the Church to Mammon. This is followed by a series of seventy-eight comparisons between the acts of the pope and the acts of Christ, suggested by and indeed an expanded version of the images in the *Passional Christi und Antichristi* of 1521 (no. 126).

154
Sir Thomas More's Letter against Frith
Sir Thomas More, *A letter of syr Tho. More Knyght impugnynge the erronyouse wrytyng of Iohan Fryth agaynst the blessed sacrament of the aultare*, London, William Rastell, 1533

Bibliography STC2, 18090; Gibson, 66; Rogers, 190; McKerrow-Ferguson, 17.

Bodleian Library, Oxford

More's *Letter against Frith*, far the shortest of his English works of controversy, is dated from Chelsea, 7 December 1532. Rastell's printing bears the date 1533.

It opens with a bravura passage on the canker and the fire of heresy and passes to Frith's work: 'a wors than this is, though the wordes be smoth and fayre, the deuyll, I trow, can not make. For herin he ronneth a great way beyond Luther, and techeth in a few leuys shortely, all the poyson that Wyclyffe, Huyskyn [ie Oecolampadius], Tyndale and Zuinglius haue taught... concernynge the blessed sacrament of the aultare, affermyng it to be not onely very brede styll as Luther doth, but also as those other bestes do, saith it is nothyng els...' The orthodox doctrine of transubstantiation is then advanced, and the letter ends with a prayer to God to 'blesse these poysened errours out of hys blynd harte, and make hym hys faythfull seruant, and sende you hartely well to fare'.

155
Frith's Answer to Sir Thomas More
John Frith, *A boke made by Iohn Frith prisoner in the tower of London answeringe vnto M mores lettur...*, 'Monster, Conrad Willems', [ie Antwerp, ?Widow of Christoffel van Ruremund, called Endhoven, 1533]

Bibliography STC, 11381; NK, 3042; *CW*, VIII, 1065–7, 1083–4, no. 31.

The British Library Board (C.12.b.9(3))

Frith's further formulation of his opinions on the Eucharist was written in the Tower after he had had access to More's *Letter*. It was smuggled out to Antwerp and published there in the second half of 1533 by an unknown printer. It proves to More, according to its author, that the Church's doctrine of the Eucharist 'was no artycle of oure faythe necessarye to be beleued vnder payne of dampnacyon'.

156
Photograph: John More's Translation of Fridericus Nausea on the Eucharist
A sermon of the sacrament of the aulter made by a famous doctoure called Fryderyke Nausea in Almayne and lately out of latyn translate into englysh by John More, London, William Rastell, 1533

Bibliography STC2, 18414; Allen, 1577; P. Hogrefe, 'John More's Translations', *Papers of the Bibliographical Society of America*, 49, 1955, 188–9; E. B. Blackburn, *Moreana*, II, 1964, 5–36.

Photograph by courtesy of the Folger Shakespeare Library, Washington DC

Sir Thomas More's son, John (c.1509–47; nos. 178, 180, 181), translated this sermon, 'meruelouse mete for the season', one Easter, presumably in 1533, just after the appearance of his father's *Letter against Frith* (no. 154) and the second part of his *Confutation* (no. 148) and just when the *Apology* (no. 165) was coming from the press. It is an exposition of orthodox doctrine on the Eucharist, translated from a sermon in the *Evangelicae veritatis homiliarum centuriae* of Fridericus Nausea (Friedrich Grawe), Cologne 1530–2. Nausea (1480–1552), born in Waischenfeld, was a noted preacher, prolific author and champion of the Church, a collaborator with Cochlaeus (nos. 127, 128). He became Bishop of Vienna in 1541 and died at Trent while the Council was in progress.

157
Joye's Supper of the Lord
George Joye, *The Souper of the Lorde, wher vnto... haue here firste the declaration of the later parte of the .6. ca. of S. Iohan...*, 'Nornburg' [ie Antwerp or London], 'Niclas twonson' [ie Symon Cock or N. Hill], 1533

Bibliography STC2, 24468; NK, 3996; A. Hume in *CW*, VIII, 1065–7, 1083, no. 29; W. D. J. Cargill Thompson, 'Who wrote *The Supper of the Lord*', *Harvard Theological Review*, LIII, 1960, 77–91; W. A. Clebsch, 'More Evidence that George Joye wrote *The Souper of the Lorde*', ibid. LIV, 1962, 63–6; Charles C. Butterworth and Allan G. Chester, *George Joye, 1495–1553...*, Philadelphia 1962.

The British Library Board (3932.a.14)

This tract is often attributed to William Tyndale, though the evidence is strongly for Joye. In his *Answer*, More inclines to the idea that it is Joye's, though he declines to make invidious distinctions between one anonymous heretic and another; he may, he feels, be dealing with Tyndale, Joye, or 'some yonge, vnlerned fole'. As the title announces, the tract deals with the right interpretation of John vi 32ff: 'My Father giveth you the true bread from heaven'; and incidentally defends Frith against 'Master Mocke', ie Thomas More. The argument is partly dependent on Zwingli (no. 137).

Three other editions were published in London in 1547.

158
Sir Thomas More's Answer to Joye
Sir Thomas More, *The answere to the fyrst parte of the poysened booke, whych a namelesse heretyke hath named the souper of the lorde...*, London, William Rastell, 1534

Bibliography STC2, 18077; Gibson, 45; cf A. Hume in *CW*, VIII, 1083, no. 29; G. Marc'hadour, *Bible*, 306ff.

The British Library Board (C.53.i.21)

The Souper of the Lorde came out on 5 April 1533, about the time More published his *Apology* (no. 165). He probably set about an answer at once, perhaps breaking off to compose his *Debellation* (no. 167). The *Answer* is dated 1534, though Rastell seems to have finished work at the end of 1533. It was More's last controversial tract; in April 1534, within a few months of its publication, he was in the Tower. He deals faithfully with his adversary's ('Master Masker') attitude to the Church's authority, refuting his 'new-fangled', individual interpretations of Scripture, thought up to buttress his errors on the Eucharist.

159
Joye Attacks Again
George Joye, *The Subuersion of Mores false foundacion...*, M.D.xxxiiij. at Emdon by Iacob Aurik [ie ?Antwerp, ?Govaert van der Haghen, 1534]

Bibliography STC2, 14829; A. Hume, in *CW*, VIII, 1084, no. 31; C. C. Butterworth and A. G. Chester, *George Joye...*, 109–13.

Durham University Library: from the Collection of M. J. Routh, 1755–1854

Joye's *Subversion* makes no reference to Thomas More's retort. It concentrates on the *Confutation* (no. 148) and the doctrine of the 'unwritten verities' of the Church, ie the doctrines not found explicitly in Scripture but handed down by tradition from the Apostles. Joye's title gives a sufficient impression of the tendentiousness and aggression which made him often at odds with his allies as well as his opponents: *The Subuersion of Mores false foundacion: where upon he sweteth to set faste and shoue under his shameles shoris* [ie props] *to under proppe the popis chirche: Made by George Ioye. More is become a vain lyer in his own resoning and arguments: and his folyssh harte is blynded. Where he beleued to haue done moste wysely there he hathe shewed himselfe a starke foole. Rom. i. Moros in Greke is stultus in Latyn/a fool in Englysshe. Viuit Dominus: cuius inuicta veritas manet in eternum.*

THE DEFENCE OF THE CHURCH

160
Photograph: **Thomas Hitton, Pseudo-Martyr**
George Joye, *Ortulus anime. The garden of the soule...*,
Antwerp, Martin de Keyser, 1530

Bibliography STC2, 13828.4; *CW*, VIII, esp. 14–17; A. Hume, ibid. 1075–6, no. 14; C. C. Butterworth and A. G. Chester, *George Joye...*, 60–7, 106–7; C. C. Butterworth, *The English Primers 1529–1645*, Philadelphia 1953, 11–23.

Photograph by courtesy of the British Library Board

Sir Thomas Hitton, a priest not a knight, came from Marsham in the diocese of Norwich and was burned as a heretic at Maidstone on 20 February 1529/30. For the Protestant exiles, Hitton was a martyr; Joye put him into the calendar of his Protestant primer in English, *Ortulus anime*, on 23 February as 'Seinte Thomas mar.' More's rage at finding Hitton so set up in opposition to St Thomas Becket is expressed with 'wit and malice hypersatanic' (Charles Lamb) in the preface to his *Confutation* (no. 148), where Hitton is called 'the dyuyls stynkyng martyr'.

161
The Burning of Richard Bayfield, 1531
Unknown artist, in John Foxe, *Actes and Monuments of the English Church*, 1563
Woodcut, 11 × 7.5 ($4\frac{3}{8} \times 2\frac{15}{16}$)

Bibliography Sir Thomas More, *Confutation*, *CW*, VIII, esp. 10–17, 1183–4; id. *Apology*, ed. Taft, 98, 105, 298–9.

The Trustees of the British Museum (English History File, Henry VIII)

Richard Bayfield, alias Somersam, was a Benedictine monk of Bury St Edmunds, converted to Lutheranism by Robert Barnes (nos. 151, 152). Detected as a heretic and forced to abjure at some time before April 1528, he then left England for the Continent, became involved in the traffic in Protestant books, and married. According to More, 'he went about two wyves, one in Brabande, another in Englande... the tone bycause he was preste, the tother bycause he was monke'. Bayfield returned to England, and was pardoned by Henry, but continued to distribute the works of Tyndale and others. As a result of the confession extracted by More from George Constantine, Bayfield was seized in the autumn of 1531 and examined before John Stokesley, Bishop of London. 'Monke and apostata, that was as an abiured and after periured and relapsed heretyke,' Bayfield was, in More's words, 'wel and worthely burned in Smythfelde', on 4 December of the same year.

Sir Thomas More's Controversy with Simon Fish

Simon Fish was a lawyer and a member of Lincoln's Inn, who had apparently been in trouble with Wolsey in 1526. In 1528, he was named in the confession of Robert Necton, bookseller, as an agent in the distribution of Tyndale's New Testament, and went into hiding. He was later persuaded to show himself to the king, who was gracious to him and gave him immunity from arrest. Fish died of the plague in 1531, after being reconciled with the Church, and his widow married James Bainham, the heretic burned in 1532.

Fish's attack was as much social as doctrinal: he saw in purgatory an institution by which the Church enriched itself and oppressed true Christians. The doctrinal issues were more fully treated by John Rastell, More's brother-in-law, and John Fisher on the Catholic side and by Tyndale and Frith on the Protestant.

162
Fish's Attack on the Clergy
Simon Fish, *A Supplicatyon for the Beggers*, [? Antwerp, ? Johannes Grapheus, 1529]

Bibliography STC, 10883; NK, 3032; *CW*, VIII, 1187–91 and A. Hume, ibid. 1071, no. 8; F. J. Furnivall, ed., *EETS*, ES, XIII, 1871.

The British Library Board (C.21.b.45)

Simon Fish's tract was addressed to Henry VIII. John Foxe says that it was distributed at Candlemas (2 February) and also that Anne Boleyn pressed it on Henry. It purports to be an open letter from the beggars of England, complaining of starvation because they are outbegged by the clergy who have got hold of half the country's wealth to support their dissolute lives. Their chief weapon and their chief money-maker, through the sale of indulgences (no. 125), is the doctrine of purgatory. The king and his Parliament must intervene, confiscate clerical property and curb their power and riches. Fish's is one of the first shots in a campaign against the spiritual jurisdiction, later to gather force through Christopher St German and others.

163
Sir Thomas More's Answer to Fish
Sir Thomas More, *The supplycacyon of soulys... Agaynst the supplycacyon of Beggars*, London, William Rastell, 1529, 2nd edition

Bibliography STC2, 18093, cf 18092; Gibson, 71, cf 72; St Thomas More, *The Supplication of Souls*, ed. Sister Mary Thecla, Westminster, Maryland 1950; St Thomas More, *Lettre à Dorp; la Supplication des âmes*, trans. G. Marc'hadour, Namur 1962, 131–274; *CW*, VIII, 1187–91, 1201–3.

The Beinecke Rare Book and Manuscript Library, Yale University

More retorts that 'the beggars' proctor' or 'the devil's proctor', as he styles Fish, has produced arguments 'so merry and so mad that it were able to make one laugh that lieth in the fire'. He defends the clergy against Fish's charges of extortion and corruption and proves to his satisfaction the existence of purgatory where souls would lie in pain for ever were it not for the alms given to the clergy so that they can deliver them from it.

More's second essay in religious controversy in English quickly went into a second edition, printed in the same month and by the same printer, More's nephew William Rastell. This copy is the one later used to set up the text of the *Supplication of Souls* for the edition of More's English *Works*, 1557 (no. 260). The printer's red chalk casting-off marks can clearly be seen.

Sir Thomas More's Controversy with Christopher St German

After More had resigned the chancellorship in May 1532, he was involved in a new dispute involving ancient discontents with clerical lives, powers, prerogatives and possessions. Hitherto his opponents had been priests in the main, and the controversy concerned with doctrine. Simon Fish's *Supplication* had been a single shot. Now there came a press campaign, apparently fostered by Thomas Cromwell and fuelled by the common lawyers, on the 'extort power' of the clergy, aimed at bringing them under the law of the realm rather than that of the pope.

When the ecclesiastical jurisdiction came thus under attack in the 1530s, More was in an impossible position: he had to defend the clergy without seeming to touch the question of the Supremacy. It seems that he thought his principal opponent a priest, or at least that he wished to be thought to think so. Almost certainly, the antagonist was one of the most learned jurists of his day, Christopher St German (?1460–1540).

Warwickshire born, St German had his legal training at the Middle Temple; his reputation rests chiefly on his *Dialogus de fundamentis legum Anglie et de conscientia* (1528), which was to become famous as *Doctor and Student*. The relevance of this book to More is in its implicit proposition that the King in Parliament has power to make laws binding on both clergy and laymen.

164
St German's Attack on the Clergy
?Christopher St German, *A Treatise concernynge the Diuision betwene the Spirytualtie and Temporaltie*, London, Robert Redman, ?1532

Bibliography STC2, 21586; McKerrow-Ferguson, 22; F. le V. Baumer, 'Christopher St German: the political Philosophy of a Tudor Lawyer', *American Historical Review*, XLII, 1940, 631–51; St German's *Doctor and Student*, ed. T. F. T. Plucknett and J. L. Barton, Selden Society, XCI, 1974; A. I. Taft, ed., in *Apology*, EETS, OS, CLXXX, 1930; J. B. Trapp, ed., in *CW*, X, forthcoming.

The Master and Fellows of St John's College, Cambridge

The first of St German's anti-clerical tracts was printed at least five times between late 1532 and 1537. It elicited the 590 or so pages of More's *Apology*. The clergy are accused of severity towards laymen and partiality to their fellows, a chief cause of discontent being the methods used by the ecclesiastical courts in the detection, trial and punishment of offenders against canon law.

165
Sir Thomas More's Defence
The Apologye of syr Thomas More knyght, London, William Rastell, 1533

Bibliography STC2, 18078; Gibson, 46; McKerrow-Ferguson, 17; A. I. Taft, ed., *EETS*, OS, CLXXX, 1930; J. B. Trapp, ed., *CW*, IX, forthcoming.

Guildhall Library, London (Cock Colln. 1.2)

Thomas More's *Apology* came out about Easter 1533, immediately preceded by the second part of his *Confutation* (no. 148), and its publication was probably simultaneous with his son John's translation of Fridericus Nausea's sermon on the Eucharist (no. 156). The *Apology* opens with a recapitulation of the controversy with Tyndale (nos. 145–8) and Fish (nos. 162, 163), and continues with a point by point refutation of the *Treatise on the Division*, defending the clergy of England against accusations of corruption and justifying especially their modes of procedure against heretics, clinging to the 'comen lawes of Christendom' in force for fifteen hundred years as against anything 'brought up for new'. More makes play with his adversary's claim to be composing strife rather than fomenting it and to be merely reporting grievances, nicknaming him 'the Pacifier' and 'Sir John Some-say'.

The most moving feature of the *Apology* is the dignified personal defence offered by More against accusations of venality and personal cruelty towards heretics.

166
St German's Retort
?Christopher St German, *Salem and Bizance*, London, Thomas Berthelet, 1533

Bibliography STC2, 21584; R. J. Schoeck and Ruth E. McGugan, eds., *CW*, X, forthcoming.

Cambridge University Library

A Dialogue betwyxte two englyshemen, wherof one was called Salem and the other Bizance, was published in answer to More's *Apology* at Michaelmas 1533. It is again anonymous, but there is no reason to doubt the attribution to St German. The title probably alludes to the plight of Jerusalem (Salem) and Constantinople (Bizance) languishing in the power of the Turks while Christendom wastes its powers in internal dissension. The final chapters deal with the lawfulness of a crusade against the infidel. In the body of the book the attack on the ecclesiastical arm is renewed.

167
Sir Thomas More's Rejoinder
Sir Thomas More, *The Debellacyon of Salem and Bizance*, London, William Rastell, 1533

Bibliography STC2, 18081; McKerrow-Ferguson, 27; Gibson, 50; R. J. Schoek and Ruth E. McGugan, eds., *CW*, X, forthcoming.

Cambridge University Library

When St German's *Salem and Bizance* was published at Michaelmas 1533, More retorted at once: 'I sodainely went in hand therewith, and made it in a breide' [in a burst]. Elsewhere he says it took him ten days. The book, again much longer than his adversary's, was in print by the beginning of November (Allhallows) 1533. More, affecting not to understand St German's title, again defends the clergy, with fewer of the brief sallies that enliven the *Apology* and little or none of the *Apology*'s personal poignancy. St German, it seems, fired off several further salvoes: *The Addicions of Salem and Bizance* (1534), *A treatyse concerning the power of the clergye and the lawes of the Realme* (?1534), *A Treatise concernynge diuers of the constitucyons prouincial and legantine* [sic] (?1535) and *An Answere to a letter* (?1535), which More allowed to pass. In the six months of freedom remaining he turned again to sacramental debate in his *Answer to a poisoned Book* (no. 158) and to devotion.

168
John Foxe (1516–87)
George Glover, 1641
Engraving 20 × 16.2 ($7\frac{7}{8} \times 6\frac{3}{8}$)

Bibliography Emden, *Oxford 1540*, 212–14; A. M. Hind, *Engraving in England*, II, Cambridge 1952, 157, 352; Strong, *Catalogue*, 123–4, pls 246–8; W. Haller, *Foxe's Book of Martyrs and the Elect Nation*, 1963.

National Portrait Gallery, London

This engraving of John Foxe is based on a portrait which exists in several versions, including a poor one at the NPG. The type was engraved for Henry Holland's *Herωologia* (1620), and again by George Glover for the 1641 edition of Foxe's *Actes and Monuments of the English Church* ('Foxe's Book of Martyrs'). The date 1587 probably represents the date of Foxe's death, rather than the year in which this portrait type was created.

Foxe, a native of Boston, educated at Oxford, resigned his fellowship of Magdalen College and went abroad in 1554, at the accession of Mary. In Strasbourg he published a first brief version, in Latin, of what was to become the 'Book of Martyrs', and at Basel, where he worked for some time as press corrector for the successor of Johann Froben, he issued an augmented version (1559). In the same year he returned to England and was ordained priest. Made a canon of Salisbury in 1563, he published in that year, at the press of John Day, his *Actes and Monuments* (nos. 149, 152, 161). There were three further editions in Foxe's lifetime.

In his first English edition, Foxe retailed a number of the stories of More's cruelty to the English heretics which had either been applied to him or invented for circulation before and after his death. Some of these were suppressed in later editions.

FAMILIA THOMAE MORI ANGL: CANCELL:
Thomas Morus A°.50. Alicia Thomæ Mori uxor A°.57. Iohannes Morus pater A°.76. Iohannes Morus Thomæ filius A°.19. Anna Grisacria Iohannis Mori Sponsa A°.15. Margareta Ropera Thomæ Mori filia A°.22. Elisabeta Dancea Thomæ Mori filia A°.21. Cæcilia Heroina Thomæ Mori filia A°.20. Margareta Giga Clementis uxor Mori filialis Condiscipula et cognata A°.22. Henricus Patensonus Thomæ Mori morio A°.40.

169

V Sir Thomas More and his Household

The firmness, serenity and fidelity of Sir Thomas More's temperament and the ordered calm of his 'private, secret and domestical life and trade', as his biographer Harpsfield was to call it, were his refuge, first in Bucklersbury and later in Chelsea, from the hurly-burly of religious controversy and public responsibility. His son-in-law William Roper tells how he was 'never in a fume', and there is much evidence of his kindness. His little patriarchal society was ordered with almost monastic regularity, Sir Thomas himself rising at 2 am and spending the time until 7 in prayer and study. As far as he could, he also passed his Fridays thus. At mealtimes, Scripture was read aloud. Erasmus described the establishment at Chelsea as Plato's Academy in Christian shape. Life there was governed by natural affection and by the threefold love of God, of self, of neighbour.

Tutors were provided for the children, so that they would learn Latin and Greek, logic, philosophy, theology, mathematics and astronomy, and Sir Thomas watched carefully over progress. Whenever he was absent, he wrote to his children, in Latin, and required that they answer faithfully in the same. His concern that his daughters should be as carefully educated as his son marks him out from his time, and he anticipates criticism of this in a letter to one of their tutors, William Gunnell. Others who regularly helped in the education of the household were Nicolaus Kratzer (no. 187), who taught astronomy and mathematics, Richard Hyrde and Master Drew. Others, like Joannes Ludovicus Vives, must have given assistance from time to time. There was music, too, and life was not all earnest: one of Sir Thomas More's favourite adjectives is 'merry', and he admired wit as much as he hated mindless pastimes like dice and cards.

Of blood relations in the household watched over by Sir Thomas and his second wife Dame Alice, there were the four children of his first marriage – Margaret, Elizabeth, Cicely and John, in order of seniority; there was also Margaret Gigs, a dear foster-daughter, and Anne Cresacre, Sir Thomas's ward. The children all married: Margaret to William Roper in 1521, Elizabeth to William Dauncey and Cicely to Giles Heron in 1525, Margaret Gigs to John Clement in 1526, and John to Anne Cresacre in 1529. John Clement was another member of the household, who had been with Sir Thomas More on his 'Utopian' mission as his 'pupil servant'. He was Cardinal Wolsey's lecturer in rhetoric and later Reader in Greek at Oxford, and also became learned as a physician. There were others, too: John Harris, Sir Thomas's amanuensis, who married Margaret Roper's maid; and Henry Patenson, his fool. And there were non-human members: Sir Thomas kept an aviary and a small menagerie, and also delighted in any strange or remarkable object.

Something of the atmosphere of Sir Thomas More's household is to be experienced from the pictures of it and its members made by Hans Holbein when he was welcomed into it for a time in 1526–8.

Of Thomas More's talent for friendship, his benevolence to rich and poor and his readiness to disregard an injury, Erasmus and others have left testimony. Sir Thomas's friends are dispersed throughout this exhibition. In this section there appear only slight evidences of his care for his friends' interests (the indenture, no. 190, concerning the mother of his late friend, John Colet), of his friendships, such as the one, lasting until the end of his life, with Antonio Bonvisi, of Lucca (no. 189), and of his encouragement of scholarly promise (Thomas Lupset, nos. 191, 192).

169
Facsimile: **Thomas More, his Father and his Household**
Hans Holbein the Younger, 1527–8 (before 7 February 1528)
Original pen and ink drawing in the Kunstmuseum Basel

Provenance Commissioned by Thomas More, perhaps at request of Erasmus; perhaps taken to Erasmus in Basel by Holbein August 1528; at death of Erasmus to Bonifacius Amerbach; Amerbach family; sold 1662 to city of Basel, with Amerbach collection.

Exhibitions Basel, *Malerfamilie Holbein* (308); *Erasmus*, 1969 (67).
Bibliography Ganz, *Handzeichnungen*, no. 24; Schmid, *Holbein*, 293ff; Morison-Barker, no. 402; Strong, *Catalogue*, 345–51; O. Pächt, 'Holbein and Kratzer as Collaborators', *Burlington Magazine*, LXXXIV, 1944, 134–9.

On the evidence of its inscriptions, Holbein's drawing must have been completed before 7 February 1528. It was certainly in Erasmus's hands in Basel by 3 September 1529, when he

171 *(enlarged)*   173 *(enlarged)*

wrote to More, as well as to Margaret Roper on 6 September (Allen, 2211, 2212), expressing admiration for Holbein's skill.

The inscriptions giving the ages of the sitters and identifying each of them were added by Nicolaus Kratzer, tutor to More's household in astronomy and mathematics (nos. 187, 188). From left, they are: Elizabeth Dauncey (daughter, b. 1506; no. 182); Margaret Clement (née Gigs, foster daughter, ?1508–70; no. 184); Sir John More (father, ?1451–1530; no. 9); Anne More, née Cresacre (daughter-in-law, 1511–77; no. 179); Sir Thomas More (1477/8–1535); John More II (son, ?1509–47; no. 178); Henry Pateuson (jester); Cicely Heron (daughter, b.1507; no. 183); Margaret Roper (daughter, 1505–44; no. 174); and Dame Alice More, widow of John Middleton (second wife).

The drawing bears two notes in another hand to the effect that the viol hanging on the wall beside the buffet should be changed into musical instruments placed on the buffet itself and that Dame Alice should sit instead of kneel. The hand is thought to be Holbein's and the proposed changes the effect of consultation with More.

170
Sir Thomas More, his Father, his Household and his Descendants
(Colour plate IV, page 90)
Rowland Lockey, *c*. 1595–1600
Vellum, 24.6 × 29.4 ($9\frac{11}{16} \times 11\frac{9}{16}$), in 17th-century walnut cabinet with double locking doors

Provenance An unidentified Lady Gerrard; bt. James Sotheby 1705 for £10.15s; Sotheby family at Ecton Hall; sold Sotheby's 11 October 1955 (67); Rev. James Edmund Strickland, by whose widow Anne Louise Strickland bequeathed to Victoria and Albert Museum 1973.
Exhibition London, New Gallery, *Royal House of Tudor*, 1890.
Bibliography E. Auerbach, *Nicholas Hilliard*, 1962, no. 262; Morison-Barker, no. 405.
Victoria and Albert Museum, London (15–1973)

George Vertue saw this miniature at Ecton Hall in 1742 and decided it was by the same hand as painted the large oil family group (no. 1) now in the NPG: he therefore attributed it to Lockey. It had previously passed for a Holbein; Horace Walpole gave it to Peter Oliver; it is now generally agreed to be by Lockey.

The miniature is more closely related to the NPG picture of 1593 than to the original Holbein type of the More household group. Eleven of its twelve figures are posed and placed identically with those in the NPG version, though their clothing and accessories are often differently coloured. They are identified by gold letters painted on their clothing and keyed to an inscription in gold along the upper edge: *A*. Johañes Morus eques auratus et iudex; *B*. Tho. Morˢ eques aur. Dns. Canc. Ang. et fil. et haer. dti. Johannis; *C*. Joh. More Ar. fil. et haer. Dti. Tho; *D*. Anna sola fil. et haer. Ed. Cresacre Ar. Vxor Joh Mor Ar. *E*. Tho. More [II] Arm. fil. et haer. Dictor. Joh. Mor. Ar. et An Vx. eius; *F*. Maria fil. Joh. Scroope Ar. frat. Henrici Dni. Scroope; *G*. Duo filii dictorum Tho. Mor. et Mar. Vx. eius [ie Thomas More III and Cresacre More]; *H*. Tres filiae Tho. Mori Dni. Cancellarij Angliae [ie Cicely Heron, Elizabeth Dauncey and Margaret Roper]. A label lettered in gold at the lower left corner reads: Thomas Morus Londini/An. Do. 1480. est natus/Scaccarij primum. tum. A.D./1529. totius Angliae/Cancellarius est factus./Henrici. 8. iussu decollatus/interijt A.D. 1535. 6 non. Jul.

It seems probable that the miniature was painted later than the NPG oil. Cresacre More, clean-shaven in the NPG picture, has a light beard and moustache. The portrait of Anne (Cresacre) More in later life and the escutcheons on the background wall of the NPG version are replaced by a 'gardenscape', with a distant view of London behind it. This takes the place of a doorway with a view through to another room in the Holbein picture. The curtain, a feature lacking in the NPG version, is parted in the centre by the hand of a twelfth figure, Henry Pateuson, More's fool, who appears in the gap. Pateuson is likewise absent from the NPG version, though he appears in the Holbein picture, standing four-square at the right centre of the group, not sidling through the curtain. The escutcheons, entirely absent from Holbein's original, are reduced from the NPG's former eight to two at the left of the miniature. These are More (with a different

174 *(enlarged)*

crest) and Cresacre quartering More (also with a different crest).

The miniature is thus, though less insistent on the Cresacre connection than the NPG oil, its prototype, also a family commemoration rather than a household group. It was probably commissioned from Lockey by Thomas More II.

171
Sir Thomas More (1477/8–1535)
After Hans Holbein the Younger, ?mid 16th century
Water-colour on vellum, diameter 6 ($2\frac{3}{8}$)

Provenance Conceivably Margaret Roper; Quicke family; J. Pierpont Morgan 1905; Christie's 24 June, 1935 (128); Sir Felix Cassell; presented by him to present owners.
Exhibitions BFAC, *Early English Portraits*, 1909; *Erasmus*, 1969 (69).
Bibliography Morison-Barker, no. 101.

Private Collection

Three miniature portraits of More are extant which can reasonably be thought to belong to the sixteenth century; there are records of another in Van der Doort's inventory of Charles I's collection (1637–40). All have been ascribed to Holbein.

172
Sir Thomas More
After Hans Holbein the Younger, 16th century
Oil, ?on gesso over silver, 3.3 × 2.8 ($1\frac{5}{16} \times 1\frac{1}{8}$)

Exhibitions Manchester, 1857; BFAC, *Early English Portraits*, 1909.
Bibliography Morison-Barker, no. 103.

His Grace the Duke of Buccleuch and Queensberry (7/31)

The latest in date of the miniatures of More which can plausibly be thought to date from the sixteenth century, though it may be later.

173
Hans Holbein the Younger (1497/8–1543)
Self-portrait, ?1543
Water-colour on playing card, diameter 3.7 ($1\frac{7}{16}$)

Provenance Horace Walpole (1717–97), Strawberry Hill.
Exhibitions BFAC, *Early English Portraits*, 1909 (23); RA, *Holbein* (191).
Bibliography Ganz, no. 150.

His Grace the Duke of Buccleuch and Queensberry (1/6)

According to Karel van Mander (*Schilderboek*, 1604), Holbein did not begin to paint miniature portraits until he had entered service with Henry VIII: his instructor in the art of 'limning' was 'the painter Lucas' (Horenbout). Of his miniature self-portrait *en peintre* four versions are extant. One, larger than the others, is in the Clowes Collection, Indianapolis (Ganz, no. 130). According to Ganz, the three small versions are copies of this. All four bear the same inscriptions H.H. A.N. 1543 ETATIS SVE. 4.5., except that, on the largest, the date is given as 1542, the year before Holbein's death at the age of forty-six in 1543. The other two small versions are in the Wallace Collection (Ganz, no. 149) and in the Mayer van den Bergh Museum, Antwerp (Ganz, no. 151).

174
Margaret Roper (1505–44) **and her Husband William Roper** (1493/8–1578)
Ascribed to Hans Holbein the Younger, ?1536–40
Two miniatures, water-colour on card, each diameter 4.5 ($1\frac{3}{4}$)

Provenance Roper family.
Bibliography Roper, xxxix–xlvii; Ganz, nos. 134–5; C. Winter, 'Holbein's Miniatures', *Burlington Magazine*, LXXXII, 1943, 266; E. E. Reynolds, *Margaret Roper*, 1960.

Metropolitan Museum of Art, New York: Rogers Fund, 1950 (50.69.2)

William Roper came of a family of wealthy Kentish landowners and was later proprietor of Well Hall, Eltham, and

the Roper property in the parish of St Dunstan's, Canterbury. In 1518 he entered Lincoln's Inn, later becoming bencher, Governor and Prothonotary. About the same time he became a member of More's household, remaining by his own account 'xvj yeares and more in house conversant with him', and marrying More's eldest and dearest child Margaret on 2 July 1521. By 1523 they had given More a grandchild, later followed by four more. The most gifted, Mary, married successively Stephen Clarke and James Basset, and translated Thomas More's *De tristitia Christi* (no. 225) into English.

Harpsfield tells how Roper espoused, more or less simultaneously, Lutheran doctrine and Margaret More, and how, after a warning from Wolsey, he was rescued by the prayers of Thomas More. Roper later took the oath of Supremacy and seems to have suffered little for his adherence to the faith or for his connexion with More's family. In 1568-9 he was in trouble for financing religious exiles. Roper was MP in 1529, 1554, 1555, and 1557-8, and was nominated by Sir Thomas White, its founder, Visitor for life of St John's College, Oxford.

Margaret, who predeceased her husband by over thirty years, was buried in the More Chapel at Chelsea. Stapleton says that she had been charged before the King's Council with 'keeping her father's head as a sacred relic, and retaining possession of his books and writings. She answered that she had saved her father's head from being devoured by the fishes with the intention of burying it...' She also said that she had almost no manuscripts that had not been published, except a few letters 'which she humbly begged to be allowed to keep for her consolation and, by the good offices of friends, she was released'.

This is the only known portrait of Roper, taken, according to the inscription, AN° AETATIS SVAE XLII. Like the husbands of More's other daughters, he does not figure in the household groups (nos. 1, 169, 170). Margaret, who is characterised A° AETATIS XXX, would have reached that age in 1536.

175
Margaret Roper's translation of Erasmus on the Lord's Prayer
A deuout treatise vpon the Pater noster ... tourned in to englisshe by a yong vertuous and well lerned gentyl-woman of .XIX. yere of age, London, Thomas Berthelet, [1526]

Bibliography STC, 10477; Gibson, 487; E. E. Reynolds, *Margaret Roper*, 1960, 39-43; J. A. Gee in *Review of English Studies*, XIII, 1937, 257-71; *Moreana*, VII, IX, XI, 1965-6.

The British Library Board (C.37.e.6)

In 1523, at the birth of Margaret and William Roper's first child, Erasmus dedicated to Margaret his commentary on the Christmas Hymn of Prudentius, and sent it with a kiss for the baby. At Basel, in the same year, he published his *Precatio dominica in septem portiones divisa*. Margaret translated it into English and it was published in early 1526 with a preface by Richard Hyrde, tutor to the household, praising Margaret's 'virtuouse conuersation, lyuynge and sad [ie steadfast] demeanoure [and] good learning'.

176
Sir Thomas More (1477/8-1535)
Hans Holbein the Younger, 1526-7
Coloured chalks on white paper, 38×25.8 ($14\frac{15}{16} \times 10\frac{1}{8}$)

Provenance Windsor Holbein drawings: ?Edward VI, c.1550; at death to Henry Fitzalan, Earl of Arundel; John, Lord Lumley, 1580; ?to Prince Henry, at whose death (1612) to Prince Charles; ceded to Earl of Pembroke in exchange for Raphael's *St George* between 1627 and 1630; Thomas Howard, 2nd Earl of Arundel; Royal Collection again by 1675; discovered by Queen Caroline, consort of George II, in a closet at Kensington Palace 1727.
Exhibition RA, *Holbein* (123).
Bibliography Parker, no. 2; Morison-Barker, no. 1.

Her Majesty the Queen (Windsor Castle 12225)

Sir Thomas More was Hans Holbein's first patron in England. Erasmus had recommended the painter and on his arrival in the late summer of 1526 he was quickly commissioned to portray More and his household. Two drawings of Sir Thomas himself (this one and no. 177) and one each of the other members of his family (nos. 9, 178, 179, 182, 183, 184) were probably made almost at once in preparation for the great family group executed by Holbein, but now lost. This 'first Windsor drawing' is paler, of slightly smaller size and of lesser quality than its companion. Its condition is also worse, it has been reworked, and it does not show the line of the collar of SS which appears in the Basel sketch (no. 169) and the oil versions. The inscription 'Sier Thomas Mooer' is in a contemporary hand.

177
Sir Thomas More
(Colour plate V, page 107)
Hans Holbein the Younger, 1526-7
Coloured chalks on white paper, 40.2×30.1 ($15\frac{13}{16} \times 11\frac{13}{16}$)

Provenance As for no. 176.
Exhibitions RA, *Holbein* (119); Brussels, *L'Europe humaniste*, 1955 (89); *Erasmus*, 1969 (65).
Bibliography Parker, no. 3; Morison-Barker, no. 2.

Her Majesty the Queen (Windsor Castle 12268)

The 'second Windsor drawing' of Sir Thomas More is a much finer production, more finished and in better condition. It is life-size, and also closer to the Basel sketch and the painted portraits in showing the line of the collar of SS as well as in other details; it has been pricked for transfer to canvas or fresco. The inscription 'Tho: Moor L<u>d</u> Chancelour' is of a later date.

178
John More (?1509-47)
Hans Holbein the Younger, 1526-7
Coloured chalks on white paper, 38.3×28.4 ($15\frac{1}{16} \times 11\frac{3}{16}$)

Provenance As for no. 176.
Exhibitions London, New Gallery, 1890; RA, *Holbein* (115).
Bibliography Parker, no. 6; Roper, 110; Harpsfield, 294-6, 329.

Her Majesty the Queen (Windsor Castle 12226)

John More must have sat to Holbein at about the same time as his father. The drawing agrees well with the figure in the

SIR THOMAS MORE AND HIS HOUSEHOLD

Colour plate IV *Sir Thomas More, his father, his household and his descendants* by Rowland Lockey (no. 170)

Basel sketch (no. 169) and in the later painted versions of the household group, except for the cap, which he does not wear in the group portraits.

Little is known of the life of Sir Thomas More's youngest child and only son, born about 1509. There is no evidence to support Sir Francis Bacon's later anecdote about his feeble-mindedness. Sir Thomas charmingly singles out a letter of John's for special praise in a letter of his own of uncertain date (Rogers, 107). In 1527, John was betrothed to, and in 1529 married, Anne Cresacre (1511–77; no. 179), Sir Thomas's ward. Three sons and a daughter of the marriage were living at John's death in 1547; one was the Thomas More who commissioned Lockey's copies of the household group (nos. 1, 170). In 1533, John More published a translation of a sermon by Fridericus Nausea (no. 156) and another of the account of the land of Prester John by the Portuguese humanist Damião a Goes. He received dedications from Simon Grynaeus (no. 180) and Erasmus (no. 181). After his father's execution, John was imprisoned in the Tower, but released unharmed because, according to Cresacre More, 'they had sufficiently fleeced him before'. He may have been implicated in the plot of the prebendaries of Canterbury against Cranmer in 1543, receiving a pardon in April 1544 for 'all treasonable words against the King's Supremacy'. John More died, presumably in Chelsea, in 1547.

Holbein has inscribed this drawing 'lipfarb brun' (complexion brown); a later hand has added 'Iohn More Sr Thomas Mores Son'.

179
Anne Cresacre (1511–77)
Hans Holbein the Younger, 1526–7
Coloured chalks on white paper, 37.5 × 26.8 (14¾ × 10 9/16)

Provenance As for no. 176.
Exhibitions RA, *Holbein* (117); Royal Academy, *British Portraits*, 1956–7 (535).
Bibliography Parker, no. 7; Roper, 110; Harpsfield, 294–6, 329.

Her Majesty the Queen (Windsor Castle 12270)

Anne Cresacre stands fourth from the left in the Basel sketch of the household group (no. 169) and the Nostell Priory copy. In the Burford Priory/NPG (no. 1) and the miniature (no. 170) composite groups, she stands second from left, between the seated figures of Sir John and Sir Thomas. This preliminary drawing by Holbein for the lost group portrait shows her seated.

Anne was the only daughter and heiress of Edward Cresacre of Barnborough, Yorkshire. She became Sir Thomas's ward as a baby, on the death of her father in 1512; and in 1527 she was betrothed to his son John (no. 178). They married in 1529 and their first son, Thomas, was born in his grandfather's house in 1531. Her portrait appears twice in the Burford Priory/NPG composite group portrait, commissioned by that son. Anne More married George West as her second husband, on 13 June 1559, and died 2 December 1577. It was she who spied Sir Thomas More's hair shirt and laughed at him for wearing it (no. 228).

180
A Dedication to John More the Younger
Platonis Opera omnia cum commentariis Procli in Timaeum et Politica, Basel, Johannes Valderus, 1534

Bibliography Adams, P1437; *RGG*3, s.v. Grynaeus; R. Pfeiffer, *History of Classical Scholarship 1300–1850*, Oxford 1976, 85, 139; Rogers, 196.

Warburg Institute, University of London

Simon Gryner (1494/5–1541) was a native of Vehringen in Hohenzollern-Sigmaringen and a fellow-pupil of Melanchthon (nos. 134, 135). He studied at Vienna and Wittenberg, early developing Lutheran sympathies. Gryner took his humanist name Grynaeus out of the *Aeneid*. He became Professor of Greek at Heidelberg in 1524 and was famous for his discovery in 1527 of the first five books of the fifth decade of Livy. Falling into disfavour for his Zwinglian views, he transferred to Basel at the invitation of Oecolampadius (nos. 138, 139). In 1531, Grynaeus visited England to search for books and manuscripts, and was probably recruited, while here, to canvass opinion on the divorce. He died of the plague in Basel, 1541.

In the epistle dedicatory, Grynaeus gives an account of his visit to England. His welcome in More's house had been secured by a letter from Erasmus, though the chancellor extracted an undertaking that he would not spread his heretical views, and kept him under surveillance personally or via his secretary, John Harris. The dedication to young John More is a token of gratitude, delicately expressed. Erasmus had intervened to prevent the embarrassment of a dedication to the ex-chancellor himself.

181
Another Dedication to John More
Aristotle, *Opera Omnia*, Basel, Johann Bebel, 1531

Bibliography Adams, A1730; Allen, 2432; Rogers, 183.

University of London Library

Erasmus dedicated four works to Thomas More and his family: the *Praise of Folly* (nos. 85, 86) to More himself; his edition of the ps.-Ovidian *De nuce* to More and his 'school'; his edition of the Christmas Hymn of Prudentius to Margaret Roper in 1523; and to John More the Younger this edition of Aristotle. He had not seen John since leaving England for the last time in 1517.

182

**182
Elizabeth Dauncey** (1506–64)
Hans Holbein the Younger, 1526–7
Coloured chalks on white paper, 37.1 × 26.2 (14$\frac{5}{8}$ × 10$\frac{5}{16}$)

Provenance As for no. 176.
Exhibition RA, *Holbein* (116).
Bibliography Parker, no. 4; Roper, 110, 115–17; Harpsfield, 311–12.

Her Majesty the Queen (Windsor Castle 12228)

Elizabeth Dauncey (Daunce), Sir Thomas More's second daughter, is the first figure standing at left in the Basel sketch (no. 169) and the Nostell Priory group. In the Burford Priory/NPG group she stands between her sisters Cicely and Margaret. Elizabeth married William Dauncey on 29 September 1525, in the chapel of Giles Alington at Willesden. On the same day and in the same place her sister Cicely (no. 183) married Giles Heron; and on the same day Sir Thomas More took up his appointment as Chancellor of the Duchy of Lancaster (no. 198). William Dauncey, son of Sir John Dauncey, Privy Councillor and Knight of the Body to Henry VIII, was MP (for Thetford) in the Reformation Parliament of 1529 (like all male members of Sir Thomas's family, except John, a minor). In 1543 he was implicated in the plot of the prebendaries of Canterbury against Cranmer, with John and others, and received pardon along with them.

A colour note *rot* (red), in Holbein's hand, is on the dress; the inscription 'The Lady Barkley' is by a later hand.

183

184

183
Cicely Heron (b.1507)
Hans Holbein the Younger, 1526–7
Coloured chalks on white paper, 38.4 × 28.3 (15 × 11⅛)

Provenance As for no. 176.
Exhibitions London, New Gallery, 1890; RA, *Holbein* (121); Royal Academy, *British Portraits*, 1956–7 (543).
Bibliography Parker, no. 5; Roper, 117–22.

Her Majesty the Queen (Windsor Castle 12269)

Cicely, third and youngest daughter of Sir Thomas More, married Giles Heron on 29 September 1525, at Willesden, on the same day and in the same place as her elder sister Elizabeth married William Dauncey and on the same day as More took up his appointment as Chancellor of the Duchy of Lancaster. Giles was the son and heir of Sir John Heron, Henry VIII's Treasurer of the Chamber, who had made his son Sir Thomas's ward. It was nevertheless against Giles that Sir Thomas, in Chancery, made a 'flatt decre'. Giles Heron sat for Thetford in the Reformation Parliament, with William Dauncey. He figures in Thomas Cromwell's 'Remembrances' (no. 245) in 1539–40, and was executed for treason in the latter year.

In the group portraits (nos. 1, 169), Cicely is the further left of the two seated daughters.

184
Margaret Gigs (Mistress Clement) (*c*.1508–70)
Hans Holbein the Younger, 1526–7
Coloured chalks on white paper, 38.5 × 27.3 (15 3/16 × 10 1/16)

Provenance As for no. 176.
Exhibitions London, New Gallery, 1890; RA, *Holbein* (122).
Bibliography Parker, no. 8; Harpsfield, 334–5; L. Antheunis, 'Quelques exilés anglais célèbres... à Louvain', *Mededeelingen van de Geschied- en Oudheidskundige Kring van Leuven*, I, 1961, 33–8; R. J. Schoeck, *N & Q*, CXCIV, 1969, 532–3.

Her Majesty the Queen (Windsor Castle 12229)

Margaret Gigs (Gigg, Giggs, Gyge) was the foster daughter of Thomas More, brought up with his family. She was later to tell how she used to misbehave a little to enjoy More's rebuke. More always made it clear that he regarded her as a daughter and employed her as his almoner. Margaret was a Greek scholar with an interest in medicine (no. 95), like her tutor, John Clement, whom she married in 1526. Their daughter Winifred married William Rastell, More's printer. Under Edward, the Clements were in exile at Louvain. Margaret was present at More's execution in 1535 and made her way to the Carthusians in prison (no. 252) to bring them food and comfort. She returned with Clement to England under Mary, but on the accession of Elizabeth both were forced into exile at Bergen and later at Malines, where she died in 1570 and John in 1571.

In the Basel drawing of the household group (no. 169), Margaret Gigs stands second from left, leaning forward to point out to John More something in the book she is holding; in the Nostell Priory oil she stands erect at the extreme left; she is omitted from the NPG oil (no. 1) and the Victoria and Albert Museum miniature (no. 170).

The 'Mother Iak', to whom the inscription in a later hand refers, was a Mistress Jack or Jackson, nurse to the infant Prince Edward.

185
Joannes Ludovicus (Juan Luis) Vives (1492–1540)
From J. J. Boissard, *Icones diversorum hominum illustrium*, Frankfurt a.M., 1628
Engraving, 14×10.5 ($5\frac{1}{2} \times 4\frac{1}{8}$)

Bibliography Emden, *Oxford 1540*, 594–6; Juan Estelreich, *Jean-Louis Vives*, exbn. at the Bibliothèque Nationale, Paris 1942; C. G. Noreña, *Juan Luis Vives*, The Hague 1970; Jesus Gil y Calpe, 'Iconografia de Luis Vives', *Cultura Valenciana*, XI, 1927, 125–30.

National Portrait Gallery, London

Born in Valencia of a celebrated Jewish *converso* family, Vives left Spain for the University of Paris in 1508, never to return. He went on to the Low Countries in 1512, being introduced to Thomas More at Bruges in 1520 by the Flemish jurist Franciscus Cranevelt (1485–1564). More admired Vives from the start and later gave him financial help. In 1522, Vives dedicated his edition of St Augustine's *City of God* (no. 268) to Henry VIII, and in 1523 came to England at the behest of More and Wolsey, who made him reader in Oxford. He found Oxford life and Oxford food boring and distasteful.

In 1524, Vives dedicated to Queen Catherine his tract *De institutione feminae Christianae* (*Instruction of a Christian Woman*; no. 186), which was translated into English by Richard Hyrde, tutor to More's children. In 1526 he spent some time in More's household. In 1527, he was appointed to teach Latin to Princess Mary, but in 1528 departed for good to the Low Countries, having fallen into disfavour along with Queen Catherine. He died in Bruges in 1540.

Vives was an enormously prolific author. All portraits of him go back to the drawing by Jan van Berghe. The image was given currency by engravings in collections such as Boissard's *Icones*, first published 1591 and many times reissued.

186
Vives on the Education of a Christian Woman
Joannes Ludovicus Vives, *A very frutefull and pleasant boke called the instruction of a christen woman...*, London, Thomas Berthelet, [?1529]

Bibliography See no. 185; Adams, V951; *STC2*, 24856–63; Foster Watson, *Vives and the Renascence Education of Women*, 1912; Vives, *Introduction to Wisdom. A Renaissance Textbook*, ed. Marian Leona Tobriner, New York 1968.

The Warden and Fellows of All Souls College, Oxford (S.R.77.d.28)

Vives's *Instruction of a Christian Woman*, dedicated to Catherine of Aragon, was first published in Latin; English, French, German, Italian and Spanish translations were issued within twenty years or so, reflecting Vives's immense reputation as an educator. The English translation was made by Richard Hyrde, 'a yong man lernyd in Greke and Latyn, with experience of physic', tutor to Thomas More's children. More had intended to translate the book himself, but merely revised and corrected Hyrde's version, first published in 1529. It had many sixteenth-century editions.

Both Vives and Hyrde probably derived their concern for women's education from More, who 'not content to have them (ie his daughters) good and very chaste, would also that they should be well learned'. Vives gives women a domestic role only, insisting on the importance of stocking their minds so that they could avoid 'fantasies' while at their household tasks and so that they could teach their children when very young. Theology and philosophy, mathematics and the like, were too hard for them and rhetoric was unsuitable, silence being so desirable in them.

187
Nicolaus Kratzer (1497–?1550)
Unknown artist, after Hans Holbein the Younger, 16th century
Oil on panel, 82.3×64.5 ($32\frac{1}{4} \times 25\frac{1}{2}$)

Bibliography Emden, *Oxford 1540*, 333; R. T. Gunther, *Early Science in Oxford*, II, Oxford 1923, 101–6, 126, 230; Ganz, *Paintings*, no. 48; Rogers, 120, 250, 254; S. Anglo, *Spectacle, Pageantry and early Tudor Policy*, Oxford 1969, 217–19; J. D. North, 'Nicolaus Kratzer – the King's Astronomer', in *Festschrift for Edward Rosen*, (*Studia Copernicana*), Wrocław, etc, forthcoming.

Private Collection

Nicolaus Kratzer, mathematician and astronomer, was born in Munich and studied in Cologne and Wittenberg before coming to England in 1517–18. In Henry's service by 1520, he met Tunstall (no. 55) in Antwerp that year and was present at one of Erasmus's sittings to Dürer for his portrait. Dürer and Kratzer later corresponded.

Thomas More's letters to his household early in 1521 call Kratzer 'a great friend of mine and very skilled in astronomy', and the German taught mathematics and astronomy to More's 'school'. He may have been admitted to Corpus Christi College, Oxford (no. 32), on 4 July 1517, but more probably merely lodged and gave lectures there until Wolsey's Cardinal College was ready. About 1523 he constructed a sundial for the university, another for Corpus Christi College, and a third (portable) dial for Wolsey. The last is extant.

Kratzer seems to have continued in royal service until the late 1540s and is presumed to have died about 1550. His struggles with the language of his adopted country are epitomised in the story of his excusing his shortcomings to Henry VIII on the ground that thirty years were not enough to learn English. It was probably Kratzer who inscribed the names and ages of the sitters on the Basel drawing of the More household group.

Holbein painted Kratzer holding in his hand a pair of dividers and an unfinished polyhedral dial, the gnomons for

187

which lie on the table, accompanied by a pivoting rule, a ruling knife, a burin, scissors, and another dialling instrument. On the wall hang a pair of larger dividers, another ruler and what appears to be a combined parallel rule and square. On a shelf behind are a cylinder dial and an unusual form of adjustable vertical dial with a semicircular scale. The present portrait is a replica of the original painted by Holbein in England in 1528 and now in the Louvre. The paper on the desk is inscribed: *Imago ad vivam effigiem expressa Nicolai Kratzeri monacensis qui bavarus erat quadragesimum primum annum tempore illo complebat 1528* (The portrait of Nicolaus Kratzer of Munich, a Bavarian, taken from life when he was completing his forty-first year).

188
Nicolaus Kratzer, 'Canones Horoptri'
Peter Meghen; decorated by Hans Holbein the Younger, 1528–9
Manuscript on vellum

Provenance ?Henry VIII; 'Johannes Bayley liber ex dono magistri Edovardi Gorge'; given to Bodleian Library by William Bailey 1602.
Exhibitions Brussels, *L'Europe humaniste*, 1955 (252); *Erasmus*, 1969 (161).
Bibliography See no. 187; *SC*, 2168; O. Pächt, 'Holbein and Kratzer as Collaborators', *Burlington Magazine*, LXXXIV, 1944, 134–9;

J. B. Trapp, 'Notes on MSS written by Peter Meghen', *Book Collector*, XXIV, 1975, 96.
Bodleian Library, Oxford (MS Bodley 504)

Kratzer's *Canones Horoptri*, a set of instructions for the use of the instrument which he calls his *horoptrum*, to be used for finding the times of sunrise and sunset, the Golden Number, the position of the sun in the zodiac, etc, was written out by Peter Meghen (nos. 38, 41, 43), decorated by Holbein and bound in green velvet as a New Year's gift for Henry VIII. Its final blank leaves were intended for associated astronomical tables.

189
Indenture between Sir Thomas More and Antonio Bonvisi
Sale of lease of Crosby Place, St Helen's, Bishopsgate, 20 January, 15 Henry VIII [1524]
Parchment, signed and sealed

Exhibitions Chelsea, 1929 (H10); Oxford Exhibition, 1935 (67).
Bibliography Catalogue of Additions to the MSS in the British Museum 1911–1915, London 1925, 491 (facsimile); John Edmund Cox, *Annals of St Helen's Bishopsgate*, 1876; Philip Norman and

188

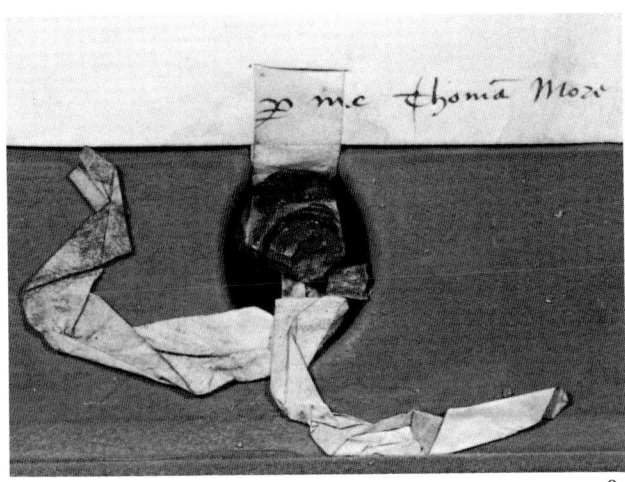

189

W. D. Caroe, *Crosby Place*, 1908; John Stow, *Survey of London*, ed. C. L. Kingsford, 1908, I, 173; *Harpsfield*, 341; R. J. Schoeck, 'Anthony Bonvisi, the Heywoods and the Ropers', *N & Q*, CXCVII, 1952, 178–9.

Thomas M. Eyston, Esq

A priory of Benedictine nuns was founded in 1212 in St Helen's, Bishopsgate, and from it, in 1466, Sir John Crosby (d.1475) obtained a lease. Perhaps from his widow it passed into the hands of Protector Richard, and it was there that he cunningly had the divided Council meet 'in protectoris aula', as More puts it in his *History of Richard III* (nos. 109, 110). In the early 1520s it was in the hands of Sir John Rest, alderman and mayor (1516) of London, from whose executors More bought the whole interest and lease on 1 June 1523. As the present deed records, he sold the lease six months later to his friend Antonio Bonvisi (no. 241).

The seal on the lease is now broken. Enough remains to make out the impression of a rounded oval armorial seal which it is reasonable to assume was More's: *Argent a Chevron engrailled between three Moorcocks Sable, crested Gules* (no. 31). This is the only known extant impression of More's private armorial seal.

190
Grant by Thomas More and others to Christopher Knyvet
Indenture between Thomas More and ten others, and Dame Christian Colet, in favour of Christopher Knyvet and his brothers
Parchment, 1519

Bibliography British Library, MS *Catalogue of Additional Charters and Rolls*, I; J. H. Lupton, in intro. to his edn. of John Colet, *Letters to Radulphus*, 1876, XXXV–XXXVII; J. B. Trapp, 'Dame Christian Colet and Thomas More', *Moreana*, XV–XVI, 1967, 107–12; id. 'A double *mise-au-point*', *Moreana*, XI, 1966, 50–1.

The British Library Board (Add. Charter 828)

This indenture confirms the rights of Christopher Knyvet and his brothers to the manors of Great and Little Weldon, Northamptonshire, after the death of Dame Christian Colet (née Knyvet). It is part of the provision made for his widowed mother by John Colet (no. 11; d.1519): she survived him by four years. Thomas More and other trustees, including members of the Mercers' Company and former members of Colet's household (notably Thomas Lupset, nos. 191, 192), sign and seal the document and Dame Christian adds her initials. More uses his pseudo-antique seal (no. 30), and Lupset either a genuine antique gem-seal or a *rifacimento all'antica*.

191
Thomas Lupset's 'Workes'
London, Thomas Berthelet, 1546

Bibliography STC2, 16932; McKerrow-Ferguson, 30; J. A. Gee, *Life and Works of Thomas Lupset*, New Haven 1928; Emden, *Oxford 1540*, 366–7.

The British Library Board (698.a.6)

Thomas Lupset (?1495–1530), 'a man most learned in Greek, Latin and theology' according to his epitaph, was born in London and died there of consumption on 27 December 1530. John Colet had taken him into his household by 1508. In 1513 he was in Cambridge, where he acted as Erasmus's assistant, and was praised by Erasmus in a letter to More: 'Lupset sees himself as reborn by my help and quite simply saved from perdition. The Masters try every way to drag the youngster back to their treadmill, for on his first day he threw away their sophistical books and bought Greek ones' (Allen, 271). From 1517 to 1519 Lupset was a student in Paris, where he saw through the press Linacre's Galen and the second edition of *Utopia* (1517), and made the acquaintance of Budé (no. 68). In April 1520 he was at Oxford, succeeding John Clement as public lecturer in Greek and Latin. He left England in 1523 for Padua, where he was a member of the household of Reginald Pole (no. 216), probably tutor to Thomas Winter (no. 192) and a friend of Richard Pace (no. 264). In 1525 he was in Venice, helping with the Aldine Galen (no. 95), and twice later he went to Paris, once to become Winter's guardian and once to persuade Pole to help Henry in the divorce. About this time he perhaps had the conversation with Pole recorded or imagined by Thomas Starkey (no. 277).

192
Thomas Lupset (?1495–1530)
Autograph letter to Thomas, Cardinal Wolsey, 4 March 1528
Manuscript on paper

Bibliography LP, IV, 2, 4015; J. A. Gee, *Life and Works of Thomas Lupset*, New Haven 1928, 128–9, 320–1.

Public Record Office, London (SP 1/47, f. 65)

In the early months of 1527/8, Lupset had come to Paris and taken over the tutorship of the Dean of Wells, Thomas Winter, Wolsey's illegitimate son. He was soon writing that Winter's lodgings were not of a sort befitting his station and that money needed to be spent on them.

VI *Politics at Home and Abroad*

On Michaelmas Day 1525 Sir Thomas More's second and third daughters married, and Sir Thomas himself was advanced to the dignity of Chancellor of the Duchy of Lancaster. Early the next year he was one of those commanded in Cardinal Wolsey's 'Eltham Ordinances' for the reform of the royal household to attend on the king at all times. His presence abroad was again required – for the signing of the Peace of Amiens, for instance, in 1527 and for the 'Ladies' Peace' of Cambrai in 1529, 'when the legues betwene the chief Princes of christendome wer renued againe and peace so long loked for restored to Christendome. Which peace our lord stable and make perpetual', as Sir Thomas put it in his own epitaph (no. 287).

The Peace of Cambrai marked the ruin of Wolsey and the collapse of his foreign policy. At the fall of the former lord chancellor in October 1529, Sir Thomas More was advanced in his stead to the 'highest office in the realm', the Duke of Norfolk (no. 207) acting on the occasion as Henry VIII's mouthpiece to express the royal sense of Sir Thomas's worthiness to occupy the chancellorship. On 3 November, a week after taking office, Sir Thomas opened the first session of the Reformation Parliament.

Of the great personages of Church and State with whom Sir Thomas More now found himself increasingly involved, our foremost recorder is again Hans Holbein. The best portraits shown here are either by Holbein's hand or copies of the images he created: the Dukes of Norfolk and Suffolk, Thomas Cromwell, later Earl of Essex, Archbishop Warham, Sir Richard Southwell, John Fisher, Bishop of Rochester. Splendid images of Thomas Cranmer, Archbishop of Canterbury, who married Henry VIII to Anne Boleyn and crowned Anne Queen, and of that other enemy to the unity of Christendom, the 'Great Turk', Suleiman the Magnificent, are also shown.

Two years after Sir Thomas More took office as Chancellor of the Duchy of Lancaster, Christian Europe had received the profoundest of shocks. Christendom was already divided by religious strife, by national enmities and by the struggle for dominance, and was also threatened by the advance of the Turks, marked by the disastrous defeat of the Hungarian armies at the Battle of Mohács in 1526. In England the progress of Lutheranism gave cause for concern. Now, in 1527, the troops of the Emperor Charles V took and sacked the Holy City of Rome itself, and confined Pope Clement VII to the Castel Sant'Angelo. The threat from this and from subsequent events is what makes Sir Thomas More welcome the Peace of Cambrai in such heartfelt terms.

In the summer of the same year, as English hostility to Spain and friendship with France grew, Henry VIII's profound wish for a male heir caused him to entertain the idea of a divorce from Catherine of Aragon, who had given him only the Princess Mary. Scruples about the validity of his marriage with the widow of his brother had been felt at the time of the event itself; now they were raised again with compelling force and 'The King's Great Matter', as it was spoken of, assumed the highest importance. Sir Thomas More's opinion was first canvassed in the summer of 1527. In the years that followed, his opposition to Henry's design to put away Catherine so as to secure a legitimate male heir was constant, if never as outspokenly expressed as John Fisher's. His loyalty to Catherine remained absolute, but he could see the danger in its being made explicit (no. 218). As the case passed from a matrimonial question to a matter of the title of Anne Boleyn's children to the throne, and then to Henry's design to be Supreme Head of the Church in England, he preserved silence. The day after the clergy of England had made submission and agreed to the Supremacy, Sir Thomas More, on 16 May 1532, by royal permission, relinquished his office of lord chancellor.

193
The 'Great' Seal of the Duchy of Lancaster
Appended to a grant to the Mayor of Thetford, Norfolk,
12 June 1532
Red wax, diameter 8.1 ($3\frac{3}{16}$)

Bibliography British Museum, MS *Catalogue of Additional Charters and Rolls*, VI, ii, 404r; British Museum, MS *Index of Seals*, A–K, 169r; W. de G. Birch, *Catalogue of Seals in the Department of MSS of the British Museum*, 1887, I, 87; Sir Robert Somerville, 'The Seals of the Duchy and County Palatinate of Lancaster', *Archives*, X, 1971–2, 146–53.

The British Library Board (Add. Charter 16575)

The Duchy of Lancaster comprised lands in every part of the country as well as including the earldoms of Hereford and Essex. The Chancellor and Council of the Duchy of Lancaster sat as an equity court in Westminster Hall, dealing with cases relating to lands held by the king in right of the Duchy. In 1525 More was first appointed Steward and three months later Chancellor of the County Palatine and of the Duchy of Lancaster and Keeper of both seals. He held the office until becoming Lord Chancellor of England in 1529.

This document has no connexion with Thomas More, but is included for its impression of the 'Great' Seal of the Duchy which More, as its Chancellor, would have used.

193

194
Photograph: **The Eltham Ordinances, 1526**
'Articles devised by the King's Highness, with the advice of his council for the establishment of good order and reformation of sundry errors and misuses in his most honourable household and chamber', Eltham, January 1526
Vellum, 1526; contemporary vellum binding.

Bibliography LP, IV, i, 1939; H. O. Coxe, *Quarto Catalogue, II: Laudian MSS*, repr. with corrections and additions by R. W. Hunt, Oxford 1973, cols. 425–6 (SC, 1474); G. R. Elton, *The Tudor Constitution*, Cambridge 1962, 90 ff; J. A. Guy, 'Wolsey, the Council and the Council Courts', *EHR*, XCI, 1976, 500.

Photograph by courtesy of the Bodleian Library, Oxford (MS Laud misc. 597)

Of several attempts at administrative reform, Wolsey's so-called Eltham Ordinances are the most important. They deal with all aspects of the royal household, of which the Council was an important part, and name twenty councillors, including More, to attend upon the king and perform the judicial and administrative work. Among those 'honourable, virtuous, sadd [reliable], wise, experte, and discreete persons' were the principal officers of state and leading civil servants, who had often to be absent. Accordingly, Wolsey reduced the Council to ten, who are 'to gyve thair contynuall attendaunce' to the king wherever he goes. More is to be one of them. However, since even some of these may have to be absent, the Ordinances continue: 'be it alwaies prouided and forseen that either the Bishop of Bathe [John Clerk], the Secretarie [Richard Pace], Syr Thomas More, and the Dean of the Chapel [Richard Sampson] or two of them at the lest alwaies be present, except the kinges grace gyve licence to any of them to the contrarie'. They shall attend the king every day at ten am and two pm 'to be in readiness, not only in case the king's pleasure shall be to commune or confer with them upon any cause or matter, but also for hearing and direction of poor men's complaints of matters of justice'. More's name also occurs amongst the persons assigned to have lodging in the king's house.

195
Confirmation of the Treaty of Amiens, 1527,
with the Gold Seal of France
Original of the ratification by Francis I of the Treaty of Perpetual Peace, signed at Amiens, 18 August 1527
Parchment

Bibliography LP, IV, ii, 3356 (6); Rymer, XIV, 218, 227 (VI, ii, 88–91); Sir H. Ellis, *Archaeologia*, XXXV, 1853, 490–1.

Public Record Office, London (E. 30/1109)

The Anglo-French Treaty of Perpetual Peace, concluded at Westminster on 30 April 1527, of which More was co-signatory, had to be ratified. Wolsey set out for France in person, with More as one of the commissioners. George Cavendish, Wolsey's gentleman usher, has described his master's triumphant journey south to Amiens in loving detail. At Amiens he met the French king ostentatiously on equal terms, and on Sunday 18 August 1527, the Treaty of Amiens was ratified, confirming and ratifying the Westminster treaties and mercantile agreement. More was one of the witnesses of the ceremony.

195

Of the series of instruments signed on the occasion, the exhibited Peace Treaty is one of the finest, because of its illuminated title-page, the Gold Seal of France and the autograph of the French king. The obverse of the seal shows Francis I sitting in majesty under a rich cloth of estate, the curtains drawn back and held open by two angels, two smaller angels assisting them at the upper end. Two lions couchant form the throne's foot-stool. The legend reads: PLVRIMA SERVANTVR FOEDERE CVNCTA FIDE. The reverse has three fleurs-de-lis on a plain shield enclosed by the collar of the Order of St Michael surmounted by the crown and the style of the French king: FRANCISCVS PRIMVS DEI GRATIA FRANCORVM REX CHRISTIANISSIMVS.

This original of the French counterpart of the treaty is preserved among the diplomatic documents of the Exchequer.

196
Margaret of Austria (1480–1530) and her Husband, Philibert II, le Beau, Duke of Savoy
Jean Marende, c.1502
Bronze medal, diameter 9.5 (3¾)

Bibliography Hill-Pollard, no. 528; *Neue Briefe*, 63–84, nos. 169B–F, 172D; Elizabeth F. Rogers, 'Margaret of Austria's Gifts to Tunstal, More and Hackett after the Ladies' Peace', *Moreana*, XII, 1966, 57–60.

The Trustees of the British Museum (1879-6-12-7)

The obverse shows, on a field semé with knots of Savoy and marguerites, busts confronted of Philibert and Margaret, encircled by the inscription PHILIBERTVS DVX SABAVDIAE VIII MARGVA[RITA] MAXI[MILIANI] CAE[SARIS] AVG[VSTI] FI[LIA] D[VCISSA] SA[BAVDIAE]. The reverse has the arms of Philibert impaling those of Margaret, with Savoy knots and marguerites in the margin and the Savoy motto FERT across the field. This is encircled with the legend GLORIA IN ALTISSIMIS DEO ET IN TERRA PAX HOMINIBVS BVRGVS (Glory to God in the highest and on earth peace to men). Margaret, only daughter of Maximilian I by Mary of Burgundy, and aunt of Charles V, married Philibert II of Savoy in 1501. When she entered Bourg-en-Bresse as Duchess of Savoy on 2 August 1502, the city presented her with a sample of the work of the local goldsmith, Jean Marende, in the form of a medal. Many bronze casts were made at the time.

Philibert died in 1504, and negotiations for a match between Margaret and Henry VII (no. 4) were opened in 1505. In 1507, Margaret was made Regent of the Netherlands and guardian of her nephew Charles. She held the appointment until her death in 1530. In 1529 she and Louise of Savoy, mother of Francis I of France, signed the 'Ladies' Peace' of Cambrai, More being present. He and the other English commissioners received gifts of silver from Margaret.

197
The Great Seal of England
'First Seal' of Henry VIII, used 1509–32. Appended, on green and white ribbon, to a treaty of alliance between Henry VIII and Christian II of Denmark, Sweden and Norway, 1523
Green wax, attached to vellum, diameter 11.6 (4½)

Bibliography British Museum, MS *Catalogue of Additional Charters and Rolls,* I; British Museum, MS *Index of Seals,* A–K, 151r; W. de G. Birch, *Catalogue of Seals in the Department of MSS in the British Museum,* 1887, I, 42; *The Great Seals of England. From the Time of Edward the Confessor to the Reign of H.M. William the Fourth,* 1837, p 8, pl XIV.

The British Library Board (Add. Charter 25959)

This document has no direct relevance to More, but is shown for its almost perfect impression of the Great Seal of England. This First Seal of Henry VIII, from the same matrix as that of Henry VII, was used by More's predecessors in the chancellorship, Warham (1509–15) and Wolsey (1515–17 October 1529). After More's successor, Audeley, had kept

196

197

it for some three months, it was broken up in 1532 and a new Second Seal delivered to him. Both the First and the Second Seal keep the Gothicism of medieval tradition going back to the days of Edward III.

The obverse shows the king, in robes of majesty, crowned, holding orb and sceptres, in a carved Gothic niche ornamented with trefoiled canopy and panelled corbel. At each side is a compartment with corbel and double arched canopy with four-light window pinnacled and crocketed; in this is a shield of arms of France and England, quarterly, and below a lion of England statant guardant; beyond this compartment is a smaller one on bracket, with a crocketed pinnacle overhead, in it a man-at-arms in armour, holding a javelin. In the field at the base on either side of the corbel is a rose, slipped and leaved. The legend reads: HENRICVS: DEI: GRA: REX: ANGLIE: ✠ : FRANCIE: ✠ : DOMINVS: HIBERNIE.

The reverse has the king riding to the right, in plate armour enriched with arms of France and England quarterly, sword, crested helmet and shield of arms as above. The horse is armorially caparisoned and plumed, and galloping on a mount covered with flowering plants, in which are three rabbit burrows, with one rabbit entering that on the right, another issuing from the centre burrow, and a third seated reguardant contourné at that on the left. The field is diapered lozengy with fleur-de-lis at each point of intersection, with a rose in each space; above the tail of the horse is a lion rampant contourné right and below the horse's head a fleur-de-lis. The legend reads: HENRICVS: : DEI : : GRACIA : : REX : : ANGLIE : : ET : : FRANCIE : : ET : : DOMINVS : : HIBERNIE. Each pair of colons encloses a rose.

198
Photograph: **Sir Thomas More receives the Great Seal, 25 October 1529**

Bibliography LP, IV, iii, 6025; Rymer, XIV, 349–50 (= VI, ii, 238–9); Halle, op.cit. (no. 108) clxxxv; Roper, 39; W. Bradford, *Correspondence of Charles V*, 1850, 293; E. Birchenough, 'More's Appointment as Chancellor and his Resignation', *Moreana*, XII, 1966, 71–8.

Photograph by courtesy of the Public Record Office, London (C.54/398)

The Close Roll memorandum records four events: (a) The delivery of the Great Seal of England by Cardinal Wolsey, on 17 October 1529, to the Dukes of Norfolk and Suffolk; (b) on 20 October, its delivery, through John Tayler, Master of the Rolls, to the king; (c) on Monday 25 October 1529, the Great Seal in the sealed bag was delivered by the king in the inner chamber by the oratory at East Greenwich to Sir Thomas More, KC, in the presence of Henry Norris and Christopher Hales, Attorney General (who was later to read More's indictment) and others, and then and there More was made Lord Chancellor; (d) on the next day, Tuesday 26 October, More took his oath as Lord Chancellor in the Great Hall at Westminster in the presence of the Dukes of Norfolk and Suffolk and many other noblemen. He then sealed a number of documents and put the Great Seal back into its bag which he sealed with his own seal. At the foot of this document the form of the Lord Chancellor's oath is given.

On the same day the imperial ambassador, Chapuys, reported to Charles V: 'Everyone is in great joy at his [More's] promotion, for besides the esteem in which he is held for his upright character, he is the most learned man in England'.

199
The Sack of Rome, 1527
Unknown artist, 16th century
Oil on panel, 54 × 137 (21¼ × 53⅞)

Exhibition Erasmus, 1969 (395).
Bibliography C. Terlinden, *Charles Quint, Empereur des deux Mondes*, Brussels 1965, 100; J. Hook, *The Sack of Rome*, 1972.

Royal Museum of Fine Arts, Brussels (687)

Charles V's power in Italy seemed to have been consolidated by victory at Pavia (1525), the capture of Francis I and the treaty of Madrid (14 January 1526), but Francis and Pope Clement VII joined in the League of Cognac against Charles, and Francis and Henry VIII signed an alliance. In Italy, Charles still held the upper hand. Rome had already once been occupied by his armies when, on 6 May 1527, imperial Spanish and German troops, many of them Lutheran, near-mutinous, unfed and unpaid, overran and brutally sacked the Holy City. Charles, though refusing to accept responsibility for the Sack, made no move to free the pope from confinement in the Castel Sant' Angelo.

All Europe was shocked by the captivity of the pope and the violation of the chief city of Christendom by the imperial army. To Thomas More the Sack was a tragedy unparalleled in recent history and a foretaste of the horrors heresy would give rise to. There is no more bitter and painful passage in his works than the pages of the *Dialogue Concerning Heresies* (no. 146) in which he recounts the events of the Sack.

200
Clement VII (1478–1534; Pope 1523–34)
Daniel Hopfer, ?1530
Etching, 22.5 × 15.7 (8 13/16 × 6⅛)

Exhibition Erasmus, 1969 (397).
Bibliography Bartsch, VIII, 492.82; Thieme-Becker, *Künstler-Lexikon*, XVII, Leipzig 1924, 474–7.

The Trustees of the British Museum (C.46*.p.3)

Clement VII, son of Giuliano de'Medici, and cousin of Leo X, was raised to the cardinalate in 1513 and succeeded Hadrian VI as pope. He was the patron of Benvenuto Cellini, Raphael and Michelangelo, among other artists. In European politics he at first supported Francis I, but after the Sack of Rome in 1527 and his own imprisonment in Castel Sant'Angelo, shifted his sympathies to Charles V. His indecisive attempts to steer a middle course in European politics and play off one power against another brought disaster. The proclamation in 1533 by Thomas Cranmer, Archbishop of Canterbury (no. 210), that Henry's marriage with Catherine was invalid was the consequence of Clement's procrastination in the matter of the divorce: it was nearly six years since this had first been mooted.

Daniel Hopfer's print, shown here in two states, is labelled 'Clement VII, the chief Bishop'. Hopfer, who had established himself at Augsburg by 1493, made woodcuts, but is best known for his skill at etched decoration on armour and as a pioneer in the development of etching as a medium for prints.

201
Clement VII
Benvenuto Cellini, 1534
Bronze medal, diameter 3.7 (1½)

Exhibition Erasmus, 1969 (398; silver example).
Bibliography Armand, I, 148.9; E. Plon, *Benvenuto Cellini...*, Paris 1883, XI.4; R. E. M. Fröhlich, *Benvenuto Cellini. Abhandlungen über die Goldschmiedekunst und die Bildhauerei*, Basel, n.d., 66–7.

The Trustees of the British Museum (M1329)

This medal celebrates the continuance of the peace established at Bologna in 1530 between Papacy and Empire by the coronation of Charles V by Clement VII. Obverse: Bust of Clement with the legend CLEMENS.VII. PONT. MAX. AN. XI. M.DXXXIIII round the edge; reverse: The Fury of War chained by Peace before the Temple of Janus, with the legend CLAVDVNTVR BELLI PORTAE (The gates of war are closed). Some examples have the signature BENVENVT[VS]. The dies are preserved in the Bargello in Florence.

Joos van Cleve was full master in the Antwerp painters' guild in 1511, and was honoured by a summons to the French court in 1530. He painted court portraits of Francis I and his queen, Eleanora, sister of Charles V. If this portrait of Henry VIII is indeed by van Cleve, it may be that the painter came to England on his own account.

The portrait is traditionally dated 1536 on the basis of the scroll held by the king, inscribed ITE IN MVNDVM VNIVERSVM ET PREDICATE EVANGELIVM OMNI CREATVRE (Mark xvi 15: Go ye into the world and preach the Gospel to every creature), a text which appears, in English, on the woodcut title-page of Coverdale's Bible of 1535 (no. 144). It may be significant that the scroll here is inscribed in Latin: the text is one regarded by the Catholic Church as supporting its apostolic authority (cf, eg, More's *Confutation*, *CW*, VIII, 614, and *Responsio ad Lutherum*, *CW*, V, 100), so that the picture might date earlier in the 1530s, when Henry was still Defender of the Faith in the sense in which he had been granted the title. Strong, defining this image as Type III, regards 1535 as acceptable on grounds of costume, and elsewhere quotes a description of Henry by the Venetian ambassador Lodovico Falier of 10 November 1531: 'His face is angelic rather than handsome; his head imperial and bald (ie cropped), and he wears a beard, contrary to English fashion' (no. 70).

201

202
Henry VIII (1491–1547; reigned 1509–47)
Joos van Cleve, ?1536
Oil on panel, 73 × 58.5 (28¾ × 23)

Provenance Earl of Arundel; by exchange to Charles I 1624; Privy Gallery, Whitehall Palace; probably bt. G. Greene 23 October 1651; recovered at Restoration and hung Whitehall; ? St James's Palace; Kensington Palace; Hampton Court by 1842.
Exhibition RA, *King's Pictures* (1).
Bibliography P. Ganz, *Burlington Magazine*, LXX, 1937, 211–17; M. J. Friedländer, *Early Netherlandish Painting*, rev. edn., IXA, 1972, pp 21, 33, 35, 66, no. 73, pl 91; E. K. Waterhouse, *Painting in Britain 1530–1790*, 3rd edn. 1969, 5; C. H. Collins Baker, *Catalogue... Hampton Court*, 1929, 25–6; Hampton Court Palace, *Handlist of the Pictures*, 2nd edn. 1958, 15; Strong, *Catalogue*, 157–8, pl 299.

Her Majesty the Queen (Hampton Court 313)

202

203
Catherine of Aragon (1485–1536)
Unknown artist, 16th century
Oil on panel, 55.9 × 44.5 (22 × 17½)

Provenance Thomas Barrett (1698–1757), Leeds Priory, Kent; Christie's 28 May 1859 (74); bt. NPG from Haines & Sons 1863.
Exhibition NPE, 1866.
Bibliography Strong, *Catalogue*, 39–40, pls 73–5; G. Mattingly, *Catherine of Aragon*, 1950.

National Portrait Gallery, London (163)

One of two identical versions of the single authentic large-scale portrait type of Catherine of Aragon; the other is in the Boston Museum of Fine Arts. The sitter wears a Spanish hood adorned with goldsmiths' work and jewels; her costume dates from about 1530.

Catherine was described by contemporaries as 'rather ugly' and 'not tall in stature, but rather short. If not handsome, she is not ugly; she is somewhat stout and has always a smile on her face'. Thomas More was more enthusiastic. He first saw Catherine on 12 November 1501, at her entry into London to be the bride of the young Prince Arthur. In his account of the entry in a letter (Rogers, 2) he wrote to John Holt, the grammarian: 'You would have burst out laughing' at Catherine's attendants who, all but three or four, looked like Ethiopian pygmies or devils out of hell. Everyone liked the look of Catherine, who was lacking in nothing that the handsomest girl should have.

Arthur died in 1502 and Catherine was finally married to his brother Henry on 11 June 1509. In his Latin verses (no. 37) celebrating the new king's coronation, More sings Catherine's praises. His panegyric reflects a loyalty to Catherine which he retained throughout his life.

204
William Warham (?1450–1532)
Unknown artist, after Hans Holbein the Younger, 16th century
Oil on panel, 82.2 × 66.3 (32⅜ × 26⅛)

Provenance Archbishops of Canterbury.
Exhibitions RA, *Holbein* (109); London County Council, Festival of Britain, 1951; Royal Academy, *British Portraits*, 1956–7 (7); NPG, *Dendrochronology*, 1977 (9).
Bibliography Emden, *Cambridge*, 618; id. *Oxford*, 1988–92; Strong, *Catalogue*, 323–4, pls 641–4; id. 'Holbein in England, III: Archbishop Warham', *Burlington Magazine*, CIX, 1967, 698–701; id. *English Icon*, 5–9, 49, 344.

His Grace the Lord Archbishop of Canterbury and the Church Commissioners

Warham is shown as Archbishop of Canterbury, to which see he was nominated in 1503. His crucifix bears his arms impaling those of Canterbury and his motto AVXILIVM MEVM A DOMINO (My aid is from the Lord). The breviary on the ledge is open at the litany of the saints. The label at top right is inscribed *Anno Domini MDXXVII aetatis suae LXX*, though the sitter was probably seven years older at the time.

Holbein's original portrait drawing of Warham is now at Windsor Castle. Two painted versions were made, one for Erasmus and the other for the archbishop's residence.

According to Strong, the first is now unidentifiable, the second is in the Louvre. The copy now at Lambeth Palace may have been commissioned to replace the latter after it was sold to Andreas de Loo between 1575 and 1590.

More and Warham must frequently have been in contact while More was making his name and Warham was already Archbishop – as well as, from 1504 to 1515, Lord Chancellor, and a generous patron of Erasmus. Early in 1517, More sent Warham a copy of his *Utopia*, with a letter (Rogers, 31), and in 1518 invoked Warham's support, as Chancellor, in his Letter to the University of Oxford (nos. 97, 98). In the last phase of More's life, the two were implicated in the affair of the Nun of Kent (no. 231) and the royal divorce. Warham's failure as Catherine's appointed advocate and his capitulation to Henry's demand for a petition of annulment to the pope would hardly have endeared his later years to More.

205
Archbishop Warham's Chantry Missal
Vellum, late 15th century

Provenance Archbishop William Warham (?1450–1532); Donald Hoye; James Dillon; James and Alexander Evers; Sir James Ware (1594–1666), who had it bound; Henry Hyde, 2nd Earl of Clarendon (1638–1709); bequeathed by Richard Rawlinson 1755.
Bibliography W. D. Macray, *MSS Rawlinsoniani*, Quarto Catalogues, V, ii, Oxford 1878, 79, no. 168; *SC*, 12031; S. J. P. van Dijk, unpublished typescript, *Handlist of the Latin Liturgical MSS in the Bodleian Library Oxford*, [1956/7], I, 172.

Bodleian Library, Oxford (MS Rawl. C.168)

Warham gave this missal to be used in the chantry founded by him near the place [*erased*: of St Thomas's martyrdom] in Canterbury Cathedral where he meant to be buried. Warham died in August 1532. His chapel was swept away at the suppression of chantries under Edward VI, and his monument removed to its present position outside the Deans' Chapel.

This manuscript is part of a missal, Sarum use, consisting of the temporale only, from the last rubric of Ash Wednesday to the Octave of Easter, the order of the mass much disturbed.

206
Stephen Gardiner, Bishop of Winchester (c.1497–1555)
Unknown artist, ?17th century
Oil on panel, 47 × 34.5 (19 × 13⅝)

Bibliography Emden, *Oxford 1540*, 227; J. A. Muller, *Stephen Gardiner and the Tudor Reaction*, 1926; *The Letters of Stephen Gardiner*, Cambridge 1933; F. Blomefield, *Collectanea Cantabrigiensia*, 1750, 209; J. Steegman, *Portraits in Welsh Houses*, I, p 31, no. 38, pl 5c; Mrs R. Lane Poole, *Oxford Portraits*, II, 266, no. 9.

Trinity Hall, Cambridge

Bishop of Winchester in succession to Wolsey from 1531 until his death, with an interval between 1551 and 1553 when he was deprived by Edward VI, Stephen Gardiner was lord chancellor under Mary. Educated in the civil and canon law and elected Master of Trinity Hall in 1525, he acted as

206

secretary to Wolsey and worked for him to secure Henry's divorce. He also served as diplomat, drafter of treaties (with Thomas More), ambassador and finally, in 1529, Principal Secretary to Henry, being replaced in this office by Thomas Cromwell in 1534. As a leader of the clerical party he at first opposed but later accepted the Supremacy, publishing his best-known work *De vera obedientia* (no. 278) in support. In 1533 he was a member of the court that dissolved Henry's marriage and one of the bishops who invited More to go with them to the coronation of Anne Boleyn. He took part in the examination of many of the reformers, to whom he was 'wily Winchester' or worse (Foxe).

This portrait was already in Trinity Hall in 1750; a good version belongs to the Marquess of Anglesey at Plas Newydd, and there is a repetition at Corpus Christi College, Oxford.

207
Thomas Howard, Earl of Surrey and 3rd Duke of Norfolk (1475–1554)
(Colour plate VI, page 125)
Hans Holbein the Younger, 1538–9
Oil and tempera on panel, 80.3 × 61.6 (31¾ × 24)

Provenance Howard family; Arundel Inventory 1655; apparently identical with picture sold Amsterdam 23 April 1732 and seen by George Vertue in London 1744; bt. Frederick, Prince of Wales (mentioned among his pictures by Vertue 1750); at Windsor early in George III's reign.
Exhibitions RA, *King's Pictures*, 1947–8 (10); RA, *Holbein* (12); RA, *British Portraits*, 1956–7 (9).
Bibliography Millar, no. 30; Ganz, *Paintings*, no. 123.

Her Majesty the Queen (Windsor Castle 59)

105

The Duke of Norfolk was one of the most powerful men of his time: Lord High Admiral, 1513–25, Lord High Treasurer, 1522–47, Earl Marshal 1533, he was closely related to the House of Tudor as well as being uncle to Henry's Queens Anne Boleyn and Catherine Howard. Holbein shows him holding his gold baton as Earl Marshal and his white wand of office as Lord Treasurer. Round his shoulders is the collar of the Garter. Behind his head is an overpainted inscription, which formerly read: . THOMAS . DVKE OF . NORFOLK . MARSHALL . AND . TREASURER OFF INGLONDE . THE . LXVI . YERE OF HIS AGE. There are two versions of this portrait at Arundel, of a lesser quality than this one, and others elsewhere.

Henry's man, Wolsey's enemy and a professed anti-clerical, Norfolk was the royal emissary, with the Duke of Suffolk (no. 208) to relieve Wolsey of the Great Seal on 17/18 October 1529. On the occasion of its transfer to More, Norfolk declared on the king's behalf 'how much all England was beholden to Sir Thomas More, and how worthy he was to have the highest room in the realm'. Norfolk remained More's friend though, in the end, at the trial in Westminster Hall on 1 July 1535, after attempting to bring More to 'forthink and repent of his obstinate opinion', he held with his master in concluding that More was rightly condemned.

208

**208
Charles Brandon, 1st Duke of Suffolk** (d.1545)
Unknown artist, later 16th century
Oil on panel, 88 × 74.4 (34⅝ × 29½)

Provenance George Lynn, antiquary (seen by George Vertue 1725, 1736); Lynn family; bt. NPG from Everard Green 1879.
Bibliography Strong, *Catalogue*, 305–6; pls 604–6.

National Portrait Gallery, London (516)

No portrait of the Duke of Suffolk in earlier life is extant. Versions exist, at Woburn Abbey and at Montacute House, of a double portrait said to show him and his wife. The portraits of Suffolk alone, as he was in 1540–5, may ultimately derive from Holbein.

Suffolk, made Henry VIII's Squire of the Body in 1509, married Henry's sister Mary, widow of Louis XII, in 1515 and was Henry's man all his life. He was royal commander on the French expedition of 1523 and More had to tell him to spare his men. With Norfolk, More and others, Suffolk was ambassador to France in 1527 (Rogers, 153; *Neue Briefe*, 153AB). An early supporter of the divorce, Suffolk was the mouthpiece of Henry's rage at the final meeting of the legatine court: 'It was never', quoth he, 'merry in England while we had cardinals amongst us'. With Norfolk, he demanded the Great Seal from Wolsey on 17/18 October 1529, and perhaps hoped to succeed him in the office to which More was then appointed. Suffolk was one of the Commissioners appointed to receive the oath to the Supremacy in 1534 (no. 237).

**209
Thomas Cromwell, Earl of Essex** (?1485–1540)
Unknown artist, after Hans Holbein the Younger,
?16th century
Oil on panel, 78.1 × 61.9 (30¾ × 24⅜)

Provenance ?Family of sitter (Lords Cromwell, later Earls of Ardglass); Southwell family, King's Weston, 1704 (seen by George Vertue c.1728, c.1795, 1796): ? sold Christie's 19 April 1833 (145); Stephen Jarrett of Crane Lodge, Wilts.; Foster sale 7 April 1853 (36); J. P. Hardy, sold Christie's 13 December 1912 (108); Pawsey and Payne; bt. NPG from A. H. Buttery 1914.
Bibliography Strong, *Catalogue*, 113–14, pls 221–4; G. R. Elton, *The Tudor Revolution in Government*, Cambridge 1953; A. G. Dickens, *Thomas Cromwell and the English Reformation*, 1959; G. R. Elton, *Policy and Police*, Cambridge 1972.

National Portrait Gallery, London (1727)

Thomas Cromwell probably sat to Holbein in 1533–4: the letter on the table is inscribed from the king 'to our trusty and right wellbeloved Counsaillor Thomas Cromwell Maister of o Jewellhouse', which he became in 1533. The original portrait is presumed lost, and the best of several copies is in the Frick Collection, New York. The present version is a copy, perhaps late; the NPG owns another workshop version (1083).

Cromwell left England young to avoid the consequences of a misdemeanour and found his way to Italy before returning to England about 1512. He 'grew continually in the King's favour' (Cavendish), and was able to advance himself after

Colour plate V *Sir Thomas More* by Hans Holbein the Younger (no. 177)

POLITICS AT HOME AND ABROAD

209

210

Wolsey's fall, so that for the next ten years he was powerful beyond any man in England except Henry. To the Catholic party an 'emissary of Satan', he gave English affairs a decisive turn by showing Henry the way to consolidate his realm through the exclusive sovereignty of the King in Parliament and his prosperity through the sale of monastic properties. Privy Councillor in 1531, he became Chancellor of the Exchequer in 1533, King's Secretary and Master of the Rolls in 1534. He was indicted for treason in 1540 and executed, his last words on the scaffold forming a striking contrast with More's: 'I am by the law condemned to die; I have offended my prince, for the which I ask him heartily forgiveness'.

210
Thomas Cranmer (1489–1556)
Gerlach Flicke, 1546
Oil on panel, 98.5 × 76.2 (38¾ × 30)

Provenance John Mitchell, of Bayfield Hall, Norfolk, by whom presented to British Museum 1776; transferred to NPG 1879.
Exhibition British Institution, 1820 (128).
Bibliography Strong, *Catalogue*, 55–6; pls 96–9; id. *English Icon*, 8, 77–81, no. 14; J. Ridley, *Thomas Cranmer*, Oxford 1962.

National Portrait Gallery, London (535)

This painting represents the earliest portrait type of Thomas Cranmer, Archbishop of Canterbury from 1533. Some later pictures show him as described by John Foxe:

'of stature mean, of complexion pure and somewhat sanguine' (ruddy), with 'a long beard, white and thick'. Cranmer here wears a signet ring with his own arms impaling those of Canterbury and the initials T.C. above. The letter on the table is addressed 'Too . . . my Lorde tharbusshope of Canterbury . . .', the book he is reading is inscribed *Epist Paul*, and one of those on the table *August[inus] de fide et operibus*, probably an allusion to the soundness of Cranmer's middle-way doctrine.

Cranmer suggested, in 1529, that the opinions of European universities should be consulted about the divorce. In 1532 he himself married, and on 23 May 1533 proclaimed the marriage of Henry and Catherine null. A few days later, he declared Henry's secret marriage with Anne Boleyn valid and he crowned Anne Queen in Westminster Abbey. Cranmer was one of More's examiners in the affair of the Nun of Kent (nos. 230–3), as well as one of the Commissioners to administer the oath of Supremacy (no. 237). He also suggested that More and Fisher should be allowed to swear a modified form of the oath, and was one of More's interrogators in the Tower.

POLITICS AT HOME AND ABROAD

211

211
Anne Boleyn (1507–36)
Unknown artist, ?late 16th century
Oil on panel, 54.3 × 41.6 (21 3/8 × 16 3/8)

Provenance Bt. NPG from Reynolds Galleries 1882.
Bibliography Strong, *Catalogue*, 5–6; pls 8–10.

National Portrait Gallery, London (668)

Inscribed ANNA BOLINA VXOR- HENRI- OCTA. 'A version, mechanical in quality, of the standard portrait', of a kind usually produced to form part of a series of kings and queens (Strong). Marino Sanuto, the Venetian diarist, described Anne as 'not one of the handsomest women in the world; she is of middling height, with a dark complexion, long neck, wide mouth, bosom not much raised . . . eyes which are black and beautiful'.
    More's opinion on Henry's taking Anne for his mistress in 1526 is not recorded, but it is clear from his conduct towards the king's bastard son by Elizabeth Blount, Henry Fitzroy, that he would not have been betrayed into public protest by his disapproval of 'pernicious and inordinate carnal love'. His espousal of Catherine of Aragon's cause, however, earned him Anne's enmity. His refusal to attend her coronation would have done nothing to soften her. When More was in the Tower, he asked Margaret Roper how Anne did: ' "In faith, father," quoth she, "never better". "Never better! Megge," quoth he. "Alas! Megge, alas! it pitieth me to remember into what misery, poore soule, she shall shortly come." ' William Roper, who tells this story, is also our authority for the statement that Henry, at first willing that More and Fisher should be allowed to swear a modified form of the oath of Supremacy, was prevailed on by Anne to insist on the full form (cf no. 238).

212
Sir Richard Southwell (1504–64)
Unknown artist, after Hans Holbein the Younger,
16th century
Oil on panel, 45.7 × 35.5 (18 × 14)

Provenance H. E. Chetwynd-Stapleton, c.1866; sold Sotheby's 21 July 1971 (41); bt. French & Co; Jean-Luc Bordeaux, Santa Monica, California; from whom bt. NPG 1972.
Exhibition NPE, 1866 (108).
Bibliography Parker, no. 38; Ganz, *Paintings*, no. 88; Roper, 84, 91; Harpsfield, 181, 192, 348.

National Portrait Gallery, London (4912)

The portrait is inscribed X°. IVLII. ANNO. H. VIII. XXVIII°. ETATIS. SVAE ANNO XXXIII – ie 10 July 1536. Its original, now in the Uffizi, was therefore painted during Holbein's second visit to England. A number of other versions exist, and Holbein's drawing is at Windsor Castle.
    Sir Richard Southwell was in trouble in 1531 as having been concerned in a murder. He became Sheriff of Norfolk in 1534, acted as an agent of Thomas Cromwell in the Dissolution of the Monasteries and was MP for Norfolk in 1539. He was knighted in 1542 and was one of the executors of the will of Henry VIII. From 1554 to 1560 he was Master of the Ordnance.

212

Both Roper and Harpsfield tell how Southwell, along with Richard Rich (no. 243) and a certain Master Palmer (probably Sir John Palmer) 'were sent to Sir Thomas More into the Tower, to fetche awaye his bookes from him. And while Sir Richard Southwell and Master Palmer were busye in the trussing upp of his bookes', Rich put his celebrated question to More about the power of King and Parliament and More replied. At More's trial, Palmer and Southwell professed to have taken no heed of this exchange, Southwell pleading that 'because he was appointed only to looke vnto the conveyaunce of his bookes, he gaue no eare vnto them' (Roper, 84, 91).

213
Suleiman the Magnificent (?1496–1566)
Melchior Lorck, 1559
Engraving, 40.5 × 28 (16 × 11¼)

Bibliography H. Harbeck, *Melchior Lorichs. Ein Beitrag...*, Hamburg 1911, p 41, no. 20; Bartsch, IX.507.13; Erik Fischer, *Melchior Lorck, Drawings from the Evelyn Collection... and ... the Royal Museum of Fine Arts, Copenhagen*, Copenhagen 1962; id. 'Melchior Lorck. En Dansk Vagants Levnedsløb i det 16 Aarhundrede', *Fund och Forskning i det k. Bibliotekets Samlinger*, XI, 1964, 33–72; C. A. Patrides, '"The Bloody and Cruell Turke": the Background of a Renaissance Commonplace', *Studies in the Renaissance*, X, 1963, 126–35; Thomas More, *Dialogue of Comfort*, CW, XII, esp. cxxii–cxxxi.

The Trustees of the British Museum (1848-11-25-22)

Suleiman I, the Magnificent, Sultan of the Ottoman Turks, the arch-enemy of Christendom, was notorious to Thomas More's age as the Great Turk. He took Belgrade in 1521, Rhodes in 1522 and soon invaded Hungary, where he inflicted a disastrous defeat on the Hungarian forces at Mohács on 28 August 1526 and sacked Buda. In 1529 he was at the gates of Vienna. More abhorred the Turk as the ally of the Reformation, the greatest external danger, temporal and spiritual, to the 'common corps of Christendom'. It is clear that Turkish atrocities were paralleled for him in the cruelties of the Sack of Rome in 1527 (no. 199). His prayer-book (no. 226) shows how often in the Tower his thoughts turned to the Turkish threat. His *Dialogue of Comfort*, set in Hungary, reflects the same concern.

The painter Melchior Lorck (Lorichs) was the foremost visual source of his time for European knowledge of the Turk. Born in Flensburg, in the Duchy of Schleswig, and trained as a goldsmith, Lorck joined the imperial embassy of Augier Ghiselin de Busbecq to Constantinople, probably in 1555, returning in 1560. The inscription on this engraving reads: IMAGO SVLEYMANNI TVRCORVM IMP. IN ORIENTE, VNICI SELIMY FILII, QVI AN. DO. MDXX PATRI IN IMPERIO SUCCESSIT: QVO ETIAM ANNO CAROLVS V MAXAEMYLIANI CAESARIS NEPOS AQVISGRANI IN OCCIDENTE CORONATVS EST CHRISTIAN. IMP. A MELCHIORE LORICH FLENSBVRGENSI HOLSATIO ANTIQVITATIS STUDIOSISS, CONSTANTINOPOLI, AN. MDLIX, MEN. FEB. DIE XV, VERISSIME EXPRESSA. (The likeness of Suleiman, Emperor of the Turks in the East, the only son of

213

Selim, who succeeded his father as Emperor in the year of Our Lord 1520 – in which year Charles V, the grandson of Maximilian, was also crowned Emperor of Western Christendom at Aix-la-Chapelle – delineated with the utmost fidelity by Melchior Lorck of Flensburg in Holstein, a great student of antiquity, on 15 February 1559, at Constantinople.)

214

214
John Fisher, Bishop of Rochester (1469–1535)
Unknown artist, after Hans Holbein the Younger,
16th century
Oil on paper, silhouetted, 21 × 19 (8¼ × 7½)

Provenance Chamberlaine, Librarian to George III; Rev. T. Bancroft 1791–2 or 1795–7; ? John Wolstenholme 1892; sold Sotheby's 1 April 1936 (6).
Exhibitions RA, *Holbein* (127); *Erasmus*, 1969 (103).
Bibliography Emden, *Cambridge*, 228–30; E. Surtz, *The Works and Days of John Fisher*, Cambridge, Mass. 1967; John Woodward, *Tudor and Stuart Drawings*, 1951, 43–4; Strong, *Catalogue*, 119–21; pls 238–40.

National Portrait Gallery, London (2821)

John Fisher was educated at Cambridge, being made Vice-Chancellor in 1501 and Chancellor in 1504, having become the first Lady Margaret Professor of Divinity in 1503. He was the patron of Erasmus, President of Queens' College and instrumental in the founding of Christ's and St John's. Appointed Bishop of Rochester in 1504, he took a leading part during the early 1520s in combating the spread of Lutheranism (nos. 121, 122) and, when the divorce was mooted, strongly opposed it. His antagonism to the Supremacy resulted in his condemnation to perpetual imprisonment in 1534 and, though the sentence was commuted, he was later confined in the Tower, in spite of his infirmity, and executed on 22 June 1535. He was canonized in 1935.

'In stature of body [Fisher] was tall and comly, exceeding the common and middle sort of men: for he was to the quantitie of 6 foote in heighte, and being therewith verie slender and leane, was nevertheless upright and well framed, straight backed, big joynted and strongly synewed. His hear by nature black ... his eyes longe and rounde, neither full black nor full graie, his nose of a goode and even proportion, somewhat wide mouthed and bigg jawed ..., his skinne somewhat tawnie mixed with manie blew vaines ...'
(British Library, MS Harley 6382).

A late eighteenth or early nineteenth-century hand identifies the NPG drawing on its reverse as by Holbein and formerly 'in Richardsons possession and from which Houbrakens print was taken'. It is derived from the drawing of *c.*1528 at Windsor Castle, of which one other early copy exists in the British Museum. The NPG copy probably formed part of the stock of a sixteenth-century workshop; it is on oiled paper, pricked along the features for tracing. Holbein's drawing, more likely made on his first visit than on his second, is the pattern for all later portraits of Fisher. A bust in the Metropolitan Museum of Art, New York, by Torrigiano, said to represent Fisher, shows a much younger man. It is likely to have been made at least fifteen years earlier.

215 (enlarged)

216

215
Paul III (1468–1549; Pope 1534–49)
?Vincenzo Belli, 1534
Bronze medal, diameter 4.3 (1¾)

Exhibition Erasmus, 1969 (495).
Bibliography Armand, II, 166.5.

The Trustees of the British Museum (506/36)

Alessandro Farnese, elected pope in the year before Thomas More was executed, was a great patron of the arts, who made Michelangelo chief architect of St Peter's, as well as a promoter of the reform of the Church from within, via ecclesiastical commissions, the restoration of the Inquisition and his advocacy of a General Council.

He sent the cardinal's hat to John Fisher (no. 214) shortly before his death; he also raised Reginald Pole (no. 216) to the cardinalate in 1536 and in 1538 promulgated the bull excommunicating Henry VIII.

This medal, probably by Vincenzo Belli, shows Paul III, newly elected pope and crowned with oak leaves on the obverse, with the legend PAVLVS III PONT[ifex] MAX[imus] ANNO I. The reverse shows the conversion of St Paul with the legend SAVLE, SAVLE, QVID ME PERSEQVERIS? (Saul, Saul, why persecutest thou me? Acts ix 4) round the rim, and VAS ELECTIONIS (A chosen vessel. Acts ix 15) in the exergue.

216
Reginald Pole (1500–58; Cardinal Archbishop of Canterbury 1556–8)
Unknown artist, 16th century
Oil on canvas, 122 × 89 (48 × 35)

Exhibition London County Council, Festival of Britain, 1951.
Bibliography Emden, *Oxford 1540*, 453–5; Rogers, 71; Strong, *Catalogue*, pl 499.

His Grace the Lord Archbishop of Canterbury and the Church Commissioners

Reginald Pole was connected, through his mother, with the royal house of York, and received early ecclesiastical preferment from Henry VIII, who sent him to Italy at his own request in 1521. He studied at Padua and, after a further period in England, at Paris. After declining the Archbishopric of York on Wolsey's fall, he was, in 1532, allowed to return to Padua. His disapproval of the divorce and of the Supremacy was formulated in his *Pro ecclesiasticae unitatis defensione* (1536), a severe critique of Henry. Paul III enlisted him to help draw up a programme of church reform and made him a cardinal in December 1536. In 1539 an act of attainder was passed against him and his family. In 1542 he was one of three legates appointed to preside at the Council of Trent; in 1547 he attempted a reconciliation of England with the papacy. He was consecrated Archbishop of Canterbury, under Mary, in 1556.

Pole's appearance in cardinal's robes in this picture indicates that the type to which it belongs was produced after 1536, in Italy. A later type is represented by the portrait in the NPG (220). Lodovico Beccadelli, Pole's private secretary, describes him as 'of the middle stature, and of a lean habit of body; he was fair, and yellow hair'd, which is the usual colour and complexion of his countrymen. The oval of his face was rather large, but enlivened with an eye benign and cheerful. His beard, when he was young, was of a very light colour.' (L. Beccadelli, *Life*, trans. B. Pye, 1766).

The inscription reads: SI SIC POLE TVAE POTVISSET MENTIS IMAGO PINGI NIL OCVLI PVLCRIVS ASPICERENT (If only, Pole, the painter had been able to show so well the image of your mind, the eye would never have beheld anything more beautiful).

Only one brief commendatory letter from Thomas More to Pole, of ?1518, is extant.

217
Letter from the Emperor Charles V to Sir Thomas More, 1531
?Autograph, Brussels, 11 March 1531
Paper, 1531

Bibliography Neue Briefe, 183A.

Haus-, Hof- und Staatsarchiv, Vienna (England Varia Fz.2)

This letter's background is 'the King's great matter', Henry's divorce. After the unsatisfactory ending of the legatine court, the clergy were accused of *praemunire*. On 11 March 1531, the Emperor Charles V, uncle to Catherine of Aragon, addressed a letter to More acknowledging his fidelity towards 'mesdits subietz' (ie Catherine). Meanwhile, Henry had sent envoys to the European universities to canvass opinion about the divorce. On 30 March 1531 More, as Lord Chancellor, had to explain the results of these 'votes' before both houses of Parliament. On 2 April Eustace Chapuys (1489–1556), imperial ambassador in London, reported that More had set forth by command in the Commons that the king pursued his divorce not out of love for some lady, but was only moved by his conscience, and further that he had informed More of the arrival of Charles's letter and of his desire to see More. The chancellor had begged him 'for the honour of God' to forbear. Though his loyalty was beyond suspicion a visit such as this might rob him of the liberty of later speaking his mind 'as he had ever done'. More begged Chapuys to keep the letter 'till some other time', since, if he received it, he must communicate it. That is the last we hear of the emperor's letter. For all we know, More may never have received it.

218
Photograph: Sir Thomas More delivers the Great Seal, 1532

Bibliography LP, V, 1075; Rymer, XIV, 433 (= VI, ii, 171).

Photograph by courtesy of the Public Record Office, London (C.54/401)

The Close Roll records that, on 16 May 1532, the Great Seal, in the custody of Sir Thomas More, Chancellor of England, enclosed in a white leather bag sealed with his own seal in wax, was delivered into the king's hands in the garden of his palace called York Place at Westminster, in the presence of the Duke of Norfolk. Then and there the same Thomas More surrendered his office of Chancellor of England into the king's hands; on Monday 20 May, at East Greenwich, the king delivered it to Thomas Audeley.

Roper tells of More's long solicitation of the Duke of Norfolk, who 'at length' obtained of the king for More 'a clear discharge of his office. Then, at a tyme convenient, by His Highnes' appointment, repaired he to His Grace to yield up unto him the Great Seal. Which, as His Grace, with thanks and praise for his worthy service in that office, courteously at his hands receaved, so pleased it His Highnes to say unto him, that for the service that he before had done him, in any suit which he should after have unto him, that either should concern his honour... or that should appertain to his profit, he should find His Highnes good and gracious lord unto him'.

On 14 June, More explains to Erasmus (Allen, X, 2659) how a chest ailment had caused him to give up his office. We do not know how far this was a diplomatic ailment. More's resignation came on the day after the Submission of the Clergy. On the same day Capello reported to the Signory of Venice: 'the cause is said to be his refusal to gratify the King by writing in favour of the divorce which His Majesty is endeavouring to dispatch with all speed' (Sanuto, *Diaries*).

VII *Sir Thomas More in the Tower*

Records remain of Sir Thomas More's imprisonment in the Tower, in the form of works of devotion which are the written testimony to how he sustained himself in the face of the ultimate spiritual peril. One is written throughout in his own hand, the only extant holograph manuscript apart from a letter or two; another is the prayer-book from which we can trace his daily petitions for strength and on behalf of his family, friends and enemies. A number of other relics are preserved.

219
Sir Thomas More's 'Treatise on the Passion'
Manuscript on paper, mid 16th century

Provenance Probably the 'Anonymi Sermo de Passione MSS' which came to the Bodleian Library 1605–11.
Bibliography CMA, I, 1698, 122, F.3.2368; *SC*, 2368; Sr Mary Thecla, 'Sir Thomas More and the *Catena aurea*', *Modern Language Notes*, LXI, 1946, 523–9; O. Pächt and J. J. G. Alexander, *Illuminated MSS in the Bodleian Library Oxford*, III, Oxford 1973, p 103, no. 1195; ed. G. E. Haupt, *CW*, XIII, 1976.

Bodleian Library, Oxford (MS Bodl. 431, ff. 1-137r)

The *Treatise* belongs to More's 'Tower works', and was included by William Rastell in *EW*. Modern scholarship is not fully agreed but there is a general consensus that it was written about the time of his imprisonment (17 April 1534). This would give the following order for the 'Tower works': *Treatise, Blessed Body, Dialogue of Comfort*, and *De Tristitia*, with the *Instructions and Prayers* interspersed.

The *Treatise* begins with a meditation on the creation and fall of angels and men and on the divine redemption through the bitter passion of Christ. Unlike many of More's other works, it is not heavy with quotations. It relies on the standard medieval work in this field, the *Catena aurea* of St Thomas Aquinas. The treason of Judas, the *mandatum* of Christ washing the feet of his disciples, and the institution of the Eucharist, on which More dwells, conclude the *Treatise*. It is thus closely linked to the treatise on the *Blessed Body* (no. 220). The text is interspersed with short prayers at the end of each chapter, demonstrating how More sought to apply each biblical citation to his own life.

220
Sir Thomas More's 'Treatise to Receive the Blessed Body of Our Lord'
Manuscript on paper, 1555

Bibliography M. R. James, *Aberdeen*, Cambridge 1932, 131f; A. G. Dickens, 'Robert Parkyn's Narrative of the Reformation', *EHR*, LXII, 1947, 58–83; id. 'R. Parkyn's MS Books', *N & Q* CXIV, 1949, 73–4; id. 'Yorkshire Clerical Documents, 1554–6', *Bodleian Library Record*, III, 1950–1, 35; id. *Tudor Treatises* (Yorkshire Archaeological Society, Record Series, vol CXXV), 1959, 18ff; ed. G. E. Haupt, *CW*, XIII, 1976.

Aberdeen University Library (MS 185, ff. 217-20)

This text, transcribed by Robert Parkyn and dated 1555, is the earliest extant version of More's *Treatise on the Eucharist*.

Two other manuscripts are in the Bodleian Library (MSS Bodl. 431 and Rawl. C.587). It illustrates the conservative nature of northern religious culture at the mid century. Since the first printed edition of the *Treatise* was to appear only two years later in *EW*, Parkyn must have had access to manuscript sources of the text.

Robert Parkyn was a Yorkshire clerical writer. He came from a yeoman family near Doncaster and became curate of Adwick-le-Street where he died in 1569. Although he conformed with the religious changes of his days, his manuscripts reveal his staunch inclinations to Catholic orthodoxy. He was very likely in contact with the Mores of Barnborough Hall, the old Cresacre estate (nos. 1,170) only five miles away, where More's son John (no. 178) had come to live with his family.

The Treatise to receive the Blessed Body of Our Lord sacramentally and virtually both was composed by More in 1534 when he was a prisoner in the Tower. It is a short and straightforward exhortation for ordinary folk.

221
Sir Thomas More's 'Dialogue of Comfort', 1534–5
A dialoge of comfort agaynst trybulacion, made by an hungaryen in laten, & translatyd out of laten into french, & out of french into English
Manuscript on paper, first half of 16th century, with later additions

Provenance The initials G. P. on the binding may be those of Sir Geoffrey Pole, brother of Reginald; the back paste-down bears the name 'Elyne Henslowe', daughter of Ralph Henslow, of Hampshire, a close friend of the Pole family.
Bibliography L. L. Martz and F. Manley, eds., *CW*, XII, 1976.

The President and Fellows of Corpus Christi College, Oxford (MS D.37)

The *Dialogue of Comfort*, written by More in the Tower, is a debate between Anthony, a wise old Hungarian, and his young nephew Vincent, under the threat of the Turkish invasion of Europe. More sets forth his advice as to how a man is to behave virtuously under suffering. The implied parallel is evident: the case of oppressed Christendom under the Great Turk serves as a lesson for English Catholics under the growing Henrician tyranny. More's lesson was that the secular ruler must not dictate the conscience of his subjects. That meant the contradiction of the maxim *cuius regio eius religio*.

222

As a prisoner facing possible torture and death, More naturally had to use precautions. Book I opens with the statement that tribulations are good for man to prove his faith. Book II adjusts this to the world as it is. In Book III, More develops the theme of the worst temptation by the 'midday devil', ie a gradual giving in to the enemy, against which only meditation on the vanity of this world and on the Redemption will suffice.

It looks as though the Corpus Christi manuscript was prepared by William Rastell for publication as part of his Great Volume of 1557. When all printing and correcting were done, Rastell perhaps gave it to Sir Geoffrey Pole.

221
Sir Thomas More's 'Dialogue of Comfort', 1553
A dialoge of comfort against tribulacion, made by Syr Thomas More Knyght, and set foorth by the name of an Hungarien, not before this time imprinted, London, Richard Tottel, 1553

Bibliography STC2, 18082; Gibson, 51; L. L. Martz and F. E. Manley, eds., *CW*, XII, 1976.

Guildhall Library, London (Cock Colln. 1.3)

According to Martz, William Rastell prepared the Corpus Christi College manuscript (no. 221) for printing. With his approval, the present Tottel edition of 1553 was published

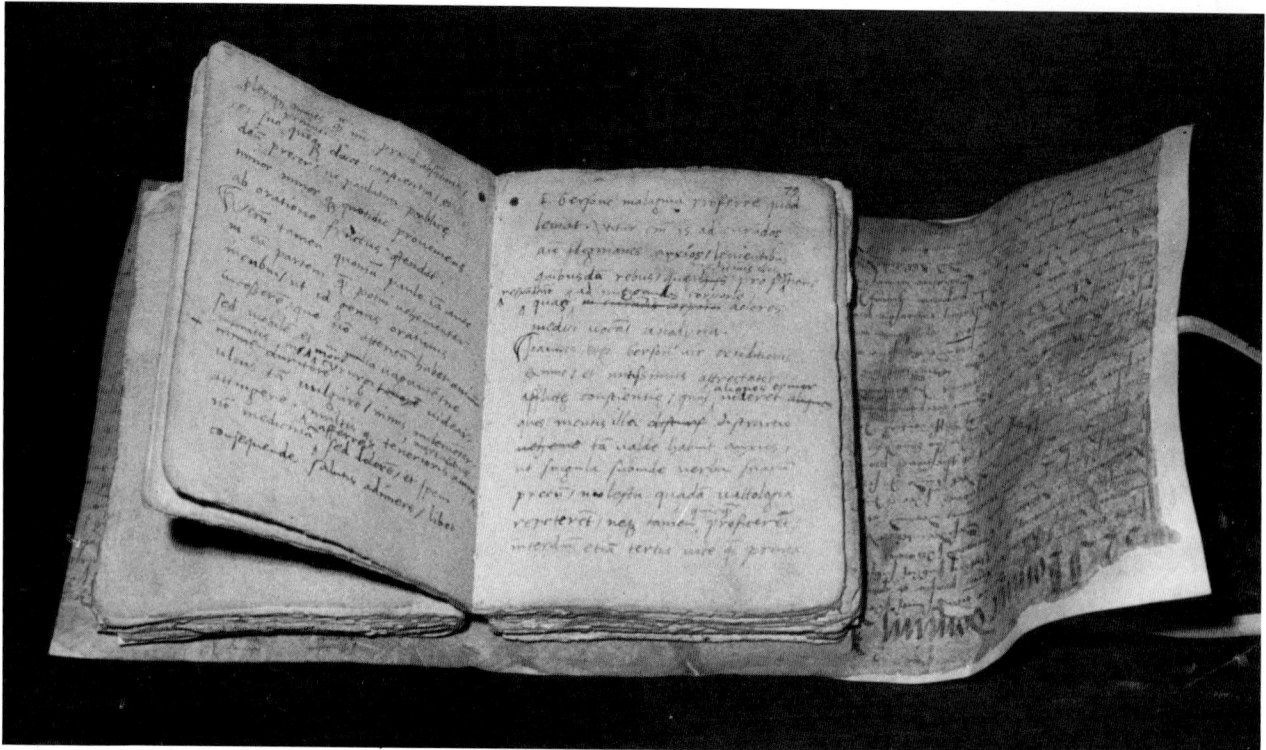

225

from another reliable manuscript, now lost. Since Tottel was also the printer of Rastell's collected edition of More's *English Works* of 1557, it was convenient to set up from his own former edition.

223
Prayers by Sir Thomas More
Collective volume of miscellaneous pieces by Robert Parkyn (d.1569), containing five prayers by More
Manuscript on paper, before 1551

Provenance Robert [Parkyn, erased and written over] Byard; Brian Cooke of Wheatley; G. E. Cooke of Yarborough; bt. 1931.
Bibliography A. G. Dickens, 'Robert Parkyn's MS Books', *N & Q*, CXCIV, 1949, 13–14; id. 'Yorkshire Clerical Documents', *Bodleian Library Record*, III, 1950–1, 34–40; id. *Tudor Treatises* (Yorkshire Archaeological Society, Record Series, vol CXXV), 1959, 18–19; D. M. Rogers, 'St John Fisher: An Unpublished Prayer to God the Father', *The Month*, n.s. VII, 1952, 106–11; G. E. Haupt, ed., *CW*, XIII, 1976.

Bodleian Library, Oxford (MS Lat.th.d.15, ff. 116v–120r)

Robert Parkyn's transcript of four of More's prayers precedes the first printed edition in Rastell's Great Volume by at least six years. More wrote these prayers – with the exception of one from his translation of Pico – 'while he was prisoner in the towre of London', as Rastell tells us. G. E. Haupt assumes that the 'Godly Meditation' ('Give me thy grace good lorde...') was written on 2 July 1535, the feast of the Visitation of the Blessed Virgin, when it would fit the canonical hours.

224
Sir Thomas More's Prayers collected out of the Psalms
Psalmi, seu Precationes D. Ioan. Fisheri Episcopi Roffensis. Accessit Imploratio divini auxilii contra tentationem ex Psalmis Dauidis, Per Th. Morum, [London, Thomas Vautrollier], 1572

Bibliography Gibson, 95; Adams, F544; Marc'hadour, *Bible*, 18, 101–2, 105–77, 369–72; G. E. Haupt, ed., *CW*, XIII, 1976.

The British Library Board (3456.a.12)

This is the third printed edition of More's 'Devoute prayer, collected out of the psalmes of David'. Although they are in Latin, William Rastell included them in *EW* (no. 260). The second edition was in the Louvain *Opera* (no. 262).

More's 'imploration of divine help' was written, like the other prayers, during his imprisonment in the Tower. It consists of selected passages from the Psalms and is thus linked with the Yale *Hours* (no. 226).

225
Sir Thomas More's 'De Tristitia Christi'
De tristitia tedio pavore et oratione christi ante captionem eius...
Holograph manuscript on paper, 1534–5

Provenance First seven gatherings removed from Tower; probably Margaret Roper; later her daughter, Mary Basset; by 1557 in possession of Pedro de Soto (c.1495–1563), who probably took it to Spain 1557, and given to Don Fernando de Toledo, whose brother, the Count of Oropesa, presented it to San Juan de Ribera, Archbishop of Valencia, who presented it to his foundation, the Royal College of Corpus Christi.
Bibliography Clarence H. Miller, ed., *CW*, XIV, 1976.

Real Colegio de Corpus Christi, Valencia

Apart from a few farewell letters, *De Tristitia Christi* is the last of More's works written under supreme psychological anguish in the Tower before his execution. It is a Latin Gospel harmony, telling the story of Christ's Agony in the Garden. More draws upon traditional sources, which find their *summa* in Jean Gerson's *Monotessaron*. He visualizes his present situation in relation to Christ's: the hesitation before accepting violent death, the soul's debate between willingness and reluctance, prayer leading to the final acceptance of God's will, and the subsequent process towards martyrdom.

The work is unfinished. When he came to the words *tum demum primum manus iniectas in Iesum* (then, after all this, did they first lay hands upon Jesus), his books, pen, ink and paper were taken from him, and soon after he was put to death.

The manuscript is More's holograph throughout, in his Latin (italic) hand with revisions and corrections. The vellum binding is enclosed in a decorative cloth cover. Later manuscript transcripts (British Library MSS Royal 17.D.XIV and Bodley 431) exist. More's granddaughter, Mary Basset (née Roper), translated *De Tristitia* from a different manuscript into English; her version was included by Rastell in *EW*.

226
The Prayer-Book of Sir Thomas More
Horae beate Marie ad vsum ecclesie Sarisburiensis, bound with *Psalterium cum Hymnis secundum usum . . . Sarum et Eboracensem*, Paris, François Regnault, 1530, and Paris, François Byrckman, 1522

Provenance Thomas More (MS annotations throughout in his hand, and on front paste-down 'Liber quondam Thomae Mori militis in multis locis manu sua propria inscriptus'); apparently remained in Catholic hands; Powys of Berwick, Shropshire, from whom to Feilding family, Earls of Denbigh, by whom sold ?1947; Beinecke Library, Yale University 1965.

Exhibitions Chelsea, 1929 (9); Oxford Exhibition, 1935.
Bibliography Thomas More's Prayer Book: A Facsimile Reproduction of the Annotated Pages..., ed. L. L. Martz and R. S. Sylvester, New Haven, Conn. 1969.

The Beinecke Rare Book and Manuscript Library, Yale University

Two books of private devotion, both imperfect, are here bound together: a *Book of Hours* and a *Psalter,* both printed at Paris for the English market and bound *c.* 1530–40. The composite volume accompanied Thomas More to the Tower in 1534 and remained with him throughout his incarceration.

The *Hours* contain the thirty-seven lines, two per page, of his 'Godly Meditation':
'Give me thy grace good lord to sett the world at nought,
To set my mynd fast vppon thee,
And not to hang vppon the blaste of mennys mowthis . . .'
It follows the canonical hours (beginning with Prime) which are accompanied by woodcuts of Christ's life, from the Nativity to the Crucifixion. This meditation on the bitter passion and death of the Saviour, More's final *imitatio Christi*, gave him strength to endure his own adversity and prepared him for his own final hour.

Some 150 marginal annotations in the *Psalter* open a vista into More's heart and mind. They 'reflect his personal griefs and fears as he prayed the Psalter and strove to comfort his soul' (Martz/Sylvester, xiii), following the spiritual progress of the psalmist out of the depths to confidence. At Psalm 37,

12–20, where the psalmist laments that he is forsaken by friends and surrounded by slander and vanity but keeps his silence, trusting that God will hear him, More wrote: 'Thus ought a meek man to behave during tribulation: he should neither speak proudly nor retort to wicked words, but instead he should bless the evil-speakers and suffer patiently either for the sake of justice if he has deserved it, or, if he has not deserved it, for the sake of God.' When More kept his own silence during his trial, he was modelling his behaviour after the psalmist (Psalm 38, 2): 'I will keep my mouth with a bridle, while the wicked is before me'.

The *leitmotif* of More's annotations is the never-ending struggle between *demones* (a word which occurs forty times in his marginal notes) and the forces of good.

227
Case of Relics associated with Sir Thomas More

a Gold crucifix, with three pendant pearls and niello back (separated)
9.5 × 5 (3¾ × 2)
?16th century

Provenance Perhaps the crucifix seen by Vertue (*Notebooks*, II, 75) in possession of Thomas More of Barnborough 1728; presented by Thomas More, SJ (1722–95) to English College of St Omers 1755; presumably removed with College to Bruges 1762; Liège 1773; Stonyhurst 1794.

b Small gold crucifix
height 4.5 (1¾)
?16th century

Provenance Given by John Gage 1826.

c Cameo of Our Lady, in a gold and white enamel setting
4.1 × 2.9 (1⅝ × 1⅛)
? 17th century

Provenance Thomas More, SJ, as above.

d Silver and crystal reliquary, with pendant bead, containing fragment of bone
height 3.8 (1½)
?16th century

Provenance Given by John Gage 1826.

e Fragment of hair shirt in silver case
3.2 × 2.5 (1¼ × 1)

Provenance Unknown.

f Gold and enamelled 'George', formerly containing a miniature of Thomas More
diameter 6.6 (2⅝)
16th century

Provenance Cresacre More (his will 1649); seen and recorded by George Vertue as above; Thomas More, SJ, as above.

Exhibitions All: Chelsea, 1929 (2); George: *Special Exhibition*, 1862 (7755); Chicago, Loyola University, Martin D'Arcy Gallery of Art, *Enamels: the XII to the XVI Century* (text by D. F. Rowe), 1970 (24).

227f

Bibliography Bridgett, 455–8; John Gerard, *Stonyhurst College Centenary Record*, Belfast 1894, 247–8; Joan Evans, *A History of Jewellery 1100–1870*, 1951, p 81, pl 38; Hugh Tait, 'Historiated Tudor Jewellery', in *The Antiquaries' Journal*, XLII, 1962, 244; R. Berliner, 'Arma Christi', in *Münchner Jahrbuch der bildenden Kunst*, 3. Folge, VI, 1955, 35–152; Y. Hackenbroch, 'Two Relics of Sir Thomas More', *The Connoisseur*, CXCIV, 1977, 43–8.

The Trustees of Stonyhurst College

Thomas More was beatified, together with John Fisher, on 29 December 1886 and canonised on 19 May 1935. Both are already named as martyrs in the constitution *Quoniam divinae bonitati* of 1 May 1579. More had intended his body to lie with those of his first and second wives at Chelsea (no. 287), but his bones were ignominiously interred in the Chapel of St Peter ad Vincula in the Tower. His head was saved by his daughter Margaret and has rested since at least 1585 in the Roper family vault in St Dunstan's, Canterbury. Other relics are preserved at Stonyhurst, at St Augustine's Priory, Newton Abbot (no. 228), at East Hendred (nos. 284, 285) and elsewhere.

The George at Stonyhurst, mentioned in the will of his great-grandson Cresacre More, may belong to the mid sixteenth century. On one side is an enamelled George and dragon, with the princess at prayer in the background; on the other a Resurrection with Christ seated on the empty tomb. He wears the crown of thorns and is surrounded by the instruments of the Passion and by the busts of Judas with a money-bag round his neck, Peter, the maidservant and ?Pontius Pilate, with ewer and basin. The object may have been a reliquary, since it contained between its two halves a miniature of More, now obliterated. The rims are enamelled with pinks and pansies, and bear the inscription O. PASSI GRAVIORA. DABIT. [DEVS] HIS QVOQVE. FINEM. (O you who have suffered worse things, He [God] will give an end to these also) – a slightly altered quotation from *Aeneid* I 199.

The crucifix with the pendant pearls has a gold and niello back, with the Greek inscription *Tou Apostolou Thoma leipsanon tode* (This is a relic of Thomas the Apostle). Crucifix and back have been separated, and are shown as two items.

228
Reliquary containing Fragment of a Hair Shirt
Unknown artist, ?17th century
Height 27.3 (10¾); breadth 21.6 (8½); depth 8.9 (3½)

Provenance According to tradition, from Margaret Roper (1505–44) to Margaret Clement (née Gigs, ?1508–70); by descent to her grandson Dr Caesar Clement, by whom bequeathed to his aunt, Mother Margaret Clement, founder of Community of St Monica's, Louvain, which came to England 1796.
Exhibition Chelsea, 1929 (1).
Literature C. S. Durrant, *A Link between Flemish Mystics and English Martyrs*, 1925, 183–223.

The Community, St Augustine's Priory, Newton Abbot

It is not known when Thomas More began to wear a hair shirt next to his skin. Stapleton speaks of his doing so 'even in youth', adding that he habitually slept on bare boards with a log for a pillow. John Bouge's letter of 1535 (no. 229) tells how Dame Alice did not discover this particular of her husband's life for nearly a year after their marriage: she begged Bouge to counsel him against wearing it, since it 'tamyd hys fflesche tyll the blod was sene in hys clothes'. Roper adds that More 'for the avoiding of singularity' did not wish his habit to be known, but that Anne Cresacre one evening 'in the sommer, as he sate at supper, singly in his doublet and hose, wearing thervppon a plaine shirte, without ruffe or collar, chancing to spye, began to laughe at it. My wife, not ignorant of his manner, perceyuinge the same, pryvily told him of it; And he, beinge sory that she sawe it, presently amended it.' The day before his death, More sent to Margaret, again according to Roper, 'his shirt of heare (not willinge to haue it seene)', accompanied by his last blessing to his family (no. 250).

The shirt is contained in a reliquary, with a portrait of Sir Thomas More, perhaps of the seventeenth century, inscribed with a brief Latin poem.

228

229
Letter from Sir Thomas More's Confessor
John Bouge, Sir Thomas More's confessor, to
Dame Catherine Manne
Manuscript on paper, 1535

Bibliography LP, Add. Vol.I, i, 357, no. 1024; J. Gairdner, 'A Letter concerning Bishop Fisher and Sir Thomas More', *EHR,* VII, 1892, 712–15; Emden, *Cambridge,* 84.

Public Record Office, London (SP1/239, ff. 223r–224v)

'In this time of tribulation and calamity of this wretched world', John Bouge (Bownge, Bunge), a Carthusian monk of Axholme, wrote a letter of spiritual advice to Dame Catherine Man (Manne). He exhorts her to keep in mind that we live in this world 'as a prisoner arraigned at the bar there' standing between two swords: 'death of body for a little while' or 'death in pain everlasting'. With this allusion to More's answer in his trial, Bouge begins to talk of More and Fisher, 'two honourable persons', whose acquaintance he had enjoyed. More had been his parishioner in London. He had christened two of his children, buried his first wife (Jane) and married him, by (Tunstall's) dispensation 'within a month' and 'without any banns', to his second (Alice). 'This Mr. More was my ghostly child; in his confession so pure, so clean, with great study, deliberation, determination and devotion, I never had many such, a gentleman of great learning, both in law, art and divinity, having no man alike now alive of a layman. Item, a gentleman of great soberness and gravity, one chief of the King's Council. Item a gentleman of little refection and marvellous diet. He was devote in his divine service and ... he wore a great hair shirt next his skin ...' (no. 228).

VIII *Succession, Supremacy and Execution*

Sir Thomas More's concern for the unity of the Christian Church and his abhorrence of individual, heretical separation, the setting up of the fallible individual judgement against the authority of the doctrine handed down and approved by the Church and her doctors since apostolic times, had been sufficiently shown by his stand against the creed of Lutheran Germany and her English disciples. His fear of civil disorder was almost as great.

The Submission of the Clergy of Canterbury to Henry's claim to the Supremacy 'as far as the law of God allows' on 11 February 1531 must have seemed to him the end of all he had fought for. A year later, on 15 May, the clergy of England made full submission to their sovereign and next day More resigned the chancellorship. He continued to write in opposition to heretical opinion, and on 1 June 1533 refused to accompany the bishops to the coronation of Anne Boleyn: 'It lieth not in my power', he told them, 'but that they may devour me; but God being my good Lord, I will provide that they shall never deflower me'.

Already 'pretie, preuie wayes how to wrap him in', to use his biographer Harpsfield's phrase for an earlier occasion, were being devised. The case of the Nun of Kent, Elizabeth Barton, whose treasonable visions concerning the royal marriage were to send her to the block in 1534, offered an opportunity to Henry and his agent, Thomas Cromwell. In the event, More's name was struck out of the bill of attainder concerning her, but other occasions were taken. William Roper, More's son-in-law, tells us of the famous 'Son Roper, I thank our Lord the field is won', as they went by water to More's examination 'before the Lords at Lambeth'. He refused to swear to the Supremacy, though willing to accept the Succession – and kept his silence about his reasons for refusal. He was sent to his last imprisonment in the Tower of London, where repeated interrogations by his successor as lord chancellor, Sir Thomas Audeley, and by Cromwell himself, and attempts to secure incriminating evidence against More and Fisher via their servants, failed to bring about the required result. Silence was his continual safeguard. At his trial in Westminster Hall on 1 July 1535, it was the perjured evidence of Sir Richard Rich, Cromwell's creature, Solicitor General and – much later – Lord Chancellor, that secured his conviction by a jury packed by Thomas Cromwell. He had time for only a few last written words to family and friends in letters which are among the most moving in the language, before he was beheaded on Tower Hill early on the morning of 6 July 1535 – the royal mercy having commuted to this the horrors of a traitor's death. Required by the king to 'use few words' at his execution, he found spirit for a characteristic jest with his escort: 'I pray you, good Master Lieutenant, see me safe up and for my coming down let me shift for myself', before his immortal statement of his life and example. A contemporary account of his death tells us of his affirmation that he died, as he had lived, 'The king's good servant, but God's first'.

230
Photograph: **Sir Thomas More to the 'Nun of Kent'**
[?1533]
Letter from Thomas More to Elizabeth Barton, the 'Nun of Kent', advising her against meddling with affairs of state

Bibliography [J. Forshall], *Catalogue of the ... Arundel MSS*, 1834, 41; *LP*, VII, 287; Rogers, 192; *SL*, 47; A. Neame, *The Holy Maid of Kent*, 1971.
Photograph by courtesy of the British Library Board
(*MS Arundel 152, f. 298r*)

Elizabeth Barton, a maidservant in Aldington, Kent, laid claim to being a prophetic visionary, and in 1527 entered the priory of St Sepulchre, Canterbury, under the spiritual guidance of the Benedictine Edward Bocking. Here her visions took on a character unfavourable to Henry's matrimonial designs and, after his marriage with Anne Boleyn, she proclaimed that, in the eyes of God, Henry was no longer king. In the latter part of 1533, Henry determined to stamp out this source of opposition, and the attempt was made to incriminate Thomas More and John Fisher in a pretended conspiracy of high treason. On 21 April 1534, the nun and four of her clerical adherents were executed. Fisher was fined and More's name was struck out of the bill of attainder which had been rushed through Parliament.

More's letter must belong to 1533, when the nun's visions had taken their most dangerous turn. It is carefully wrought, reminding her of the execution of the 'late Duke of Buckingham' and counselling her not to talk 'of eny such maner thinges as pertayne to princes affairs ... but onely to talke ... of suche maner thinges as maye to the soul be profitable'.

231
Sermon against the 'Nun of Kent' and her Adherents
Manuscript on paper, 1533

Bibliography LP, VII, 72 (iii); L. E. Whatmore, 'The Sermon against the Holy Maid of Kent and her Adherents, delivered at Paul's Cross, November the 23rd, 1533, and at Canterbury, December the 7th', *EHR*, LVIII, 1943, 463–75; Dom David Knowles, *Religious Orders in England*, III, Cambridge 1959, 182–91.
Public Record Office, London (SP 1/82, ff. 85v, 91r)

The confession of the nun (no. 232) provided an opportunity, immediately seized by Cromwell, to publicise and denounce her offences. Within two or three days a 'sermon' was drafted, for John Capon (alias Salcot), Abbot of Hyde and Bishop-elect of Bangor by grace of Anne Boleyn, to read at Paul's Cross on 23 November 1533. The nun, two Benedictine monks (Bocking and Dering), two Friars Observants (Richard Risby and Hugh Riche), and two secular priests (Richard Masters, of Aldington, and Henry Golde, of Aldermary) were put to public humiliation and the nun had to read a confession. A fortnight later, the same 'sermon' was read at Canterbury, by Dr Nicholas Heath (*c.*1501–78; later Archbishop of York and Lord Chancellor) again in the presence of the nun and her adherents. The exhibited manuscript was used for both these propaganda sermons, rehearsing 'this false, forged and feigned matter' of the nun, then exposing the imposture of her revelations. As we know from More's letter to Cromwell (no. 233), he himself was present at Paul's Cross.

232
Form of Confession by the 'Nun of Kent'
Manuscript on paper, 1533

Bibliography LP, VII, 72 (ii); G. R. Elton, *England under the Tudors*, 2nd edn. 1974, 138.
Public Record Office, London (SP 1/82, f. 87)

In July 1533 Archbishop Cranmer was commanded by the king, via Cromwell, to examine Elizabeth Barton and deviously secured her incrimination of herself and others: she confessed that she had 'never Hadde Vision in all her Lyff, but all that ever she said was fayned of her owne ymagynacion'. In September, the Attorney General was rounding up selected victims among her associates at Canterbury: first Bocking and Headley, then Masters and Dering. By 12 November, the nun was in prison. She was several times interrogated by the Council, in the Star Chamber and then before a great assembly of lords spiritual and temporal for three whole days. Audeley accused her of fomenting rebellion and urging the deposition of the king and the gathering cried 'To the stake with her'.

We cannot know what the present undated form of confession is worth. In the first place, her admissions were forced in circumstances that would have intimidated a 'right simple woman'. Early in her career, Warham, Wolsey, Fisher and More thought favourably of her, and Henry granted her an audience. Later, More's letter to her witnesses his caution and later still he praises Cromwell for 'bringing forth to light such detestable hypocrisy' (no. 233).

233
Photograph: **Sir Thomas More to Thomas Cromwell**
More to Thomas Cromwell, the King's Secretary, justifying himself with regard to the implications of the 'Nun of Kent', [?1534 March]

Bibliography [J. Forshall], *Catalogue of the ... Arundel MSS*, 1834, 41; *LP*, VII, 287; Rogers, 197.

Photograph by courtesy of the British Library Board (MS Arundel 152, ff. 296r–299v)

This is the third of four extant letters from More to 'Master Secretary', all written within the six weeks preceding his imprisonment.

He details his communications with the 'lewd [untutored] Nun of Canterbury', from the time, eight years ago, when the king had first asked his opinion, until the recent talk of her revelations concerning the king's marriage, protesting that he himself has neither done, said, nor thought evil in this matter and has the firm intent so to bear himself in every man's company, that neither good man nor bad, neither monk, friar nor nun, nor other man or woman in this world shall make him digress from his faith to God and his prince.

234
Sir Thomas More's Last Letter to Henry VIII
More to Henry VIII, protesting his loyalty and fidelity in the matter of the 'Nun of Kent', Chelsea, 5 March [1534]
Manuscript on paper, 1534

Bibliography [Joseph Planta], *Catalogue of the MSS in the Cottonian Library ... 1802*, 596; *LP*, VII, 288; Rogers, 198.

The British Library Board (MS Cotton Cleopatra E.VI, ff. 176r–177v)

The last of six extant letters by More to Henry VIII begs the king to trust his honesty and sincerity in declaring his whole communication with 'the wykked woman of Canterbery' to Cromwell; the clearness of his conscience knows that in all the matter his mind and intent is so good. If the king, after weighing the matter, still suspects him to 'be a wretche of such a monstrouse ingratitude, as coulde .. digresse fro [his] bounden dutie of allegeaunce', then he desires no more than to lose all he has. His only comfort would be 'that after my short life and your long ... I should onys mete with your Grace agayn in hevyn' where the king 'shold surely se there than, that (how so ever you take me) I am your trew bedeman now and ever have bene'. He begs for protection from the bill 'put ... in to your high Cort of Perleament agaynst me', and for protection against slander.

235
Photographs: **Fragments from William Rastell's 'Life of Sir Thomas More'**
(Inside back cover)

Provenance John Theyer, antiquary (1597–1673); Thomas Howard, 2nd Earl of Arundel (1586–1646); bt. British Museum 1831.
Bibliography [J. Forshall], *Catalogue of the ... Arundel MSS*, 1834, 41f; F. Van Ortroy, ed., in *Analecta Bollandiana*, XII, 1893, 248–70; Harpsfield, 219–52.

Photographs by courtesy of the British Library Board (MS Arundel 152, ff. 246r–247v(A); 307r–308r(B); 309r–312r(C))

Lawyer and printer like his father, William Rastell had published almost all More's works in English issued during More's lifetime. Rastell married Winifred Clement, daughter of John Clement and Margaret Gigs (no. 184). Returning from his refuge at Louvain to London at the beginning of Mary's reign, he resumed his distinguished legal career, becoming a judge. On 3 January 1563 he fled again to Louvain where he was buried in St Peter's Church beside his wife in 1565. Probably during his first exile he found time to write the voluminous *Life of More* of which transcripts, sent home to England and extant in three Arundel fragments, are the only remains. They are written in two different hands.

Fragment B begins with the 'Nun of Canterbury' and the king's attempt at attainting More of misprision of treason, mentions his letters to Cromwell and to the king (nos. 233, 234) and deals with Fisher's and Wilson's refusal to swear the amplified oath (no. 237). It exposes six corrupt Acts of Parliament passed in those years (eg Act of Treasons, More's Attainder, Act of Supremacy), the execution of the Carthusians and the legal interpretation of the word 'maliciously' as void.

The page shown from Fragment C (Rastell's *Life*, Book III, Chapter 55) opens with an account of the contemptuous burial of Fisher's naked corpse and the setting up of his head upon London Bridge, whence it was cast into the Thames so that More's head could be set up in its place on 7 July 1535.

236
Grant of Land in Chelsea to John Clement and Others
Original indenture, dated 25 March, 25 Henry VIII [1534]
Manuscript on parchment

Exhibitions Oxford, *Erasmus*, 1936; Oxford, *Erasmus and his Friends*, 1969 (133).
Bibliography W. H. Turner and H. O. Coxe, *Calendar of Charters and Rolls Preserved in the Bodleian Library*, Oxford 1878, 148; *Catalogue of Additions to the MSS in the British Museum 1911–1915*, 1925, 491; J. D. M. Derrett, 'More's Conveyance of his Lands and the Law of Fraud', *Moreana*, V, 1965, 19–26.

Bodleian Library, Oxford (Charters Middlesex 90/London Ch.misc.a.2)

More clearly foresaw his approaching ruin. He therefore thought it prudent to protect his family by making over his property at Chelsea to ten trustees: John Clement (MD, husband of More's foster-daughter Margaret Gigs; no. 184); Henry Say; Walter Marshe, mercer of London; John

Heywood (the dramatist, married to William Rastell's sister); Richard Heywood (his brother); William Rastell (More's nephew, lawyer and printer of *EW*; no. 260); John Marshe; John Watson; Thomas Sharpe; Richard Symkys and their heirs and assigns.

237
The Oath of Supremacy
Warrant for the Great Seal, giving two forms of the oath, both signed by the king with his sign manual ('Henry rex'), 1534
Parchment

Bibliography LP, VII, 1379 (1); J. J. Scarisbrick, *Henry VIII*, 1968, chap 10; S. E. Lehmberg, *The Reformation Parliament 1529–1536*, Cambridge 1970, 182–216; G. de C. Parmiter, 'A Note on Some Aspects of the Royal Supremacy of Henry VIII', *Recusant History*, X, 1970, 183–92; G. R. Elton, *Policy and Police,* Cambridge 1972, 228–30.

Public Record Office, London (C82/690, no. 2)

The way towards Supremacy was long and involved, a year-long campaign against the Church. In March 1534, the First Act of Succession (25 H.VIII, c.22) passed Parliament. It renounces Henry's marriage with Catherine, accepting that the king's marriage with Anne Boleyn is 'consonant to the laws of Almighty God' and that Henry's heirs of that marriage alone are to be successors to the crown. Penalties are imposed in three degrees: those who by an exterior deed deprive the king of his title, to be guilty of treason; those who maliciously utter anything against this statute, to be guilty of misprision of treason; and the whole population to 'make a corporal oath' of keeping not only the succession as here established, but 'the whole effects and contents of this present act'; refusal of the oath to be punishable as misprision of treason. The form of the oath, to be administered by a commission comprising Cranmer, Audeley, and the Dukes of Norfolk and Suffolk, is not given in the Act.

On Monday 13 April 1534, More was summoned 'before the Lords at Lambeth'. Shown the oath 'under the Great Seal', 'after which redde... and the othe considered with the acte' [of Succession], More explained, 'my conscience so moued me in the matter, that though I wolde not denie to swere to the succession, yet vnto the othe that there was offred me I coulde not sware, without the iubardinge of my soule to perpetuall dampnacion' (More to Margaret, *c.* 17 April 1534; Rogers, 200). For this he was imprisoned. This document is not the form of the oath offered to More, which is unknown. It is taken from the Chancery Warrants which constitute the Crown's authorisation, given by Henry's sign manual, of the Lord Chancellor to affix the Great Seal. It thus comes nearest to the form shown to More.

238
Thomas Cromwell to Thomas Cranmer
Corrected draft, partly in Cromwell's hand [?17] April 1534
Manuscript on paper

Bibliography LP, VII, 500; R. B. Merriman, *Life and Letters of Thomas Cromwell*, I, 1902, p 381, no. 71.

Public Record Office, London (SP 1/83, f. 98r–v)

After refusing the Oath of Supremacy, More had signified his willingness to swear to the Act of Succession, though not to its preamble. He had also refused to give a reason for his refusal. Cranmer suggested to Cromwell that a modified oath to the Succession only would not be refused by More and Fisher; if the king pleased, the actual form of their oaths might even be suppressed.

Cromwell replies here that he has shown Cranmer's letter to the king who takes the opposite view: this expedient would occasion 'all men to refuse the whole or at least the like', it might be taken as a confirmation of the pope's authority and a reprobation of the king's second marriage. Therefore the king 'in no wise wills but that they shall be sworn as well to the preamble as to the Act of Succession'.

Thus far, the text of the letter is written in a clear and calm hand. From now on we find extensive, hasty and heated corrections by 'Master Secretary'. He underlines the essential message: the king trusts and expects Cranmer's 'approved wisdom and dexterity' to bring Fisher and More to swear the full oath. He has difficulty in finding the right word in his interlinear corrections: the king, adamant, 'specially trusts that ye will in no wyse suppose, attempt or move him to the contrary, for [...] that manner of swearing, if it should be suffered, might be an utter destruction to his whole cause and also to the effect of the law made for the same'.

239
The Attainder of Sir Thomas More
Act of November 1534 (26 Henry VIII, c.23)
Manuscript on paper, second half of 16th century

Bibliography LP, VII, 1381 (9); *Statutes of the Realm*, III, 1817, 528; J. D. M. Derrett, 'More's Attainder and Dame Alice's Predicament', *Moreana*, VI, 1965, 9–20; J. R. Lander, 'Attainder and Forfeiture, 1453 to 1509', *Historical Journal*, IV, 1961, 119–51.

Public Record Office, London (SP 1/86, ff. 182–4)

By refusing the oath offered to him on 13 April 1534 which implied the royal Supremacy, More had contravened section IX of the Act of Succession. He was accordingly imprisoned for misprision of high treason, a misdemeanour leading also to the forfeiture of his goods. Foreseeing what might happen to him, More had beforehand distributed part of his estate by conveyance in order to secure the welfare of his family (no. 236). His movable goods and revenues of his lands were not immediately seized by the Crown. During that 'half-and-half existence' (Derrett) part of More's movable property was spirited away.

The seventh session of the Reformation Parliament (3 November – 18 December 1534) passed Acts for the Attainder of Fisher and More (c.22, 23). More's Attainder is recorded in the Parliament Roll as number 4 of that session and will thus have been passed during November. Attainder was the most solemn penalty known to the Common Law. It involved the extinction of all civil rights and capacities, thus rendering the offender *civiliter mortuus*, with consequent forfeiture and escheat of lands and the 'corruption of his blood'.

240
Photograph: **Lady More's Petition to Henry VIII**
Lady Alice and Sir Thomas More's children sue to the king for his pardon and release [1535, *c.* beginning of January]
Manuscript on paper, second half of 16th century

Bibliography [J. Forshall], *Catalogue of the... Arundel MSS*, 1834, 41; *LP*, VII, 1591; J. Bruce, *Archaeologia*, XXVII, 1838, 369; Rogers, 212; J. D. M. Derrett, 'More's Attainder and Dame Alice's Predicament', *Moreana*, VI, 1965, 9–20.

Photograph by courtesy of the British Library Board (MS Arundel 152, ff. 300v–301r)

The original is not extant. After More had been in the Tower 'by the space of eighte monethes and above in greate continuall sicknes of bodye and hevines of harte', his wife, Lady Alice, and More's children 'in lamentable wise' petitioned the king for pardon and release. Henry had allowed Lady More to retain her husband's goods and the revenues of his lands (£60 per year) though forfeit by his refusal of the oath. However, the former forfeiture has been confirmed. All the 'faire substance' More's wife brought him is spent in the king's service and she 'ys likelie to be holye vndone', and his poor son 'standinge charged and bownden for the paymente of greate sommes of money due by the saide Sir Thomas vnto your grace standithe in dangeor to be cast aweye'. Sir Thomas himself, after his long true service to the king, is likely in his age and continual sickness for lack of comfort and good keeping shortly to be destroyed. They beseech the king to grant this their petition. It remained unheard.

241
Photograph: **Sir Thomas More to Antonio Bonvisi**
Letter from More thanking Bonvisi for forty years of friendship, written from the Tower of London, *c.* June 1535
Manuscript on paper, second half of 16th century

Bibliography LP, VIII, 987; *CMA*, II, 6582.212; G. F. Warner and J. P. Gilson, *British Museum Catalogue of Western MSS in the Old Royal and King's Collections*, 1921, I, 253; Rogers, 217; *SL*, 65; Desmond Ford, 'Good Master Bonvisi', *Clergy Review*, N.S. XXVII, 1947, 228–35.

Photograph by courtesy of the British Library Board (MS Royal 17 D XIV, ff. 438r–439v)

'Good Master Bonvisi', More's friend for forty years, was a merchant of Lucca who had settled in London. In 1524 More sold him the lease of Crosby Place (no. 189). In the early twenties More had broached to his friend his anxiety at the growth of heresy, and also discussed the papal primacy with him. When More was in the Tower, Bonvisi sent him a warm camlet (angora) gown and gifts of wine, meat and oranges. When More was 'shut up so close in prison... that he had no pen nor ink [he] wrote with a coal a pistle in Latin... to his old and dear friend'. It shows for the last time More's command of a highly polished and elegant Latin style. He plays again with the motif of Fortune and her brittle gifts which he contrasts with their life-long constant friendship, and he bids farewell to his dearest friend, the 'apple of his eye'. He signs 'T.Morus', adding 'I should in vain put to it *yours*, for thereof can you not be ignorant, since you have bought it with so many benefits. Nor now am I such a one that it forceth whose I am'.

242
Interrogation of Servants in the Tower
'Answers by confession of Richard Wilson, servant to Mr John Fisher', of John à Wood, servant to More, and of George Golde, servant of the Lieutenant of the Tower (Sir Edmund Walsingham), before Sir Edmund Walsingham and Thomas Legh, 7–11 June 1535
Manuscript on paper

Bibliography LP, VIII, 856.

Public Record Office, London (SP 1/93, f. 52r)

On 7 June 1535 and the four following days an attempt was made to secure from the servants in the Tower evidence that would convict More and Fisher. Henry Polstede, Cromwell's man, and John Whalley, later paymaster of the works at Dover, were witnesses to the interrogation. The answers, recorded by John ap Rice, notary public, cover twenty-one pages. Their import is that Succession and Supremacy were touched upon many times but that the prisoners did not reveal their intentions, beyond refusing the oath. Fisher leaned much on the word 'maliciously' in the Act and More kept silent. Many small tokens of friendship (oranges, boiled meat brought by Margaret Roper, a bottle of wine from Bonvisi, or a dish of jelly) passed beteween them, and they had exchanged a number of letters 'some with ink and some with coal'. Apparently all persons mentioned in these answers as having had contact with the two (John the Falconer, William Thorneton) were likewise immediately interrogated.

243
Conversation between Sir Thomas More and Richard Rich in the Tower
'The effect of the [colloquy] between Richard Ri[che] and the said Sir Thomas More in the presence of [Sir] Edmund Walsingham, Richard Southwell, [blank] Palmer and [blank] ?Berleght' [12 June 1535]
Manuscript on paper

Bibliography LP, VIII, 814 (ii); E. E. Reynolds, *The Trial of St Thomas More*, 1964, 166–7; id. 'An unnoticed Document', *Moreana*, I, 1963, 12–19; J. D. M. Derrett, 'The "New" Document on Thomas More's Trial', ibid. III, 1964, 5–19; and E. E. Reynolds's reply, ibid. 20–2; B. Byron, 'The Fourth Count of the Indictment of St Thomas More', ibid. X, 1966, 33–46; Mary E. Coyle, *Sir Richard Rich*, Harvard University PHD thesis, 1967.

Public Record Office, London (SP 2/Folio R, f. 25r)

The present document was evidently used for drafting More's indictment (no. 246). The Rich interview took place the day after the interrogation of the servants had come to an end (no. 242). The occasion is clearly part of a carefully devised plan by Cromwell to procure some sort of evidence for formal conviction, either by direct statements from themselves, or by evidence of witnesses.

Rich attempts to move More to conform. Failing, he tries to ensnare him by the putting of cases. Would More accept Rich for king if Parliament so decreed? More assents and puts the counter-case: would Rich believe that God were not God if Parliament so decreed? Rich denies this, Parliament having no power to make such an act. Rich's second case and

Colour plate VI *Thomas Howard, 3rd Duke of Norfolk*, by Hans Holbein the Younger (no. 207)

More's reply are lost from this document, the paper being damaged. It is vital to the Crown case and we know it only from Roper and the Indictment. Here Rich concludes by remarking on More's unchangeable mind and corroborating his 'concealment to the question that has been asked of him'.

244
Interrogation of Sir Thomas More in the Tower
Interrogatory ministered to Sir Thomas More by Thomas Bedyll, Dr Aldridge, Dr Layton, Dr Carwen, in the presence of Harry Polstede, John Whalley, and John ap Rice, notary public; with More's answers, 14 June 1535
Manuscript on paper

Bibliography LP, VIII, 867 (ii); *State Papers*, I, 1830, 431ff.

Public Record Office, London (SP 6/7, f. 11r)

Three days after the interrogation of the servants (no. 242) and two days after the encounter with Rich, More and Fisher were questioned again by Thomas Bedyll, clerk of the Council, Dr Robert Aldridge, king's chaplain, Richard Layton, later Master in Chancery, and Dr Richard Carwen. More was interrogated twice that day, on his communications and correspondence with others regarding the Succession, the Supremacy and the Act of Treason, and on his silence.

This was the last of More's four interrogations in the Tower. The others had been on 30 April, 7 May and 3 June. They had all failed in their purpose. The prisoner made no statement that could legally be used against him.

245
Thomas Cromwell's 'Remembrances'
(Inside front cover)
Manuscript on paper, [June] 1535

Bibliography [J. Planta], *Catalogue of MSS in the Cottonian Library...*, 1802, 519; *LP*, VIII, 892; R. B. Merriman, *The Life and Letters of Thomas Cromwell*, 1902, I, 122; G. R. Elton, *Policy and Police*, Cambridge 1972, 409.

The British Library Board (MS Titus B.I, f. 475r)

Thomas Cromwell's 'Remembrances' are notes 'to be remembered at my next going to the court', extending over many years. The present document is not the first mention of More in them. In it we find: 'To know his [the king's] pleasure touching Master More, [and in Cromwell's hand] and declare the opinion of the judges thereon, & what shall be the King's pleasure'; 'Item when Master Fisher shall go to execution with also the other' [?More]; 'What shall be done farther touching Master More'.

The page is of the utmost importance for the understanding of More's indictment, trial and execution, although it does not seem to be mentioned by More's biographers. The document must be dated before 22 June 1535 (Fisher's execution) and apparently after 17 June (Fisher's trial), ie with certainty *before* a court was set up for the trial of More by the Special Commission of *oyer and terminer* (26 June; no. 246). It would thus establish, partly in Cromwell's own hand, that More's condemnation and execution were a foregone conclusion, decided by Henry VIII and implemented by Cromwell.

This is corroborated by a circular letter, under Henry's sign manual, dated Westminster, 25 June 1535 (again one day *before* More's court was appointed), instructing a councillor to declare to the people at the assize the treasons of the late Bishop Fisher and More, who had been 'the root and spring' of the confusions, so that the common people should hold Fisher and More 'like most recent traitors both in heart and deed, in more hatred, contempt and detestation' (*LP*, VIII, 921, 1).

246
The Indictment of Sir Thomas More
(A) *Special Commission of Oyer and Terminer for Middlesex*, dated Westminster, 26 June 1535; and (B) *Bill of Indictment* from the *Baga de secretis*, 1535
Manuscript on parchment

Bibliography LP, VIII, 974 (i), (iii); L. W. V. Harcourt, 'The Baga de Secretis', *EHR*, XXIII, 1908, 508–29; G. de C. Parmiter, 'The Indictment of St Thomas More', *Downside Review*, LXXV, 1957, 149–66; id. 'Tudor Indictments, illustrated by the Indictment of St Thomas More', *Recusant History*, VI, 1961, 141–56; G. R. Elton, 'Thomas Cromwell's Decline and Fall', in *Cambridge Historical Journal*, X, 1951, 182; J. D. M. Derrett, 'The Trial of Sir Thomas More', *EHR*, LXXIX, 1969, 449–77; Harpsfield, 267–76.

Public Record Office, London (KB 8/7/3, mm. 1–3, 7)

The first document is the official enrolment of the letters patent by which Henry VIII formed a Special Commission of *oyer and terminer* for Middlesex to 'hear and determine' More's cause. This allowed the Crown to complement the court by members of the right persuasion.

The commission was directed to nineteen members of the Council and justices: Lord Chancellor Audeley, the Duke of Norfolk (Anne Boleyn's uncle), the Duke of Suffolk (the king's brother-in-law), Henry Earl of Cumberland (Lord Privy Seal), Thomas Earl of Wiltshire (Anne's father), George Earl of Huntingdon, Henry Lord Montague, George Lord Rochford (Anne's brother), Andrew Lord Windsor, Thomas Cromwell ('Master Secretary' of the king), Sir William Fitzwilliam (treasurer of the household), Sir William Paulet (comptroller of the household), Sir John Fitzjames, Sir John Baldwin, Sir Richard Lister, and the four Justices of the King's Bench, Sir John Porte, Sir John Spelman, Sir Walter Luke, and Sir Anthony Fitzherbert.

The second document is the original *billa vera* of More's indictment, 'preferred' (laid before) the Grand Jury of sixteen members named in the commission. After the formal commencement and the statement of the relevant acts, it gives the particulars of More's offence, ie: *a*. That on 7 May 1535, More, when examined in the Tower before Cromwell and others, remained maliciously silent, saying only 'I will not meddle with any such matters, for I am fully determined to serve God, and to think upon His Passion and my passage out of this world'. *b*. That on 12 May, he had maliciously refused to acknowledge the king as Supreme Head and had sent letters to Fisher, encouraging him in his malicious refusal and comparing the Act to a two-edged sword. *c*. That on 26 May, More had given counsel to Fisher in writing, and in his interrogation deprived the king of the said title by his silence. *d*. That on 12 June, More, in a colloquy with Richard Rich (no. 243), had said that no subject could give his consent to the enactment of the king's Supremacy through Parliament and therefore that he would not be bound by the Act; and that More had asserted that although the king might be accepted for that in England, yet he was not in most parts abroad.

In the conclusion More was charged that he falsely, traitorously, and maliciously, by craft imagined, invented, practised and attempted utterly to deprive the king of his title, ie Supreme Head on earth of the Church of England. The jury endorsed this document 'true bill'. More stood indicted of treason by maliciously denying the royal Supremacy.

On 1 July More was brought for trial to Westminster Hall. When he had defended himself on the first three counts, Rich was called and 'burdened his soul with perjury in order to procure the verbal details of treason which would secure a conviction at law' (Elton). Of the witnesses present in More's cell, the Lieutenant of the Tower, Walsingham, was spared; Southwell (no. 212) and Palmer refused to corroborate Rich's 'evidence', excusing themselves.

The jury found a verdict of 'Guilty'. Audeley was so eager to pass sentence that he had to be stayed by More: 'My Lord, when I was toward the law, the manner in such a case was to ask the prisoner before judgement, why judgement should not be given against him'. And when Audeley allowed him to speak, More answered: 'Seeing that ye are determined to condemn me (God knoweth how), I will now in discharge of my conscience speak my mind plainly and freely touching my indictment and your Statute withal'. He declared that he had all the councils of Christendom in support of his conscience, not just the council of one realm.

247
Photograph: **Margaret Roper to Sir Thomas More** in the Tower [?May 1534]
Manuscript on paper, mid 16th century

Bibliography CMA, II, 6582.212; G. F. Warner and J. P. Gilson, British Museum Catalogue of Western MSS in the Old Royal and King's Collections, 1921, I, 253; LP, VII, 746; Rogers, 203.

Photograph by courtesy of the British Library Board (MS Royal 17 D XIV, f. 454r)

After refusing to take the Oath of Supremacy (no. 237), More was sent to the Tower (17 April 1534). Margaret Roper then sent him 'a letter wherein she seemed somewhat to labour to persuade him to take the oath (though she nothing so thought) to win thereby credence with Master Thomas Cromwell, that she might the rather get liberty to have free resort unto her father (which she only had for the most time of his imprisonment)' as William Rastell tells us. More replied (Rogers, 202) that he had clearly and repeatedly told her that he would disclose to no one the 'causes of his conscience'.

Margaret answers with the present letter, trusting in God to preserve him and remembering 'your lyfe past and godly conversacion, and wholesome counsaile, and vertuous example'. She signs: 'Your owne most loving obedient daughter and bedeswoman, Margaret Roper, which desireth above all worldly things to be in John Woodes stede to do you some service'. John à Wood was More's servant in the Tower. To his care we owe the preservation of More's 'Tower works' (nos. 219–26).

248
Photograph: **Margaret Roper to Sir Thomas More** in the Tower [1534], thanking him for his letter, his words, his example
Manuscript on paper, mid 16th century

Bibliography CMA, II, 6582.212; G. F. Warner and J. P. Gilson, British Museum Catalogue of Western MSS in the Old Royal and King's Collections, 1921, I, 253; LP, VII, 117; Rogers, 209.

Photograph by courtesy of the British Library Board (MS Royal 17 D XIV, ff. 454v–455r)

Rastell tells us that this letter was written in 1534. Margaret thanks her 'awne most enterly beloved father' for 'the inestymable comforte my poore harte recevythe in the redyng of your moste lovyng & godly letter representyng to me the clere shynyng brytnes of your soule the puer temple of the holy spyryte of god ...'. She cannot hear what moved them to shut him up again and supposes they thought it not possible 'to inclyne you to there wyll, excepte hit were by restrenynge you from the church & the company of my good mother your dere wyff and vs your chyldren'. She will not forget that he told them in the garden that these things were likely enough to chance shortly after and has many times rehearsed, for her own comfort and that of divers others, his 'fashions and words ye had to vs when we were laste with you for which, I trust by the grace of God, to be the better whyle I lyve & when I am departed owt of this frayle lyff.'

249
Sir Thomas More to Margaret Roper from the Tower
Report of his interrogation before the Council, on Friday 30 April, written 2–3 May 1535
Manuscript on paper, mid 16th century

Bibliography [J. Forshall], Catalogue of the ... Arundel MSS, 1834, 41; LP, VIII, 659; Rogers, 214; SL, 63.

The British Library Board (MS Arundel 152, ff. 294r–295r)

More gives a minute account of the proceedings, so that Margaret may 'neither conceive more hope ... nor more grief and fear than the matter giveth of'. In the afternoon of Friday 30 April [1535], he was brought before 'Master Secretary' (Thomas Cromwell), 'Master Attorney' (Sir Christopher Hales), 'Master Solicitor' (Richard Rich), Thomas Bedyll (Clerk of the Privy Council) and Sir John Tregonwell in the Council chamber. Cromwell interrogated. Had he seen the new statutes (Act of Supremacy; no. 237)? Yes, but he had 'never marked nor studyed to put in remembrance' their effect. Had he not read the first Statute of the Supremacy? Yes. What did he think of it? He had trusted the king would never have commanded any such question to be demanded of him. Cromwell demands a 'more full answer', but More replies that he will 'never meddle in the worlde again ... but that [his] hole study shulde be upon the passyon of chryst and [his] owne passage owt of thys world.' Cromwell reminds More of his obedience to the king, declaring that More's demeanour was likely to make other men obstinate. More answers 'I do nobody harme, I say none harme, I thynk none harme, but I wish everybody good. And yf thys be not ynough to kepe a man alyve in good faith, I long not to live', adding that he is dying already. Finally Cromwell demands if he finds any fault in the statutes, but More refuses to answer.

250
Sir Thomas More's Last Letter to Margaret Roper
from the Tower 5 July 1535
Manuscript on paper, mid 16th century

Bibliography CMA, II, 6582.212; G. F. Warner and J. P. Gilson, *British Museum Catalogue of Western MSS in the Old Royal and King's Collections*, 1921, I, 253; *LP*, VIII, 988; Rogers, 218; *SL*, 66.

The British Library Board (MS Royal 17 D XIV, ff. 426v–427r)

In his last letter, More sends his paternal blessing to his beloved daughter, Margaret Roper, and, through her, to her husband William, their little boy (Thomas, b. *c.* 1534) and all theirs, 'and all my children (Elizabeth, Cicely and John) and all my god children and all our freindes'. Next, he sends his greetings and such small tokens of fatherly love as were left to him in close imprisonment to his other children: to Cicely (Heron) a handkerchief, to Elizabeth Dauncey 'the picture in parchemente' given to him by Lady Conyers. He speaks of his imminent execution on 'a daye very mete and conveniente' for him to go to God, 'for it is S.Thomas evin and the vtas of Sainte Peter'. He recalls Margaret's 'doughterly love and deere charitie' when she kissed him last without 'laisor to looke to worldely curtesys' as he came from judgement at Westminster. Finally, he remembers his youngest child and only son, John and 'his naturall fashion', alluding to John's kneeling amongst the throng after the trial for his father's blessing (Stapleton), and his good wife. He admonishes him to respect his will concerning his disposition of lands in favour of Elizabeth Dauncey. And he concludes: 'And our Lorde blisse Thomas and Austen and all that thei shall have'.

251
Photograph: **Act of Annulment**
Act of 4 February 1536 (27 Henry VIII, c. 58)

Bibliography LP, X, 243 (31); *Statutes of the Realm*, III, 1817, 629; [J. Forshall], *Catalogue of the... Arundel MSS*, 1834, 41f; J. D. M. Derrett, 'More's Conveyance of his Lands and the Law of Fraud', *Moreana*, V, 1965, 19–26.

Photograph by courtesy of the British Library Board (MS Arundel 152, ff. 305v–306v)

On 4 February 1536, the Reformation Parliament passed 'an Act annullying as well a Dede of Feoffement as also an Indenture fraudeilently made by Sir Thomas More Knight of his purchased landes in Chelseth or elleswhere in the Countye of Middlesex'. Both those deeds were dated 25 March 1534, when he conveyed his lands to trustees (no. 236). The present act annulled those conveyances. Roper tells us that the act achieved only a partial success, in so far as More, only two days after those conveyances, had, on second thoughts, granted a substantial part of his Chelsea property to his daughter Margaret and her husband William Roper entirely and with direct effect. Thus, whereas the act annulled the first conveyance, it did not touch the second, and the Ropers continued the enjoyment of their rights in that respect.

252
The Trial and Martyrdom of the English Carthusians, 1535
Unknown artist, 1555
Engraving, 42.5 × 52.75 (16¾ × 20¾)

Bibliography Rastell Fragments, in Harpsfield, 235–6; Maurice Chauncy, *Historia aliquot saeculi martyrum Anglorum*, Louvain 1550; David Knowles, *Religious Orders in England*, III, Cambridge 1959, 229–33, App. III, 471f.

The Trustees of the British Museum (1854-11-13-151)

In the spring of 1534, John Houghton, Prior of the London Charterhouse, refused to swear to the first Act of Succession and was sent to the Tower with the procurator Humphrey Middlemore. They were shortly released, but in spring 1535 Houghton and other priors were tried under the Treason Act which had come into force on 1 February and found guilty on 29 April, after Cromwell had threatened the jury. On 4 May, Margaret Roper was in the Tower with More. Together they watched the Carthusians and Richard Reynolds brought down to be laid on hurdles and dragged to Tyburn for the horrors of the death decreed for traitors. More, who had no reason to suppose that he would not suffer the same death, 'as one longinge in that iourneye to have accompanied them, said... "Loe, doest thow not see, Megge, that thes blessed fathers be nowe as chearefully goinge to their deathes as bridegromes to their Mariage?"' (Roper).

On 25 May, Middlemore and William Exmewe, with Sebastian Newdigate, a former courtier and favourite of Henry's, were arrested and, refusing to acknowledge the Supremacy, were imprisoned in barbarous conditions in the Tower. They were tried for treason, found guilty and executed on 19 June. Fisher had been tried two days before their execution and was himself executed three days after it, on 22 June.

This anonymous engraving in six compartments, after the account in Maurice Chauncy's *Historia aliquot saeculi martyrum Anglorum* of 1550, shows the sufferings of the Carthusians, and the Tyburn of York.

253
The 'Paris News Letter'
Manuscript on paper, 1535

Bibliography Catalogue des MSS Français, Ancien fonds, I, 1868, 292; Harpsfield, 253–66; J. D. M. Derrett, 'Neglected Versions of the Contemporary Account of the Trial of Sir Thomas More', *Bulletin of the Institute of Historical Research*, XXXIII, 1960, 202–23.

Bibliothèque Nationale, Paris: Cabinet des Manuscrits (MSS franç. 2981, ff. 44–45)

The name *Paris News Letter* is given to a number of closely related accounts of More's trial and death which were circulated in French in Paris within a fortnight or so (23 July 1535) of the latter event. Its author's identity remains unknown. Perhaps he was a diplomat, since he had means to transport this account with extraordinary speed to Paris.

252

It was widely distributed and immediately translated into German, Spanish and Italian as well as into Latin (nos. 254, 255, 256).

The account is concerned with More's trial, and reports his execution only briefly. It quotes the dialogue with his judges often verbatim, beginning with Norfolk's attempt at persuading More to conform, and gives More's answers to the first three counts of his indictment (no. 246): *a*. he has never *denied* the king's supremacy and cannot be punished for his silence; *b*. in his correspondence with Fisher he has not counselled him but asked Fisher to inform his own conscience; *c*. the comparison of the statute to a double-edged sword has not been agreed upon between them. The fourth article, the Rich interview, is completely omitted. After mentioning the jury's verdict of 'Guilty', the *News Letter* concludes with More's final encounter with Margaret and his last words on the scaffold, praying God to send the king good counsel and protesting that he dies 'the king's good servant but God's first'.

254
Philippus Montanus, 'Expositio fidelis'
Expositio fidelis de morte D. Thomas Mori & quorundam aliorum insignium virorum in Anglia [Basel, Hieronymus Froben], 1535

Bibliography Gibson, 423; Adams, M 1761; Allen, XI, App. XXVII, 368–78; J. D. M. Derrett, loc. cit. (no. 253); E. E. Reynolds, *The Trial of St Thomas More*, 1964, 4–8.

The British Library Board (1130.e.4)

The *Expositio* was printed, without place of publication or printer's name, by Jerome Froben (son of Johann), in whose house Erasmus was then living. Hence it was long ascribed to the Dutch scholar. It takes the form of a letter from one 'P.M.' to an unidentified 'Caspar Aggripinus', and was reprinted by Johann Steels at Antwerp in 1536. Nicolaus Episcopius reprinted it, from Steels, in his *Thomae Mori Lucubrationes*, Basel 1563 (no. 261). From Episcopius we learn that 'P. M.' was Philippus Montanus (*c*. 1496–1576), the former servant-pupil of Erasmus.

The *Expositio* is dated from Paris, 23 July 1535, and consists of three parts: *a*. An account of More's trial, taken over from the *Paris News Letter* (no. 253); *b*. A narrative of the deaths of the Carthusians and Fisher; *c*. Reflections on these, with a faint apology for Henry VIII.

255
A German Translation of the 'Expositio fidelis'
Glaubwirdiger bericht von dem Todt des Edlen Hochgelerten Herrn Thome Mori und anderer herlicher Menner in Engellandt getödtet durch ein Epistel eynem guten freundt zugeschickt auss Latein in Teutsch vertholmetschet, Freiburg i. B., Johann Faber, 1535

Bibliography Gibson, 423; H. de Vocht, *Acta Thomae Mori* (Humanistica Lovaniensia, VII), Louvain 1947, 59f.

The British Library Board (697.c.43)

Interest in the deaths of More and Fisher is witnessed by the speedy publication of at least four translations into German, two of the 'Paris News Letter' (no. 253) and two of the *Expositio fidelis* (no. 254). *Glaubwirdiger bericht* (a trustworthy account) is the first of the latter, made by Gregorius (Jörg) Wickram (*c*. 1505–60), humanist, poet, town clerk of Colmar and a relative of Geiler von Kaisersberg. It was published at the turn of the year 1535–6, without printer's name or place of publication, but has been assigned to Johann Faber of Freiburg i. B., formerly of Basel. He moved at the Reformation to Freiburg, where he printed a number of Erasmus's works.

256
A Second German Translation of the 'Expositio fidelis'
Ein glaubwirdige anzaygung des todts Herrn Thomae Mori unnd anderer trefflicher männer inn Engelland geschehen im jar M.D. xxxv, [Augsburg, Heinrich Steiner], 1536

Bibliography Gibson, 423; Adams, M 1760; Morison-Barker, no. 601; C. Dodgson, 'A Pretended Illustration of the Death of St Thomas More', *Maso Finiguerra*, I, 1936, 44–5.

The British Library Board (699.g.36)

The second of the German translations of the *Expositio fidelis* (no. 254), anonymous and independent of the other, appeared in 1536, again with no place of publication or printer's name. It can be assigned to the press of Heinrich Steiner (d.1548) at Augsburg. Steiner's publications were widely aimed at the popular market, assisted by attractive woodcuts and decorative borders for which he employed notable artists like Burgkmair, Schäufelein, Breu and Weiditz. The present booklet has two scenes of execution by guillotine. The blocks had earlier been employed to illustrate the martyrdom of SS James the Greater and Matthew and are here applied to More and Fisher respectively.

257
A Heroic Poem on the Death of Sir Thomas More
Incomparabilis doctrine, trium item linguarum peritissimi viri D. Erasmi Roterodami, in sanctissimorum martirum Rofensis Episcopi, ac Thomae Mori ... Heroicum Carmen ..., Hagenau, Valentin Kobian, 1536

Bibliography Gibson, 514; J. Jortin, *Life of Erasmus*, II, 1758, 289; Preserved Smith, *Erasmus*, New York 1923, 418; D. T. Starnes, 'A Heroic Poem on the Death of Sir Thomas More', *Texas University Bulletin, Studies in English*, IX, 1929, 69–81.

The British Library Board (G.1577)

In September 1536 Hieronymus Gebweiler edited this Latin poem of 144 lines, ascribing it on the title-page to Erasmus, an attribution still disputed. A second edition appeared three months later at Louvain under the name of Johannes (Janus) Secundus, *Naenia in mortem Thomae Mori*. The poet (1511–36; author of the celebrated *Basia*) urges his readers 'weep with me over the slain bard, the great singer'. Henry's marriage with Anne has brought about More's execution. Praising Catherine, Secundus reproves Henry for sanctimoniously changing religion so as to cloak his adultery. After extolling More as the ornament of his kingdom, the model of equity among judges, he consoles mourning Margaret, foreseeing that one day the two martyrs, Fisher and More, will be sanctified.

258
Odinet Godrand, 'Expositio passionis Thomae Mori, 1535'
Manuscript on paper, 16th century

Provenance Entries of receipt from the Receiver General Bourelier, 1577–8; Sotheby's 10 July 1871.
Bibliography LP, VIII, 997; *Catalogue of Additions to the MSS in the British Museum 1854–75*, 1877, 552; Morison-Barker, no. 602.

The British Library Board (MS Add. 28786, ff. 1–17r)

Odinet Godrand, born in Dijon, distinguished and talented, was later raised to the presidency of the Burgundian parliament. In his native town the College of Jesuits was named after him for his great benefactions. He died in 1581.

His description of More's death forms the first item in this collective volume. As appears from the inscription, HVMANISSIMO VIRO AC IVSTISSIMO SENATORI DOMINO IACOBO GODRANDO PATRI SVO ODINETVS GODRANDVS MORTEM THOME MAVRI EXPONIT, 1535, it was written shortly after More's execution for the information of Godrand's father, a Burgundian senator, with a gouache representation of the event on folio 4r.

259
Sir Thomas More led to Execution
Antoine Caron, *c*.1591
Oil on panel, 114.5 × 142.75 (45½ × 56¼)

Bibliography J. Ehrmann, 'Antoine Caron', *Burlington Magazine*, XCII, 1950, 36; id. *A. Caron, peintre à la cour des Valois, 1521–99*, Geneva-Lille 1955, 29–30, 45; Morison-Barker, no. 606.

Musée du Château de Blois

There is no extant picture which can certainly be said to show Thomas More in his last hours. The *Glaubwirdige Anzaygung* (no. 256) has a vade-mecum woodcut of an execution; the manuscript of Odinet Godrand (no. 258) a fictitious rendering. The event was also shown in the frescoes by Pomarancio in the English College at Rome, executed about 1580 and destroyed about 1800, of which the sole remaining record is the engraving by G. B. Cavalieri in *Ecclesiae Anglicanae Trophaea ...*, Rome 1584. An engraving of More's execution, based on Cavalieri, was included in Richard Verstegan's *Theatrum crudelitatum*, Antwerp 1592. The picture by Antoine Caron (1521–99) may be a translation into the painter's classicizing visual language of the scene as More is led back to the Tower after his trial. Margaret Roper has broken through the guards to embrace the bearded figure of her father in the foreground. The execution can be seen in the background. There is nothing against the identification of Caron's subject, which may stand until a better is proposed.

SUCCESSION, SUPREMACY AND EXECUTION

259

IX *The Posthumous Reputation of Sir Thomas More*

William Roper, Sir Thomas's son-in-law, preserves a family tradition that when the Emperor Charles V heard the news of More's execution, he called the English ambassador (according to Roper it was Sir Thomas Elyot (no. 279)), to him and said:

'My Lord Embassador, we vnderstand that the Kinge, your master, hath put his faithfull seruaunt and grave, wise Councelour, Sir Thomas Moore, to deathe'. Wherunto Sir Thomas Elliott awnswered that he vnderstood nothing thereof. 'Well', said the Emperour, 'it is too true. And this will we say, that if we had bine master of such a servante, of whose doings our selfe haue had these many yeares no small experience, we wold rather haue lost the best city of our dominions then haue lost such a worthy councellour'.

The story may be apocryphal, but the valuation is hardly too low. Sir Thomas More was famous in his lifetime as the pattern of the active humanist life ruled by virtue and learning. His Latin works, especially *Utopia*, were read and admired and the commendatory letters prefixed to them gave the author's name an added resonance. There were other written panegyrics, which continued to be read long after their subject's death, many of them incidental, like Richard Pace's (no. 264) and Joannes Ludovicus Vives's (no. 268), the Latin epigrams of John Constable (no. 267) or the Latin exercises of Robert Whittinton (no. 266). The splendid letter by Erasmus to Ulrich von Hutten, a full-length portrait in little (no. 265), was written to order and is complete in itself.

During Sir Thomas More's lifetime stories (and calumnies) circulated by word of mouth. His sayings were treasured in his circle and his writings preserved, as far as possible, in his family. It was not until the coming of a more favourable climate under Mary that Sir Thomas More's nephew, William Rastell, who had also been his uncle's printer, put together the great folio of More's *English Works* (1557; no. 260). Six years later, at Basel, a collection of his Latin works was published (no. 261) and in 1565–6 no fewer than four separate impressions of the Latin *Opera omnia* came out at Louvain (no. 262). A third edition of the Latin *Opera* was published in Frankfurt a.M. in 1689 (no. 263).

Meantime, a fresh dimension of outrage had been added to accounts of Sir Thomas More by the narratives of his trial and death which immediately followed the execution – the *Paris News Letter*, the *Expositio fidelis* and their translations, and the *Carmen heroicum* (nos. 253–8). So great was the feeling that Henry's agents in France and Germany had special orders to advance the view that Sir Thomas More had been justly condemned as a traitor. Later than these accounts of Sir Thomas More's death came formal eulogies such as George Lily's (no. 269), in collections of the lives of great men.

Later still, about the time that Rastell was putting together his 'great volume', came biographies, first in English and later in Latin, Spanish, Italian and German. William Roper's was the first (no. 271), followed by Nicholas Harpsfield's (no. 272), for which Roper had intended his *Life* as a preparatory sketch. These two English *Lives* circulated only in manuscript: Roper's was not printed until 1626, Harpsfield's until 1932. Meanwhile, the Latin *Life* by Thomas Stapleton (no. 273) was printed in Douai: it remained the dominant account for the Continent and forms the basis for the Spanish and Italian *Lives* by Fernando de Herrera (1592) and Domenico Regi (1675) respectively. It was also drawn on by the unknown author, Ro. Ba. (no. 274), of the most finished of the English biographies, written about 1599 but not printed until 1950, and by Cresacre More (no. 276).

All these lives dwell at least as much on the holiness of their subject as they do on his humanist accomplishments and his political eminence. Rastell and Stapleton preserve letters and papers in family possession at their time.

Perhaps the best estimate of Sir Thomas More is his own: the epitaph he composed after he had resigned office (no. 287). It is a profoundly moving and eminently just plea to be judged after his righteous dealing and the cleanness of his hands.

260
Sir Thomas More's English Works
The workes of Sir Thomas More Knyght sometyme Lorde Chauncellor of England, wrytten by him in the Englysh tonge, London, John Cawood, John Waly and Richard Tottel, 1557

Provenance Sir William Roper.
Bibliography STC2, 18076; Gibson, 73; A. W. Reed, introduction to *English Works*, vol. I, 1931.

The President and Fellows of St John's College, Oxford

The pious care of William Rastell (?1508–65) is responsible for the first collected edition of More's *English Works*. Rastell put together those works of his uncle that had previously been published, he preserved and published for the first time a good deal which would otherwise have been lost, and he corrected and restored faulty or incomplete works.

Under Edward VI, William Rastell had left England in 1549 with his wife and her parents for religious reasons. During his exile at Louvain he prepared his uncle's works for the press. Back home in England (1553), he commissioned Cawood, Waly and Tottel to print and publish 'this commodious and profitable boke'. The volume's 1491 pages in black-letter type helped to win for their author the respect of Ben Jonson, who considered More a model of pure and elegant English style. When the printing was finished 'the last day of April 1557', Rastell dedicated the 'Great Volume' to Queen Mary in order to preserve the 'great eloquence, excellent learning and moral virtues contained in the books', lest they should 'in time percase perish and utterly vanish away'. Dr Samuel Johnson devoted a quarter of his *History of the English Language*, which served as an introduction to his great *Dictionary*, to illustrative quotations from More's *English Works*.

261
Sir Thomas More's Latin Works
Thomae Mori, Angliae ornamenti eximii, Lucubrationes, ab innumeris mendis repurgatae..., Basel, Nicolaus Episcopius the Younger, 1563

Bibliography Gibson, 74; Adams, M 1752.

Guildhall Library, London (Cock Colln. 1.3)

This handsome octavo volume appeared only six years after Rastell's English edition. It contains the two books of *Utopia* with the usual prefatory letters, More's and Lily's *Progymnasmata*, Latin *Epigrams*, his translations from Lucian, along with More's *Declamatio* in response to Lucian, and a number of letters to which are added Erasmus's famous biographical sketch of More in his letter to Hutten (no. 265) and G. Covrinus Nucerinus's letter to Philip Montanus, the so-called 'Paris News Letter' on the execution of More and Fisher (no. 253).

262
Sir Thomas More's Latin Works
Thomae Mori Angli, Viri Eruditionis pariter ac virtutis nomine clarissimi, Angliaeque olim Cancellarii, Omnia, quae hucusque ad manus nostras pervenerunt, Latina Opera..., Louvain, Jan Bogard, 1565

Bibliography Gibson, 75–6; Adams, M 1749.

The Master, Fellows and Scholars of Pembroke College, Cambridge

Four editions of More's Latin works were printed by Jan Bogard and Pieter Zangrius at Louvain in 1565–6. They are simultaneous issues and almost identical but for the different printer's device, imprint, year of publication, etc. This second Continental edition of the Latin works of More, made within a year or two of the first, and four times issued, almost simultaneously, is an index of the demand for More's writings during the first years of the Elizabethan exile. The Louvain editions include More's epitaph for himself and his first wife (no. 287); *Utopia*; More's farewell letter to Antonio Bonvisi; the *Progymnasmata* and *Epigrammata*; the translations from Lucian; the Latin *Historia Richardi Regis*; *Responsio ad Lutherum*; *Expositio Passionis Christi*; *Quod pro fide mors fugienda non est*; and *Precationes ex Psalmis collecta*.

263
Sir Thomas More's Latin Works
Thomae Mori Angliae quondam cancellarii Opera Omnia... Praefixae de Vita & Morte Thomae Mori, Erasmi et Nucerini Epistolae, ut et doctorum virorum de eo Elogia, Frankfurt a. M. and Leipzig, Christian Gensch, 1689

Bibliography Gibson, 77.
Private Collection

The third of the Continental editions of More's Latin works adds to the contents of the 1565–6 edition the Latin life by Thomas Stapleton (no. 273), Erasmus's letter to Hutten (no. 265), the *Expositio fidelis* (no. 254), and other Latin letters and *Elogia*.

264
Richard Pace on Thomas More
From Richard Pace (c. 1483–1536), *De fructu qui ex doctrina percipitur*, Basel, Johann Froben, 1517

Bibliography Emden, *Oxford*, 1417; Richard Pace, *De fructu...*, ed. and trans. Frank Manley and Richard S. Sylvester, New York 1967; E. Surtz, 'Richard Pace's Sketch of Thomas More', *Journal of English and Germanic Philology*, LVII, 1958, 36–50

The British Library Board (G.6177)

Richard Pace's first contacts with the circle that became Thomas More's were made in Italy: about 1499 he was at Padua and must have met Tunstall. Later, in Italy, he gained the respect of Erasmus and lost it again in 1509 for entering service with Christopher Bainbridge, Archbishop of York, and spending the rest of his life as secretary and diplomat. In 1519 he succeeded Colet as Dean of St Paul's. His health failed in 1529–30, and he lived his last years in retirement. His *De fructu* is a humanist *disputatio*, a debate among the liberal arts, written for St Paul's School. It contains an encomium of More, whom Pace seems first to have met in 1514. More is praised for the superhuman intelligence and supra-grammatical art by which he can take in meaning, especially in Greek, at a glance. He is too brilliant for his own good, a great Graecist, superbly eloquent in both Latin and English, a laughing philosopher, who arouses the envy of dull men.

265
Thomas More, a Pen-Portrait by Erasmus
Letter to Ulrich von Hutten, 23 July 1519, in *Farrago noua epistolarum Des. Erasmi ad alios & aliorum ad hunc...*, Basel, Johann Froben, 1519

Bibliography Allen, 999; trans. F. M. Nichols, *The Epistles of Erasmus*, III, 1918, 387–401; trans. Barbara Flower in J. Huizinga, *Erasmus of Rotterdam*, 1952, 231–9.

The President and Fellows, Queens' College, Cambridge

Erasmus, asked by Ulrich von Hutten (no. 123) for a full-length portrait of his friend Thomas More, accepted what he protests to be a task too great for his feeble pen. To begin with outward appearance, More's middling height, neat build, clear complexion, light brown hair, light beard and grey-blue eyes made him handsome as a young man and good-looking in maturity. His habitual expression corresponds to his character; it is open and pleasant, neither solemn nor silly. When he walks, particularly, his right shoulder seems rather higher than his left, his hands are a little clumsy, and he takes little or no care for his appearance. More's health is good rather than robust and he can look forward to a long life. Like his father, he prefers water as a drink, but will take beer or sip wine for courtesy's sake. Unfussy about his food, he eats from choice beef, salt-fish, coarse bread, milk foods, fruit and eggs.

As for his speech, his voice is clear and penetrating rather than soft or pleasant-sounding, and he cannot sing though he loves music. He dresses plainly and never wears his gold chain if he can avoid it. He dislikes court life as much as he values equality, freedom and lack of formality, so that Henry VIII has had virtually to drag him into his entourage. He dislikes mindless pastimes like ball games, dice and cards but he loves the creations of nature, animate and inanimate. He keeps an ape, a fox, a beaver, a weasel and his home is a cabinet of curiosities.

Friendship is Thomas More's greatest gift: he seems formed for it and he cultivates it constantly, with perfect courtesy and charm. He loves jokes, wit, intelligence in any company, male or female; he can lighten the most melancholy mood or the most tedious occupation, but he is the reverse of a buffoon. Above all he keeps his own independent and humane judgement.

From his earliest years More had read omnivorously in classical literature, but embraced the illiberal profession of a lawyer and made a great success of it. As a young man he lectured on St Augustine (no. 20) and gave himself to the study of piety. He married because he chose to be a chaste husband rather than an unchaste priest. His household he rules firmly but lightly, so that there is no dissension there. He provides suitably for all and gives away the rest of his money generously.

As a lawyer More always put his clients' interests before his own and as a judge he always sought the fair and equitable solution. Then he was the common advocate of all who needed help, and so he has remained. After he had twice shown himself a splendid ambassador, Henry got him to court, in spite of his resistance, for he had determined to surround himself with men of weight, learning, sagacity and integrity. More still manages, with all his burdens, to find time for his friends and for literature. He loves paradox and has indulged his love in the translation of Lucian and the writing of *Utopia*.

Thomas More is a superb extempore speaker, quick witted, strong of memory, acute in argument. As John Colet used to say to me, England, rich as she is in talents, has only one genius and that is More. Finally, he is truly pious and a living refutation of those who believe that true Christians are found only in monasteries.

266
'A Man for all Seasons'
Vulgaria Roberti Whitintoni Lichfeldiensis, et de institutione grammaticulorum Opusculum..., London, Robert Pynson, 1520

Bibliography Emden, *Oxford*, 2039–40; *STC2*, 25570; Beatrice White, ed., Whittinton and Stanbridge's *Vulgaria*, EETS, OS, 187, 1932; R. S. Sylvester, 'The "Man for all Seasons" again: Robert Whittington's Verses to Sir Thomas More', *Huntington Library Quarterly*, xxvi, 1963, 147–54.

University Library, Exeter: from the Parish Library, Crediton

Collections of English passages for translation (*vulgaria*), chosen to illustrate correct Latin usage, were issued by several English grammarians of More's time. Robert Whittinton (*c.* 1480–*c.* 1548) first published his with Wynkyn de Worde in 1520. It was many times reprinted during the 'grammarians' war', in which Whittinton opposed himself to William Lily (no. 15) among others. As an exercise in the use of the 'laudatory genitive' (*post possessorem signans laudem*) Whittinton sets the passage: 'Moore is a man of an aungels wyt, & syngler lernyng. He is a man of many excellent vertues (yf I shold say as it is) I knowe not his felowe. For where is the man (in whome is so many goodly vertues) of y^t gentylnes, lowlynes, and affabylyte. And as tyme requyreth, a man of marveylous myrth and pastymes, & somtyme of as sad gravyte, as who say a man for all seasons.' Whittinton also published, in his *Opusculum* of 1519, two Latin epigrams eulogising More (as did John Constable, no. 267), but his English encomium – echoing the words of Erasmus in the preface to the *Praise of Folly*, 1511 – is the one that has lived.

267
John Constable's Poems to Thomas More
Ioannis Constablii Londinensis et artium professoris epigrammata, London, Richard Pynson, 1520

Bibliography STC, 5639; R. S. Sylvester, 'John Constable's Poems to Thomas More', *Philological Quarterly*, XLII, 1963, 525–31.

The British Library Board (C.57.c.9)

John Constable (fl. 1520) was a pupil of William Lily's (no. 15) and took Lily's part in the 'grammarians' war' of 1519–20 against Robert Whittinton (no. 266). Constable and Whittinton were united in their valuation of Thomas More. Constable's two epigrams are another testimonial to that learned and eloquent 'glory of London and shining star of Britain', ever occupied in philosophy, rhetoric, poetry, divinity, whose learned daughter (Margaret) is worthy of her great father.

268
Sir Thomas More, as seen by Joannes Ludovicus Vives
St Augustine, *De civitate Dei*, ed. J. L. Vives, Basel, Johann Froben, 1522, p. 41

The Master, Fellows and Scholars of Pembroke College, Cambridge

In the introduction to his edition of the *City of God*, St Augustine's greatest work and one of Thomas More's favourites, Vives makes a quotation from Lucian. He uses More's Latin translation of the dialogue known as the *Calling up of the Dead*. This gives him the opportunity of dilating upon the virtues of the translator, his acute intelligence, his extensive learning, his mastery of eloquence, his prudence, integrity, moderation and *suavitas*, the evenness of his temper.

269
George Lily's Eulogy of Sir Thomas More
In Paolo Giovio, *Descriptio Britanniae, Scottiae, Hyberniae et Orchadum*, Venice, M. Tramezzino, 1548

Bibliography Emden, *Oxford 1540*, 357; P. Giovio, *Gli elogi degli uomini illustri*, a cura di Renzo Meregazzi, 1972, 1–30 (on *Elogia*), 113, cf 464.

The British Library Board (981.d.5)

This brief laudatory life was first printed in the *Descriptio Britanniae* of Paolo Giovio, Bishop of Nocera (1483–1552). It is the work of Giovio's collaborator in the *Descriptio Britanniae*, George Lily, son of William Lily (no. 15). George Lily also supplied Giovio with notices of Colet, William Lily, Grocyn, Linacre, Lupset, Pace, Fisher and William Latimer. He lays stress both on More's humanistic and official distinction and on his martyrdom. In the earlier eulogies of More and Fisher in Giovio's *Elogia virorum literis illustrium* (1st edn. 1546, 56), the emphasis is on More the martyr, with Latin verses by various hands to the same effect added in later editions.

George Lily was educated at Magdalen College, Oxford, possibly entered the household of Cardinal Pole (no. 216) in 1532, went with Pole to Padua and Venice, and continued in his service thereafter. He was outlawed from England in 1543 but returned with Pole under Mary in 1554 and was later Canon of St Paul's in London and of Canterbury.

270
Ellis Heywood's Dialogue
Heliseo Heivodo [Ellis Heywood], *Il Moro*, Florence, Lorenzo Torrentino, 1556

Bibliography Adams, H 531; Gibson, 350; *Il Moro. Ellis Heywood's Dialogue in Memory of Thomas More*, ed. and trans. with introduction by Roger Lee Deakins, Cambridge, Mass. 1972.

Guildhall Library, London (Cock Colln. 1.2)

Il Moro is an imaginary dialogue between Thomas More and six friends on the nature of true happiness. Lorenzo is for riches, Carlo for honour, Pietro for love, Alessandro for knowledge, Leonardo argues that happiness is relative to the individual and Paolo that it is vain to pursue it. More then brings these warring opposites into equilibrium in the concept of a contentment perfect in itself since it rests in the subduing of human appetite by reason to accord with divine will. The setting is More's garden at Chelsea, after dinner, where More is represented in tranquil retirement after he had resigned the chancellorship (1532). His death is mentioned only in the closing sentences.

Ellis Heywood (1530–78) was Thomas More's grand-nephew, son of the playwright John Heywood and brother of Jasper Heywood, the translator of Seneca. Ellis joined the entourage of Cardinal Pole (no. 216), to whom *Il Moro* is dedicated, after taking his Oxford degree in 1552. It is not clear when and where he learned his Italian or why he wrote his dialogue in that language. He seems to have stayed in England after Mary's death and left it only in 1564, when he joined the Jesuits.

271
William Roper's 'Life of More'
Manuscript on paper, late 16th century

Provenance Entered British Museum with Harleian Collection 1754–5.
Bibliography Gibson, 117–20; Robert Nares, *Catalogue of the Harleian MSS*, III, 1808, 347; ed. E. V. Hitchcock, *EETS*, OS, CXCVII, 1935 (base text).

The British Library Board (MS Harl. 6254)

Roper has stated his own case: 'there is no one man living that of him [More] and his doings understand so much as myself, for that I was continually resident in his house by the space of sixteen years and more'. His story was written about 1557, some twenty years after More's death, in the days of Queen Mary. One has also to take into account its character as an imaginative work of art. It was not intended by Roper as a freestanding and complete *Life* to be published, but rather as notes for Nicholas Harpsfield (no. 272). These notes remained (and were widely circulated) in manuscript. They were first printed at 'Paris' (ie St Omer) in 1626.

272
Nicholas Harpsfield's 'Life of More'
Manuscript on paper, third quarter of 16th century

Provenance Dedication, signed N[icholas] H[arpsfield] L.D. to Will[iam] Roper, undated; 'This booke was founde by Rich: Topclyff in Mr Thomas Moare studdye emongs other bookes at Greenstreet Mr Wayfarers house wher Mr Moare was apprehended the xiiijth of April 1582'.
Bibliography James, *Emmanuel*, 1904, 69; ed. E. V. Hitchcock,

EETS, OS, CLXXXVI, 1932 (base text); Chambers, 31 ff; Emden, *Oxford 1540*, 268–9.

The Master and Fellows of Emmanuel College, Cambridge (MS 76 (1.3.24)

Nicholas Harpsfield (1519–75) was educated at Winchester and New College, Oxford. He emigrated under Edward VI to Louvain, returned under Mary, was deprived under Elizabeth and imprisoned in the Tower 1559–74.

Harpsfield's *Life of More* lacks a title, but was written under Mary *c.* 1557. It is praised by Chambers as 'the first formal biography in the English language', compiled from More's autobiographical pieces, from the letters of Erasmus, from the Continental accounts of More's trial and death and, most important of all, from the notes given to him for this purpose by William Roper (no. 271). While Roper's *Life*, perfect as it is, is little more than the personal memoirs of a family member, Harpsfield tells his story after diligently collecting and critically sifting all the sources he could lay his hands on.

Harpsfield's *Life*, like those of Roper and of Ro: Ba:, circulated only in manuscript; it was not printed until 1932. The inscription by Topclyffe, the priest-catcher, concerns Thomas More II, grandson of Sir Thomas (nos. 1, 170).

273
Thomas Stapleton's 'Life of Thomas More'
Thomas Stapleton, *Thomae Mori Vita*, in his *Tres Thomae*, Douai, J. Bogard, 1588

Bibliography Gibson, 121–4; French trans. 1849; English trans. by P. E. Hallett 1928; ed. E. E. Reynolds, 1966; Marvin R. O'Connell, *Thomas Stapleton and the Counter Reformation*, New Haven 1964.

Bodleian Library, Oxford (8° C.267.Art.)

Thomas Stapleton (1535–98) of Winchester and New College, Oxford, was born during the month in which More was executed, 'as if divine providence had purposely dropped from heaven an acorn in place of the oak that was felled' (Thomas Fuller). At the beginning of Mary's reign he became prebendary of Chichester and took refuge in the Netherlands at Elizabeth's accession, keeping in close contact with the other refugees of the More circle. Unfortunately, he did not write his life of More until he was in his fifties and his memories of what he had learned from them were no longer fresh. His *Life* relies on three main sources: Harpsfield's biography; documents and letters that he had obtained from Dorothy Colley (a former maid of Margaret Roper's) and, no doubt, her husband, More's secretary, John Harris; and the stock of More anecdotes current among the Continental exiles.

Stapleton was called by Anthony à Wood 'the most learned Roman Catholic of his time', author, according to a later calculation, of a million words in English and five million in Latin. He was professor of theology in the University of Louvain and at Douai.

There was a second edition of the *Vita Mori* (Cologne, 1612) and it was reprinted both separately at Graz in 1689, and forming part of More's (1689) and Stapleton's own (1620) Latin *Opera omnia*.

274
Ro: Ba:'s 'Life of Sir Thomas More'
The Life of Syr Thomas More, Somtymes Lord Chancellour of England, by Ro: Ba:, 1599
Manuscript on paper, early 17th century

Bibliography H. J. Todd, *Catalogue of... the Library at Lambeth Palace*, 1812, 22–3; M. R. James and Claude Jenkins, *MSS in the Library of Lambeth Palace*, II, Cambridge 1931, 278–82; ed. E. V. Hitchcock and P. E. Hallett, *EETS*, OS, CCII, 1950 (base text).

His Grace the Lord Archbishop of Canterbury and the Trustees of Lambeth Palace Library (MS 179, ff. 199r–243r)

After Roper, Harpsfield and Stapleton, Ro: Ba:, whose identity is unknown, was the fourth English biographer of More. Writing in 1599, he combines the 'insular' (Roper–Harpsfield) and the 'refugee' streams (Harris, Clement, Rastell, Bonvisi, feeding Stapleton). His composite life is more than a mere compilation; it is, in some respects, the best biography of More (Chambers), in particular in its anecdotes. At least eight manuscripts of Ro. Ba. are extant; an incomplete text was printed by Christopher Wordsworth in his *Ecclesiastical History*, II, 1839, but there was no satisfactory edition until 1950.

275
'The Booke of Sir Thomas Moore', a Play
Manuscript on paper, *c.* 1595

Bibliography Ed. F. P. Wilson and A. Brown (Malone Society), 1961; E. M. Thompson, *Shakespeare's Hand in the Play of Sir Thomas More*, papers by A. W. Pollard, W. W. Greg and others, Cambridge 1923; R. W. Chambers, *Man's Unconquerable Mind*, 1939, 172–249; R. C. Bald, 'The Booke of Sir Thomas Moore and its Problems', *Shakespeare Survey*, II, 1949, 44–65; K. P. Wentersdorff, *The Date of the Additions in the Booke of Sir Thomas Moore*, Nashville 1969; S. McMillin, 'The Book of Sir Thomas Moore: a theatrical view', *Modern Philology*, LXVII, 1970, 10–24.

The British Library Board (MS Harl. 7368, f.21v)

The play of 'Sir Thomas Moore' was written by a group of Elizabethan dramatists of whom William Shakespeare was one. The manuscript, now severely damaged, shows evidence of seven different hands. Several folios have been removed, others added. The text is equally a patchwork; whole passages have been revised and dialogues added. The play may have been a cooperative effort by Anthony Munday, Henry Chettle, Thomas Heywood, an unknown playhouse scribe, William Shakespeare and Thomas Dekker. In addition, various notes and deletions are by the censor, Edmund Tilney, Master of the Revels 1579–1610.

The play incorporates the London tradition of the city's great hero which had remained alive in spite of all Henrician efforts to stamp it out and in spite of Foxe's tales of cruelty and Halle's sneers. More remains 'the best friend that the poor e'er had'. The censor intervened for political considerations in view of the disturbed state of the country following the anti-alien riots of 1593 or the Essex rebellion of 1601. Thus the 'Evil May Day' scenes (no. 108) came under his veto.

The exhibited folio (21v) gives a scene towards the end of

the play, when Lady More, the daughters and William Roper have come to the Tower to take leave of the prisoner before his imminent execution. Even then, it is More who makes them good cheer:

> 'Be comforted, good wife, to liue and looue my children;
> For with thee leaue I all my care of them.–
> Sonne Roper, for my sake that haue loou'de thee well,
> And for her vertues sake, cherishe my childe.–
> Girle, be not proude, but of thy husbands looue;
> Euer retaine thy vertuous modestie;
> That modestie is such a comely garment
> As it is neuer out of fashion, fits as faire
> Vppon the meaner woman as the empresse;
> No stuffe that golde can buye is half so riche,
> Nor ornament that so becomes a woman.
> Liue all and looue together, and therby
> You giue your father a riche obsequye.'

276
Cresacre More's Life of his Grandfather
[Cresacre/Thomas More], *The Life and Death of Sir Thomas Moore*, 'Written by M.T.M.', [Douai, Balthasar Ballère or Bellère, *c.* 1631]

Bibliography STC2, 18066; Allison and Rogers, 548; Gibson, 106; M. A. Anderegg, *An Edition of Cresacre More's Life of Sir Thomas Moore*, Yale University dissertation, 1972.

Guildhall Library, London (Cock Colln. 1.4)

For more than two centuries this biography was the best known and most frequently read of the early lives of More; it is extant in more than ten manuscripts. Yet its authorship, genesis, composition and publication have remained clouded over for long.

The M.C.M.E., who signed the dedication to Queen Henrietta Maria, is Master Cresacre More Esquire (1572–1649; nos. 1, 170), youngest son by Mary Scrope of Thomas More II (1531–1606), son of John More Jr. and Anne Cresacre. Cresacre, More's great-grandson, attributed the work to his elder brother, Father Thomas More IV (b. 1565), who had died at Rome in 1625, but is generally credited with its authorship himself; it is possible that he edited his brother's draft. The reissue of 1642 and the second edition of 1736, like the German translation of 1741, name Thomas as author, and it was only in 1828 that the Reverend Joseph Hunter attributed the work to Cresacre. It was composed between 1615 and 1620. Cresacre's dedicatory letter to the queen refers to 'the hope-full yssue': Prince Charles was born 29 May 1630.

The biography is a highly derivative work, incorporating the whole of Roper (no. 271) and a good deal of Stapleton (no. 273), adding anecdotes, historical facts from Halle (no. 108) and Stow, and using its own distinctive tone to present a well-rounded portrait, only surpassed and supplanted 250 years later by Bridgett.

277
Thomas Starkey on the Proper Structure of a Commonwealth
Thomas Starkey, *A Dialogue between Cardinal Pole and Thomas Lupset*, with the draft of a dedicatory Letter to Henry VIII

Autograph manuscript, ?1533–5
Paper

Bibliography Emden, *Oxford 1540*, 537–8; J. M. Cowper, ed., *England in the Reign of Henry VIII*, EETS, ES, XXXII, pt 2, 1871; K. M. Burton, ed., *A Dialogue between Reginald Pole and Thomas Lupset*, 1948; J. A. Gee, *Life and Works of Thomas Lupset*, New Haven 1928, 147–56; G. R. Elton, 'Reform by Statute: Thomas Starkey's *Dialogue* and Thomas Cromwell's Policy', *Proceedings of the British Academy*, LIV, 1968, 165–88.

Public Record Office, London (SP 1/90)

Thomas Starkey (?1499–1538) studied at Oxford while Thomas Lupset (nos. 191, 192) was there and was Reginald Pole's (no. 216) chaplain or secretary in early 1530. In 1532 he moved to Padua with Pole, returning to England early in 1535. His imaginary dialogue between Pole and Lupset, as the draft letter to Henry VIII tells, is a three-part discussion of the right ordering of a commonwealth, the ills of England and what should be done about them. Written and revised over a period of years and existing in autograph manuscript only, it was not published until 1871. Starkey was among the younger humanists whose preoccupation with the well-ordered Christian state and their willingness to work towards that end link them with Thomas More's *Utopia*. He also hoped to bring Pole to favour Henry's cause, a hope that was dissipated when Pole published his denunciation of Henry's viewpoint, *Pro ecclesiasticae unitatis defensione*, in 1536.

278
Stephen Gardiner, 'De vera obedientia'
London, Thomas Berthelet, 1535

Bibliography STC, 11584; McKerrow-Ferguson, 19.

The Master and Fellows of St John's College, Cambridge (A.6.18)

Stephani Winton. episcopi de vera obedientia oratio was Gardiner's considered statement on the division between the ecclesiastical and the lay power and comes down on the side of Henry as Supreme Head of the Church in England. An English translation was three times issued in 1553 – from 'Roane' (twice) and from 'Rome, before ye castle of S. Angel' (actually London). The binding of this copy bears the arms of John Williams, Bishop of Lincoln (1582–1649/50), whose gift of money financed the building of St John's College Library.

279
Sir Thomas Elyot (*c.* 1490–1546)
Hans Holbein the Younger, 1533–4
Coloured chalks on pink-primed paper,
28.6 × 20.6 (11¼ × 8⅛)

Provenance As for no. 176.
Exhibition RA, *Holbein* (160).
Bibliography Parker, no. 15; S. E. Lehmberg, *Sir Thomas Elyot, Tudor Humanist*, Austin, Texas 1960; J. M. Major, *Sir Thomas Elyot and Tudor Humanism*, Lincoln, Nebraska 1964.

Her Majesty the Queen (Windsor Castle 12203)

Sir Thomas Elyot came of a Wiltshire landowning family and had a legal training in the Middle Temple, becoming Clerk to the Justices of Assize and to the King's Council. He was knighted in 1530. From 1516 to 1524 he was at Oxford, where he took the degrees of BA and BCL, and was probably taught Greek and medicine by Thomas Linacre (no. 95). More and Elyot shared a passion for Greek and Lucian (nos. 83, 84), as well as an interest in Pico della Mirandola (nos. 22–5) and St Cyprian (no. 25). Elyot seems to have shared in the life of More's household, to which his wife, Margaret à Barrow, belonged. His chief published work was *The Boke named the Gouvernour*, first issued in 1531.

Holbein's drawing, inscribed 'Th: Elliott Knight' in a later hand, shows the subject long-haired and without a beard, in accordance with the style that was passing out of fashion.

280
Sir Thomas Elyot to Thomas Cromwell
Autograph, London, ?1536
Manuscript on paper

Bibliography LP, XIII, ii, 854; Lehmberg, 153–5; K. J. Wilson, ed., 'The Letters of Sir Thomas Elyot', *Studies in Philology*, LXXIII, no. 5, 1976, 30–3.

The British Library Board (MS Cotton, Cleopatra E.IV, f. 260)

In the *Boke named the Gouvernour* (1531), Elyot defined friendship as 'a blessed and stable connexion of sondrie willes, makinge of two parsones one in hauinge and suffringe.' In 1536 he wrote to Cromwell thanking him for his 'honourable and gentill report to the Kinges Majesty on Wenesday last passid in my fauor . . .'. The occasion of the letter is not known. Elyot goes on: 'I therefore beseich your goode lordship now to lay apart the remembrance of the amity between me and Sir Thomas More, which was but *usque ad aras*, as is the proverb, considering that I was never so moche addict unto hym as I was unto truthe and fidelity toward my soveraignc lordc, as goddc is my juge.' The letter concludes with a request for a share in the lands of the suppressed monasteries.

281
Martyrdom of St Thomas Becket
Unknown artist, 12th–13th century
Enamel, 13.3 × 8.2 (5¼ × 3¼)

Bibliography T. Borenius, *St Thomas Becket in Art*, 1932; with Supplement in *Archaeologia*, LXXXIII, 1933, 171–86; Marie-Madeleine Gauthier, 'Le meurtre dans la cathédrale, thème iconographique médiéval', *Thomas Becket. Actes du Colloque internationale de Sédières, 1973*, ed. R. Foreville, 1975, 247–53; *Neue Briefe*, 84–91.

Victoria and Albert Museum, London (4041–1856)

The martyrdom in 1170 of St Thomas Becket was among the scenes most popular with the late twelfth and early thirteenth-century enamellers of Limoges. Some forty examples are preserved of plaques showing the martyrdom of a bishop or archbishop by knights. They date from about 1195–1200, the time of the translation of the relics of St Thomas Becket to the 'Trinity Chapel' in the choir of Canterbury Cathedral. Some may represent the martyrdom

284

of St Savinian, St Ethelbert, St Theodore of Croyland or another.

Thomas More's devotion to his name saint and the premier saint of England is well known. In 1530, Sir Thomas and Lady More were received into the fraternity of Christ Church Canterbury for their reverence to St Thomas. He writes to Margaret that he wishes to die 'on S. Thomas evin' (the eve of the feast of the Translation). Harpsfield (no. 272) compares the two and Stapleton associates them both with St Thomas the Apostle (no. 273).

282
Sir Thomas More and St Thomas Becket
Unknown artist, 17th century
Silver medal, diameter 3.75 (1 7/16)

Bibliography Medallic Illustrations, I, 36. 24; Morison-Barker, no. 302.

The Trustees of the British Museum (Med.Ill.I.36.24)

Nothing is known of the circumstances in which this medal was made. This seems to be the only extant example. The obverse has the legend EFFIGIES THOMAE MORI MARTIRIS ANGLI ('The likeness of Thomas More, the English martyr') encircling a portrait of More of the type established in the early seventeenth century by Anton Wiericx and Willem and Magdalena van de Passe. On the reverse, St Thomas Becket, wearing mitre and holding cross and book, with the inscription S. THOMAS ARCHIEP[ISCOPVS] CANTVAR[IENSIS] MART[YR] AN[NO] 1171.

283
Sir Thomas More
Unknown artist, ?16th–17th century
Bronze medal, diameter 6 (2 3/8)

Provenance Sir Mark Masterman Sykes (1771–1823); Edward Hawkins, (1780–1867), at whose death to British Museum.
Bibliography Medallic Illustrations, I, 34.23; pl II, 8; Sir George Hill, *Medals of the Renaissance*, Oxford 1920, 151; Morison-Barker, no. 301; J. B. Trapp, '*Suavius olet*: a Bronze Medal of Thomas More and its Motto', and 'Postscript', *Moreana*, IV, 1964, 40–1 and VI, 1965, 45–50.

The Trustees of the British Museum (Med.Ill.I.34.23)

This medal also exists in one example only. The obverse portrait is the only profile head of More. It is surrounded by the legend THOMAS MORVS ANGLIAE CANCELLARIVS. On the reverse is a cypress stump, with an axe sticking in it and the rest of the tree felled at the side, with the motto SVAVIVS OLET (It smells the sweeter [for death]). The emblem and motto are applied to More by the Abate Filippo Picinelli of Milan (1604–78), who wrote extempore Latin eulogies of More and Fisher. Both emblem and motto appear on the engraved title-page of some editions of the Italian life of Thomas More by Domenico Regi, first published at Milan, in 1675. The medal may date from the late sixteenth century, but is more likely to belong to the seventeenth.

284
Drinking Cup said to have belonged to Sir Thomas More
?17th century
Oak with silver bands, height 15 (6); diameter: top 8.7 ($3\frac{3}{8}$); bottom 13.6 ($5\frac{3}{8}$)

Provenance Eyston family.
Exhibition Chelsea, 1929 (8).
Bibliography E. V. Hitchcock, preface to Roper, viii; Bridgett, 458.

Thomas M. Eyston, Esq

The cup may be older than its three bands of silver which, on the evidence of their hallmarks, belong to *c.* 1670. The inscription round the rim of the top band, 'The Can of Sir Thomas More Lord Chancellor of England in King Henry 8th time', is in a nineteenth-century imitation Gothic script.

285
Walking Staff said to have belonged to John Fisher
Wood, with metal ferrule and silver band near top, length 84 ($33\frac{1}{8}$)

Provenance Charles Eyston, antiquary (1667–1721), by whose will to Eyston family.
Bibliography E. V. Hitchcock, preface to Roper, viii.

Thomas M. Eyston, Esq

The band is inscribed 'The Walking Staff of/John Fisher, Cardinal,/and Bishop of Rochester;/who suffered on the 22" of June 1535. Aged 76 Years and 9 Months'. Accounts of Fisher's execution mention the staff upon which he leaned, though the more authentic indicate that he was carried to the scaffold in a chair, on account of his physical weakness.

286
Double Portrait of Sir Thomas More
Unknown artist, 17th–18th century
Oil on canvas, 22.8 × 30.5 (9 × 12)

Provenance Throckmorton family; by marriage to Eyston family.
Bibliography Morison-Barker, pp 45–6; Stapleton, 188.

Thomas M. Eyston, Esq

This is a late version of a devotional image, showing More in official dress and as he prepared for death. The latter image may be related to the one which Margaret Gigs (Clement) showed Stapleton. A miniature in the possession of the Melander Shakespeare Society shows him in similar dress and there is a version of the image at Rome.

287
Sir Thomas More's Epitaph in Chelsea Old Church, 1532

Bibliography Allen, 2831; Rogers, 191; *SL*, 46; *EW*, 1421–2; Harpsfield, 279–81; Thomas More, *Latin Epigrams*, ed. L. Bradner and C. A. Lynch, Chicago 1953, no. 242.

Thomas More's last extant letter to Erasmus was written some time between March and June 1533. It gives news of old friends and enemies: Warham, Archbishop of Canterbury (no. 204), is dead; Tunstall (no. 55) is hard pressed in the north and More is out of touch with him; Tyndale (nos. 143–9) is troubled by Melanchthon's (nos. 134, 135) influence with the king of France. A few have put it about that More's resignation of the chancellorship on 16 May 1532 was forced and that he suppressed the fact. He has therefore decided to declare himself to the public and to posterity in an epitaph, of which he encloses the Latin text. The epitaph, profoundly moving, was reprinted with an English translation, probably by William Rastell, in *EW*:

'Sir Thomas More being lorde Chaunceller of England, gaue ouer that office (by his great sute & labour) the .xvi. day of may, in the yere of our lord god a.1532. and in the .xxiiii. yere of the raigne of king Henry the eight. And after in that somer, he wrote an epitaphy in latin, and caused it to be written vpon his tombe of stone, which himself (while he was lord Chanceller) had caused to be made in his parishe church of Chelsey (where he dwelled) thre smal Miles from London. The copye of which epitaphy here foloweth...

"Thomas More, a Londoner borne, of no noble famely, but of an honest stocke, somewhat brought vp in learning, after that in his yong dayes, he had ben a pleader in the lawes of this hall certaine yeres, being one of the vndershrieues of London, was of noble kinge Henry the eight (which alone of all kinges worthely deserued both with sweorde and penne, to be called the defender of the faith, a glory afore not herd of) called into the court, & chosen one of the counsel, and made knight: then made first vnder treasorer of englande, after that Chanceller of ye Duchy of Lancaster, and last of all (with great fauour of his Prince) lord Chaunceller of England. But in the meane season, he was chosen speker of the parlement, & besides was diuers times in dyuers places the kinges enbassator, and last of all at Cameray (ioined felow and companion with Cuthbert Tonstal chief of that embassy than Bishop of London, and wythin a while after Bishop of Durham, who so excelleth in learning wit and vertue, that the whole world scant hath at this daye any more lerned wiser or better) where he both ioyfully saw & was present embassator, when the legues betwene the chief Princes of christendome wer renued againe and peace so long loked for restored to Christendome. Which peace oure lord stable and make perpetual.

When he had thus gone throughe thys course of offices or honours, that neither that gracious prince could disalow his doinges, nor was he odious to the nobilite, nor vnplesant to the people, but yet to theues, murderers and heretikes greuous, at laste John More hys father knight, and chosen of the Prince to be one of the iustyces of the kynges benche a ciuil man, plesant, harmless gentil, pitiful, iust, & vncorrupted, in yeres old, but in body more than for his

286

yeres lusty, after that he parceiued his sonne lord Chaunceller of Englande, thinking hymselfe nowe to haue liued long inough, gladly departed to god, his sonne than, his father being dead, to whome as long as he liued being compared, was wont both to be called yong, & himself so thought to, missing now his father departed, and seing .iiii. children of his own, & of their offspringes xi. began in his own conceit to waxe old. And this affect of his was increased, by a certayne sickly disposicion of hys brest, euen by & by folowing, as a signe or token of age creping vpon him. He therfore irke and wery of worldly busines, giuing vp his promocions, obtained at last by ye incomparable benefite of his most gentil prince (if it please god to fauour his enterprise) that thing which from a childe in a manner alway he wished & desyred, that he might haue some yeres of his life fre, in which he litle and litle withdrawing himself from the business of this life, might continually remember the immortalite of the lyfe to come. And he hath caused this tombe to be made for himselfe (his firste wiues bones brought hither to) that might euerye day put him in memory of death that neuer ceaseth to crepe on hym. And that this tombe made for him in his life time be not in vaine, nor that he fere death comming vpon him, but that he may willingly for the desire of Christ, die, & find death not vtterly death to him, but ye gate of a welthyer life, helpe hym (I besech you good reader) nowe with your praiers while he liueth, & when he is dead also."

Under this epitaphy in prose, he caused to be written on his tombe, this latten epitaphy in versis following, which himself had made .xx. yeres before', for Jane Colt:
' "Here lieth Ione ye welbeloued wife of me Thomas More, who haue apointed this tombe for Alis my wife and me also, the one being coupled with me in matrimony, in my youthe brought me forth thre daughters & one sone, ye other hath ben so good to my children (which is a rare praise in mothers in law) [ie stepmothers] as scant any could be better to her own. The one so liued with me, & the other nowe so lyueth, that it is doubtfull whether thys or the other were derer vnto me. Oh howe well could we thre haue liued ioined together in matrimony, if fortune and religion wolde haue suffred it. But I beseche our lord that this tombe and heauen may ioine vs togither. So deathe shall give vs, that thyng that life could not." '

The epitaph can still be read, incised on a slab of black marble within an architectural framework bearing the arms of Sir Thomas More and the Colt family, in Chelsea Old Church. It has been recut at least once and moved to its present position from its original site in the More family chapel.

140

List of Lenders

Her Majesty the Queen   9, 67, 72, 176–9, 182–4, 202, 207, 279
Aberdeen University Library   220
The Warden and Fellows of All Souls College, Oxford   94, 186
Archives du Nord, Lille   30
The Visitors of the Ashmolean Museum, Oxford   7
Bayerische Staatsbibliothek, Munich   119
The Beinecke Rare Book and Manuscript Library, Yale University   163, 226
Bibliotheca Apostolica Vaticana   117
Bibliothèque Nationale, Paris: Cabinet des Manuscrits   100, 253
Musée du Château de Blois   259
Bodleian Library, Oxford   15, 16, 45, 77, 78, 95, 97, 99, 102, 122, 150, 154, 188, 194, 205, 219, 223, 236, 273
City of Bristol Museum and Art Gallery   113
British and Foreign Bible Society, London   142
The British Library Board   14, 19, 22, 24, 37, 39, 49, 79, 85, 96, 98, 108, 110, 116, 120, 128, 129, 136, 143, 144, 147, 153, 155, 157, 158, 160, 162, 175, 190, 191, 193, 197, 224, 230, 233–5, 240, 241, 245, 247–51, 254–8, 264, 267, 269, 271, 275, 280
The Trustees of the British Museum   23, 34, 51, 52, 58, 60, 64, 66, 73, 74, 76, 88, 89, 114, 115, 124, 126, 131, 135, 149, 152, 161, 196, 200, 201, 213, 215, 252, 282, 283
His Grace the Duke of Buccleuch and Queensberry   172, 173
Cambridge University Library   56, 83, 104, 132, 148, 151, 166, 167
His Grace the Lord Archbishop of Canterbury and the Church Commissioners   204, 216
His Grace the Lord Archbishop of Canterbury and the Trustees of Lambeth Palace Library   80, 82, 107, 274
J. R. Chichester-Constable, Esq   55
The Governing Body of Christ Church, Oxford   43
The College of Arms, London   109
Corpus Christi College, Cambridge   20
The President and Fellows of Corpus Christi College, Oxford   32, 33, 91–3, 221
The Devonshire Collection, Chatsworth: The Trustees of the Chatsworth Settlement   59, 75
Durham University Library: from the Collection of M. J. Routh, 1755–1854   118, 159
Edinburgh University Library   127
The Master and Fellows of Emmanuel College, Cambridge   272
Thomas M. Eyston, Esq   189, 284–6
Fitzwilliam Museum, Cambridge   35, 125
Folger Shakespeare Library, Washington DC   156
Musée national du Château de Fontainebleau   65
Galleria Nazionale d'Arte Antica, Rome   53
Glasgow University Library   133
Guildhall Library, London   40, 44, 46, 47, 101, 103, 140, 146, 148, 165, 222, 261, 270, 276
Haus-, Hof- und Staatsarchiv, Vienna   29, 217
Historisches Archiv der Stadt, Cologne   69
The Speaker of the House of Commons   111
Henry E. Huntington Library and Art Gallery, San Marino, California   81
Bibliotheek, Katholieke Universiteit Leuven   57
Kunstmuseum Basel   139
Kunstmuseum Winterthur   137
The Worshipful Company of Mercers, London   12, 13, 106
Merton Collection (Trustees of the late Lady Merton's Will Trust)   57A
The Warden and Fellows of Merton College, Oxford   90
Metropolitan Museum of Art, New York: Rogers Fund, 1950   174
National Portrait Gallery, London   1, 2, 4–6, 11, 26, 36, 42, 71, 123, 168, 185, 203, 208–12, 214
The Master, Fellows and Scholars of Pembroke College, Cambridge   262, 268
Private Collections   17, 171, 187, 263

Public Record Office, London   28, 48, 105, 112, 192, 195, 198, 218, 229, 231, 232, 237–9, 242–4, 246, 277
The President and Fellows, Queens' College, Cambridge   265
The Earl of Radnor   54
Real Colegio de Corpus Christi, Valencia   225
Royal Museum of Fine Arts, Brussels   199
The John Rylands University Library of Manchester   145
The Community, St Augustine's Priory, Newton Abbot   228
The Master and Fellows of St John's College, Cambridge   121, 164, 278
The President and Fellows of St John's College, Oxford   260
The Marquess of Salisbury   38
The President and Court of Governors of Sion College   25
The Society of Antiquaries of London   8, 141
Staatliche Münzsammlung, Munich   130, 138
The Trustees of Stonyhurst College   31, 227
The Governors of Sutton's Hospital in the Charterhouse   21
Thyssen-Bornemisza Collection, Lugano   70
The Armouries, H. M. Tower of London   61, 62
The Master and Fellows of Trinity College, Cambridge   10
Trinity Hall, Cambridge   206
Universitätsbibliothek Basel   84
University College London   134
University College, Oxford   41
University Library, Exeter: from the Parish Library, Crediton   266
University of London Library   68, 181
Victoria and Albert Museum, London   3, 27, 63, 87, 170, 281
Warburg Institute, University of London   180
The Dean and Chapter of York   18

Index

References are to catalogue numbers; Roman numerals indicate illustration in colour, italics indicate illustration in black and white

Abbot, George 80
Aegidius, Petrus *See* Gillis, Peter
Aggripinus, Caspar 254
Agricola, Rudolf 54
Ahasuerus 74
Aldridge, Robert 244
Alington, Giles 182
Alleyn, Sir John 27
Amaurotum 52
Amerbach, Basilius 86, 89
Amerbach, Bonifacius 169
Amiens, Treaty of 195
Ammonius, Andrea 107
Anne Boleyn 143, 145, 162, 206, 207, *211*, 212, 230, 231, 237, 246, 257
Anne de Bretagne 103
Annulment, Act of 251
Anselm, St 79
Antichrist 126
Antwerp 42, 48, *49*, 50, 53, 54, 106, 143–5, 147, 151, 153, 155, 157, 159
Anydrus, River 52
Apelles 89
Aragon *See* Catherine of Aragon
Aristotle 22, 94, 95, 124, 181
Arthur, Prince 94, 203
Arundel, Earl of 202, 207
Asper, Hans 137, *139*
Audeley, Sir Thomas 197, 218, 232, 237
Augsburg Confession 130, 134
Augustine, St 20, 33, 41, 90, 185, 210, 265, 268
Aurik, I. 159

Ba:, Ro: *See* Ro: Ba:
Bacon, Sir Francis 178
Badius Ascensius, Jodocus 83, 84
Baga de secretis 246
Bailey, William 188
Bainbridge, Christopher 264
Baker, Thomas 76
Baldung Grien, Hans 114, 115, 123, 136
Baldwin, Sir John 246
Ballère, Balthasar 276
Bancroft, Richard 80
'Baravellus, Ferdinandus' 118
Barbara, St 62
'Barkley, Lady' 182
Barlow, Thomas 122
Barlowe, Jerome 150
Barnborough, Yorks. 1, *179*, 220
Barnes, Robert 144, 148, 151, 152, 161
Barrett, Thomas 203
Barrow, Margaret à 279
Barton, Elizabeth 204, 210, 230–5
Basset, Mary 174, 225
Batmanson, John 102
Bayfield, Richard 161
Bayley, John 188
Beatus Rhenanus 58
Beaumont, William, Viscount 105
Bebel, Johann 46, 181
Beccadelli, Lodovico 216
Beckford, William 34
Bedyll, Thomas 244, 249
Belli, Vincenzo 215

Bergen 184
Berghe, Jan van 185
Berleght 243
Berthelet, Thomas 25, 166, 175, 186, 191, 278
Beza, Theodore 149
Bible
    Alcalà Polyglot 39
    Coverdale's *144*, 202
    Erasmus's New Testament *38*–40, 53, 75, 142, 143
    Joye's New Testament 143
    Lollard 143
    Luther's New Testament 115, 116, 142–4
    'Matthew's' 144
    Tyndale's New Testament 127, 141–4
    Vulgate 38, 39, 142, 144
Bibliander, Theodor 137
Bild, Beat *See* Beatus Rhenanus
Billa vera 246
Birckmann, F. *See* Byrckman
Blount, Elizabeth 211
Bocking, Edward 230–2
Bogard, Jan 262, 273
Boissard, J. J. 123, 185
Bonvisi, Antonio 189, 241, 242, 262, 274
Booke of Sir Thomas Moore 275
Bora, Katharina von 113
Bouge, John 228, 229
Bramante 59
Brandon, Charles *See* Suffolk, Duke of
Breu, Jörg, Jr 256
Brie, Germain de *See* Brixius
'Brightewell, Richard' *See* Frith
Brixius, G. 103, 104
Bruges 42, 69
Brunfels, Otto 136
Brussels 48
Buckingham, Duke of 230
Budé, Guillaume 54, 67, 68, 123, 191
Bugenhagen, Johann *131*, 132, 133, 135
Bullart, I. 53
Bullinger, Heinrich 137
Burgkmair, Hans 60, 256
Busleyden, Jerome 54, 55, 57
Byrckman, F. 226

Cabbala 22
Cambrai 42, 55, 196
Cambridge University 32, 214
    Christ's College 214
    Pembroke College 32
    Queens' College 214
    St John's College 32, 214, 278
    Trinity Hall 206
Canterbury
    Cathedral 205, 281
    St Dunstan's, Roper Vault 227
Cantiuncula, Claudius 46
Capello 218
Capon, John 231
Carmen heroicum 257
Caron, Antoine 259
Carthusians 21, 136, 184, 229, 235, *252*, 254

Carwen, Richard 244
Cassiodorus 128
Catherine of Aragon 35–8, 62, 67, 185, *203*, 204, 210, 211, 217, 237, 257
Catherine Howard 207
Cavalieri, G. B. 259
Cavendish, George 195, 209
Cawood, John 260
Cecil, William (Burghley) 47
Cellini, Benvenuto 66, 200, 201
Cervicornus, E. 144
Chansonette, C. *See* Cantiuncula
Chapuys, Eustace 198, 217
Charles I 34, 98, 171, 202, 276
Charles II 72
Charles V, Emperor 29, 30, 48, 50, 55, 57, 61, 63, *64*, 65, 76, 149, 196, 198–202, 213, 217
Chaudière, G. 68
Chauncy, Maurice 252
Chelsea, More Chapel 174, 287
Chettle, Henry 275
Christian II of Denmark 197
Clarke, Mary *See* Basset
Claymond, John 91–3
Clement VII, Pope 76, 125, 199, 200, *201*
Clement, Caesar 228
Clement, Elizabeth *See* Rastell
Clement, John *51*, 78, 191, 235, 260, 274
Clement, Margaret 1, 78, 95, *169*, *184*, 235, 236, 260, 286
Clement, Mother Margaret 228
Clement, Thomas 78
Clement, Winifred 235
Clerk, John 194
Cleve, Joos van 65, 202
Clifford, John 48
Clouet, Jean 68
Cochlaeus, Johannes 127–9, 132, 143, 156
Cock, Symon 147, 151, 157
Cognac, League of 199
Colet, Dame Christian 11, 190
Colet, Sir Henry 11
Colet, John 3, 11, 12, 13–16, 22, 38, 39, 41, 57A, 96, 106, 107, 191, 264, 265, 269
Colley, Dorothy *See* Harris
Cologne 69, 116, 143
Colt, Jane *See* More
Constable, John 266, 267
Constantine, George 161
Constantinople 166, 213
Conyers, Lady 250
Copp, Johann 125
Cordelière 103
Cornaro, Francesco 6, 42
Corvus, Johannes 32, 67
Cotton, Sir Robert 37
Court of Arches 107
Coverdale, Miles 144
Covrinus *See* Nucerinus, G. Covrinus
Cranach, Lucas, the Elder 113–15, 126, 131, 135, 142
Cranach, Lucas, the Younger 131, 134, 135
Cranevelt, Francis 185
Cranmer, Thomas 178, 182, 200, *210*, 232, 237, 238

142

INDEX

Cresacre, Anne   *See* More
Cresacre, Edward   179
Cromwell, Thomas   144, 149, 183, 206, *209*, 212, 231–5, 238, 242, 243, *245–7*, 249, 252, 280
Crosby Place   189, 241
Cumberland, Henry Earl of   246
Cyprian, St   25, 279

Dauncey, Elizabeth   IV, *1*, *169*, 170, *182*, 183, 250, 275
Dauncey, Sir John   182
Dauncey, William   182, 183
David   125, 144
Day, John   168
De' Medici
   Giuliano   200
   Lorenzo il Magnifico   75
   See also Clement VII and Leo X, Popes
Dekker, Thomas   275
Demosthenes   140
Dering   231, 232
Diet of Worms   116, 126
Dobneck, Johann   *See* Cochlaeus
Doctors' Commons   55, *107*
Dorp, Martin van   54, 94, 95, 100, 101
Doue (Dewe), Robert   97
Dumont, Philippe   *See* Montanus
Dürer, Albrecht   50, 58, 87, 88, 134, 187

Eck, Johann   119, *129*, *130*
Edward I   80
Edward III   197
Edward IV   5, 19, 109
Edward VI   184, 205, 206, 260, 272
Eleanor of France, Queen   202
Elizabeth of York   5, 19, 71, 72
Elizabeth I   55, 184, 262, 272, 273, 275
Eltham Ordinances   194
Elyot, Sir Thomas   25, 279, 280
Emser, Hieronymus   129
Endhoven, C. van   155
Episcopius, Nicolaus   254, 261
Erasmus   10, 11, 14–16, 21, 25–8, *38*, 41, 44, 50, *53*, 54, 57, 57A, 59, 67, 76, *87*, *88*, 89, *91*, 93, *94*, 97, *100*, 102–4, *114*, 116, 123, 134, 137, 169, 176, 178, 180, 181, 187, 191, 204, 214, 217, 254, 255, 257, 261, 263, 264, 267, 272, 287
   Library   84
   Antibarbari   54
   New Testament   *See* Bible
   Institution of a Christian Prince   54
   Edition of St Jerome   53
   Letter to Hutten   123, 265
   On the Lord's Prayer   175
   On Prudentius   175
   De libero arbitrio   133
   Lucian   83, 84
   Paraphrase of Romans   53
   Praise of Folly   53, 85, 86, 266
Esdras   144
Essex, Earl of   275
Esther   74
Ethelbert, St   281

Euclid   78
Evelyn, John   43
'Evil May Day'   108, 275
Exchequer   195
Exmewe, William   252
Expositio fidelis   254–6, 263
Expositio passionis Thomae Mori   258
Exsurge Domine   116
Eyston family   284–6

Faber, Johann   255
Falier, Lodovico   202
Farley, Henry   8
Farnese, Alessandro   *See* Paul III, Pope
Feilding family   226
Ficino, Marsilio   22, 23
Field of the Cloth of Gold   42, 65, *67*, 68
Fish, Simon   162, 163, 165
Fisher, John   3, 32, 116, 118, 121, 122, 127, 129, 210, *214*, 215, 227, 229, 230, 232, 235, 238, 239, 242, 244–6, 252–5, 257, 261, 269, 283, 285
Fitzherbert, Sir Anthony   246
Fitzjames, Sir John   246
Fitzroy, Henry   211
Fitzwilliam, Sir William   246
Flaxman, John   3
Flicke, Gerlach   210
Fortune   66, 82
Fowler, Alice   133
Fowler, John   133
Fox, Richard   *32*, 33, 93
Foxe, John   145, 149, 152, 161, 162, 168, 206, 210, 275
Francis I   6, 65, *66*, 67, 195, 196, 199, 200, 202, 254, 287
Frith, John   153–5, 157
Froben, Hieronymus   57A, 254
Froben, Johann   39, 40, 45, 46, 57A, 86, 102, 168, 254, 264, 268
Froschauer, C.   144
Fuller, Thomas   273

Galen   94, 95, 191
Gardiner, Stephen   152, 206, 278
Garrard, Thomas   152
Gebweiler, Hieronymus   257
Geiler von Kaisersberg, Johann   255
Geisshüssler, Oswald   *See* Myconius
Gensch, Christian   263
Geoffrey of Monmouth   10
George, St   60, 62, *227*
George of Saxony   127
Gerson, Jean   225
Gheet, Jan de   49
Ghiselin de Busbecq, Augier   213
Gig(g)s, Margaret   *See* Clement
Gillis, Peter   II, 48, 50, *51*, 53, 54
Giovio, Paolo   269
Gipkym (Gipkyn), John   8
Giulio Romano   75
Giustinian, Sebastiano   6, 42
Glaubwirdige anzaygung   256, 259
Glaubwirdiger bericht   255
Glover, George   168

Godrand, Jacques   258
Godrand, Odinet   258, 259
Goes, Damião a   178
Golde, George   242
Golde, Henry   231
Golden Fleece, Order of   4, 63, 64
Gonzaga, Ferrante   64
Gourmont, Gilles de   45, 85
Graces   23
Grafton, Richard   108, 110
Grapheus, Johannes   162
Graunger, Agnes   *See* More
Graunger, Thomas   9
Grawe, Friedrich   *See* Nausea
Gray, Daniel   80
Great Seal
   of England   *197*, 198, 218, 237
   of France   *195*
'Great Turk'   *See* Suleiman I
Grocyn, William   11, 20, 57A, 90–2, 107, 269
Grunenberg, Johann   126
Grüninger, Johann   18
Grynaeus, Simon   78, 178, 180
Gualtieri, L.   *See* Spirito
Gwalther, Rudolf   137
Gyge, Margaret   *See* Clement

Hadrian VI, Pope   *76*, 200
Haghen, G. van der   159
Hales, Alexander of   77
Hales, Sir Christopher   198, 249
Hales, Christopher   137, 139
Halle, Edward   108, 275, 276
Haneton, Philippe   30
Hansa   67, 69
Hardyng, John   109, 110
Harpsfield, Nicholas   9, 95, 107, 174, 212, 271–4, 281
Harris, Dorothy   133, 273
Harris, John   *1*, 133, 180, 273, 274
Heath, Nicholas   231
Heivodo, Heliseo   *See* Heywood
Henrietta Maria   98, 276
Henry VII   I, 3, *4*, 19, 27, 32, *71*, 72, 103
Henry VIII   III, 3, 5, 6, 19, 29, 34, *35*, 37, 38, 41–3, 57, *61*, 62, 65, *67*, 70, *71*, 72–4, 95, 97, 105, 110–12, 116, 129, 141, 145, 149, 152, 162, 173, 185, 187, 188, 196, 197, 199, *202*, 204, 207–10, 212, 215–18, 221, 230, 232, 234, 235, 237, 238, 240, 245, 246, 249, 252–4, 257, 262, 275, 277, 278, 280, 287
   Assertio septem Sacramentorum   75, 95, *117*, 118–21, 140
Henslowe, Elyne   221
Hercules   64
Heresy   141
Heron, Cicely   IV, *1*, *169*, 170, 182, *183*, 250, 275
Heron, Giles   182, 183
Herwagen, Johann   78
Hewester   69
Heywood
   Ellis   270
   Jasper   270

143

INDEX

Heywood *contd*
    John   236, 270
    Richard   236
    Thomas   275
Hill
    Nicolas   157
    Richard   82
Hillen, Michael   121
Hitton, Thomas   160
Hoccleve, Thomas   19
Holbein
    Ambrosius   45, 51, 52
    Hans, the Elder   51
    Hans, the Younger   III, V, VI, 1, 9–11, 26, 34, 40, 45, 46, 51, 57A, 70, 71, 72, 74, 86, 88, 89, 124, 125, 144, 169, 170, 171, 172, *173*, 174, 176–9, 182–4, 187, 188, 204, 207–9, 212, 214, 279
Holland, Henry   168
Holt, John   203
Hoochstraten, Johannes   145, 153
Hooker, John   32
Hopfer, Daniel   199
Horenbout, Gerard   43
Horenbout, Lucas   35, 36, 43, 173
Houghton, John   252
Howard, Thomas   *See* Norfolk
Huntingdon, Earl of   246
Husee   69
Huszgen, Johann   *See* Oecolampadius
Hutten, Ulrich von   10, 21, 57A, 123, 136, 261, 263, 265
Hydra   64
Hyrde, Richard   175, 185, 186
Hythlodaeus, Raphel   46, 48, *51, 52*, 54

'Iak, Mother'   184
Indictment, More's   246
Indulgences   75, 125
Instrument, Publick   141
Intercursus magnus   48, 106
Intercursus malus   106

Jabach, Everard   57A
Jack(son), Mistress   184
Jakes, Thomas   105
James the Greater, St   256
James the Less, St   256
James I   8
Jane Seymour   34, 70, 71, 72
Janus, Temple of   201
Jerningham, Sir Richard   61
Jerome, St   33, 53, 57
Jerome, William   152
Jerusalem   166
John Chrysostom, St   41, 92
John the Falconer   242
John Fisher, St   *See* Fisher
Johnson, Samuel   260
Jonson, Ben   260
Joye, George   143, 144, 157–60
Juan de Ribera, St   225
Judas   219, 227
Julius II, Pope   13, *59*, 75
Jupiter   87

Justice   74
Justinian, Emperor   18, 54

Kappel, Battle of   137
Kervert, J.   68
Keyser, Martin van   143, 147, 151, 160
Knight   69
Knox, John   149
Kobian, Valentin   257
Kratzer, Nikolaus   169, *187*, 188
Kynen, Rutger   49

Lamb, Charles   160
Lancaster, Duchy of   193
Lancaster, House of   4, 27, 37
Lanfranc   79
La Sauch, Jehan de   30
Latimer, William   57A, 269
Layton, Richard   244
Le Boucq, Jacques   42
Lee, Edward   22, 102
Lee, Joyeuce   236
Leemput, Remigius van   71, 72
Legh, Thomas   242
Leo X   39, *75*, 76, 95, 117, 122, 125, 200
Leoni, Leone   64
Lichfield, John   98
Liège   116
Lily, George   269
Lily, William   14, 15, 96, 266, 267, 269
Linacre, Thomas   57A, 90, 91, 93–6, 191, 269, 279
Lister, Sir Richard   246
Listrius, Gerardus   86
Livy   180
Lockey, Rowland   IV, 1, 170, 178
London humanists   41
London
    Bridewell Palace   74
    Charterhouse   21, 102, 252
    Lincoln's Inn   9, 17, 174
    London Bridge   7, 8
    New Inn   17
    St Lawrence Jewry   20, 90
    St Paul's Cathedral   7, *8*, 11, 12
    St Paul's Cross   *8*, 116, 117, 122, 152
    St Paul's School   7, 8, 11–16, 96, 264
    Smithfield   161
    Southwark   7
    The Tower   7, 155, 227
    Tyburn   252
    Westminster Abbey   7
    Westminster Palace   7
    Whitehall Palace   71, 72
    York Place   71
Loo, Andreas de   204
Lorck, Melchior   213
Lotther, M., Jr   142
Louis XII   208
Louise of Savoy   196
Louvain   116, 184
Louvain, *Collegium trilingue*   57, 100
Lovell, Sir Thomas   99
Lucian   41, 53, 83, 84, 261, 262, 265, 268, 279

Luke, St   38
Luke, Sir Walter   246
Lupset, Thomas   90, 191, 192, 277, 289
Luther, Martin   39, 41, 75, *113*, 114, 115, 116–23, 126, 129, 131–6, 138, 140, 144, 146, 153, 154, 262
    See also Bible
Lutheranism   174, 214
Lützelburger, Hans   124, 125

Madrid, Treaty of   199
Malines   57, 184
Manasseh   125
'Man for all seasons'   85, 266
Manne, Dame Catherine   229
Manutius, Aldus   94
'Marburg' Series   145, 153
Marende, Jean   196
Margaret, St   33
Margaret of Savoy (Austria)   4, 63, 106, *196*
Marshe, John   236
Marshe, Walter   236
Martens, Dirk   16, 44, 54
Mary, Virgin   33, 226
Mary Magdalen, St   33
Mary (sister of Henry VIII)   208
Mary, Queen   55, 168, 184, 185, 206, 216, 235, 260, 269–73
Mary of Burgundy   196
'Masker, Master'   158
Massys, Quentin   II, 50, 53, 54, 87, 88
Masters, Richard   231, 232
Matthew, St   256
Maximilian I, Emperor   4, 49, *60*, 61–3, 65, 123, 196, 213
Meghen, Peter   38, 41, 43, 188
Meit, Conrad   63
Melanchthon, Philipp   57A, 126, 131, *134*, 135, 142, 180, 287
Mercers, Company of   12, 13, 106
Merchants Adventurers   106
Mesa, Bernard de   30
Meyer, Adalbert   46
Michelangelo   59, 200, 215
Michiel, Master   *See* Sittow
Middlemore, Humphrey   252
Middleton, Alice   *See* More
Middleton, John   169
'Mocke, Master'   157
Mohács, Battle of   213
Montague, Henry Lord   246
Montanus, Philippus   254, 261
More family, of Barnborough, Yorks.   1, 220
More, Agatha   10
More, Agnes   9, 10
More, Dame Alice   1, *169*, 228, 229, 240, 275, 281, 287
More, Anne   IV, *1*, *169*, 170, 178, *179*, 228, 250
More, Austin   250
More, Cresacre   IV, *1*, 22, 170, 178, 227, 276
More, Edward   10
More, Elizabeth   10

More, Jane 229, 262, 287
More, Joan (Stafferton) 10, 17
More, Johanna 9
More, Sir John IV, *1*, 9, 10, 17, 81, 105, 111, *169*, 170, 287
More, John (son of Sir John) 10
More, John II IV, *1*, 156, 165, *169*, 170, *178*, 179, 181, 182, 184, 220, 240, 250, 276
More, Mary IV, *1*, 170, 276

More, Sir Thomas
LIFE (chronological order)
  Birth 10
  Admission to Lincoln's Inn 17
  Member of Parliament 32, 111, 112
  Living at The Old Barge 83, 85
  Interpreter 106
  First Royal Commission 105
  Second marriage 229
  Admitted to Doctors' Commons *107*
  Utopian mission 29, 42, 48, 51, 54, 55
  Evil May Day 108, 275
  Mission to Calais 28, 53
  King's Councillor 28, 120, 229
  Mission to Charles V 29, 30
  Mission to Bruges 185
  Prays for W. Roper 174
  Speaker of House of Commons 111, 112
  Indenture with A. Bonvisi 189
  High Steward of Oxford University 99
  Steward and Chancellor of the Duchy of Lancaster 128, 182, 193
  Has lodging in the king's house 194
  In Eltham Ordinances 194
  Mission to Amiens 42, 208
  Co-signatory of Treaty of Amiens 195
  Mission to Cambrai 42, 55, 196
  Lord Chancellor 42, 198
  On royal divorce 217
  Informed of Emperor's letter 217
  'Cruelty' to heretics 168
  Resigns as Lord Chancellor 218, 287
  And Nun of Kent 230, 232, 234, 235
  Conveys lands 236, 239, 251
  Foretells imprisonment 248
  'Before the Lords at Lambeth' 237
  Refuses Oath of Supremacy 237–9, 247
  Cranmer suggests modified Oath 238
  Prisoner in Tower 211, 220, 223, 240, 247
  Applies Bible to own life 219, 226
  Advice on virtue 221
  Goods forfeited 240
  Urged by Margaret to take Oath 247
  Attainder 235, 239
  Consoles family 248, 275
  Compares Act of Succession to 'two-edged sword' 229, 246, 253
  First interrogation 244, 249
  Second interrogation 244
  Did not counsel Fisher 246, 253
  In 'Cromwell's Remembrances' 245
  Condemnation and execution a foregone conclusion 245
  Third interrogation 244
  Interrogation of servants 242
  Rich interview 243, 246
  Fourth interrogation 244
  Publicly condemned as traitor before court is set up 245
  His court appointed 245
  Grand Jury appointed 246
  Trial 207, 246
  Indictment 243, 246
  Urged by Norfolk to conform 253
  Keeps silence 226, 242, 243, 246, 249
  Condemned upon Rich's perjury 246
  Jury's verdict: 'Guilty' 253
  Stays Audeley in passing sentence 246
  Answers to indictment 253
  All councils of Christendom on his side 246
  Final encounter with John and Margaret 250, 253
  Dies 'the king's good servant, but God's first' 253
  Execution 215, 253, 257, *259*, 261, 271, 273
  Head on London Bridge 235
  Accounts of death 253–8, 272
  Indenture and feofment annulled 251
  Sanctification foreseen by J. Secundus 257
  Beatification and Sanctification 227

MISCELLANEOUS
  Anecdotes 273, 276
  Arms *31*, 170, *189*, 287
  And Civil Law 18
  And City of London 108
  Dedications to 128, 181
  Devotion 229, 281
  As ornament of the kingdom 257
  And Fortune 82
  Friend of poor 275
  And Hansa 69
  Household IV, *1*, *169*, 170, 187
  Learning 15, 90, 229
  Library 77–80, 224, 226
  Model of elegant English 260
  Portraits of Frontispiece, IV, V, *1*, *26*, *51*, *169*, 170, *171*, *172*, *176*, *177*, *228*, *282*, *283*, *286*
  Relics 227
    Head 174
    Cup *284*
    George 227
    Hair shirt 179, 227, *228*, 229
  And Roman coins 30, 57
  Secretary: John Harris 273
  Seals *30*, *31*, *189*
  Servant: John à Wood 242
  Translation by 186

WORKS
  Autograph *107*, *120*, *225*
  English Workes, 1557 222–5, 235, 236, 260
  Lucubrationes, 1563 100, 223, 261
  Opera, 1565–6 262
  Opera, 1689 263, 273
  Answer to a Poisoned Book 158, 167
  Apology 148, 156, 158, 164–7
  Book of the Fair Gentlewoman 82
  Confutation 79, 148, 151, 156, 160, 165, 202
  Debellation 158, 167
  De Tristitia Christi 174, 219, *225*, 262
  Dialogue of Comfort 95, 213, 219, *221*, 222
  Dialogue Concerning Heresies 146, 199
  Epigrammata 37, 40, 45, 53, 57A, 58, 96, 103, 203, 261, 262
  Epitaph 262, 287
  Lectures on Augustine 20, 265
  Life of Picus 22, 223
  Lucian 83, 84, 261, 262, 265, 268, 279
  Merry Jest 81
  Prayers 213, 219, 223, *226*
  Precationes ex Psalmis 224, 262
  Progymnasmata 261, 262
  Quod pro fide mors fugienda non est See *De Tristitia Christi*
  Responsio ad Lutherum 118, 119, 129, 133, 202, 262
  Richard III 109, 110, 189, 262
  Rueful Lamentation 5, 19
  Supplication of Souls 163
  'Tower works' 219, 247
  Treatise on the Passion 219, 220
  Treatise to receive the Blessed Body 219, 220
  Utopia 40, 44–7, 51, 52, 54, 57A, 68, 123, 191, 262, 265, 277

LETTERS
  Latin 263
  Bonvisi 241, 262
  Brixius 104
  Bugenhagen 133
  Charles V 217
  Cromwell 231–3, 235
  Dorp 76, 94, 95, 100, 101
  Erasmus 287
  Fisher 246
  Frith 154–6
  Henry VIII 234, 235
  Holt 36
  John More II 22, 178
  Margaret Roper 237, 247–50
  Monk 11, 102
  Nun of Kent 230–2
  Oxford University 32, 97, 98, 204
  Pole 216
  Wolsey 120

BIOGRAPHIES AND EULOGIES
(chronologically, by author)
  Pace 264
  Erasmus 123, 261, 263, 265
  Whittinton 266
  Constable 267
  Vives 268
  More (Epitaph) 262, 287
  George Lily 269
  Ellis Heywood 270
  Roper 20, 21, 32, 175, 211, 212, 218, 228, 243, 250, 251, 271, 272, 274–6
  Harpsfield 9, 95, 107, 174, 212, 271–4, 281
  Rastell 235
  Stapleton 98, 174, 228, 250, 276, 281, 286, 263, 273, 274
  Play of Sir Thomas Moore 108, 275

INDEX

More, Sir Thomas *contd*
  Ro: Ba: 274
  Cresacre More 276
  Regi 283
  Picinelli 283
More, Thomas II IV, *1*, 80, 170, 178, 179, 250, 272, 276
More, Thomas III IV, *1*, 170
More, Thomas IV 276
More, Thomas X, of Barnborough 227
More, Thomas XI, SJ 31, 227
More, William 9
Moro, Il 270
Moses 144
Munday, Anthony 275
Murner, Thomas 116, 120, 129
Myconius, Jakob 86
Myconius, Oswald 86
Mylner, U. 15

Naenia in mortem Thomae Mori 257
Nausea, Fridericus 156, 165, 178
Neve, Johannes 49
Newbold, William 13, 106
Newdigate, Sebastian 252
Niccolò Fiorentino 23
Norfolk, Duke of VI, 198, 207, 208, 218, 237, 246, 253
Norris, Henry 198
Notary, Julian 81
Nucerinus, G. Covrinus 261, 263
Nun of Kent *See* Barton, Elizabeth

Oath of Supremacy *See* Supremacy
Oecolampadius, Johannes 86, *138*, 139, 154, 180
Oliver, Peter 170
Opitiis, Benedictus and Georgius de 49
Oropesa, Count of 225
Otho the Monk *See* Brunfels
Oxford University 97–9, 185, 191
  Cardinal College 187
  Corpus Christi College 32, 33, 38, 43, 91–3, 187, 206
  Magdalen College 269
  St John's College 174
Oyer and terminer, Special Commission of 245, 246

P.M. *See* Montanus, Philippus
Pace, Richard 29, 30, 46, 97, 117, 122, 191, 194, 264, 269
'Pacifer' *See* St German, Christopher
Padua, University 55, 57, 58, 94, 103, 191, 216, 264, 269, 277
Palmer, Thomas 212, 243, 246
Paris News Letter 253–5, 261
Parkyn, Robert 220, 223
Parliament, 1504 32
Parliament, 1523 42, 111, 112
Parliament, Reformation 42, 239, 251
Passe, Magdalena and Willem van de 282
Passional Christi und Antichristi 126, 153
Patenson, Henry IV, 1, *169*, 170

Paul, St 144, 215
Paul III, Pope *215*, 216
Paulet, Sir William 246
'Paul's Cross' *See* London, St Paul's Cross
Pavia 58, 199
Peacham, Henry 74
Peasants' War 133
Pelikan, Konrad 137
Pentecost 144
Peter, St 144, 227, 250
Petrus, Henricus 128
Philibert II of Savoy *196*
Philip of Burgundy and Castille 4
Philip II of Spain 7, 64
Picinelli, Filippo 283
Pico della Mirandola, Gianfrancesco 22, 24
Pico della Mirandola, Giovanni 22, *23*, 24, 25, 279
Pietro, Gabriele di 70
Pilate, Pontius 227
Pirckheimer, Willibald *58*
Plana, Gerard de 30
Plato 22, 124, 180
Play of Sir Thomas Moore 108, 275
Plutarch 54, 93
Pole, Sir Geoffrey 221
Pole, Reginald, Cardinal 191, 215, *216*, 221, 269, 270, 277
Poliziano, Angelo 22, 54
Polstede, Henry 242, 244
Pomarancio, Il 259
Pomeranus, Johannes *See* Bugenhagen, Johann
Powys family 226
Porte, Sir John 246
Prebendaries of Canterbury, Plot of 178, 182
Prester John 178
Proclus 78, 180
Prudentius 175
Pynson, R. 15, 56, 104, 118, 119, 266, 267

Quentel, Peter 129
Quintus Curtius 54

Raphael 59, 200
Rastell family 274
  Elizabeth 184
  John 22, 96, 146
  William 82, 84, 146, 148, 154, 156, 158, 163, 165, 167, 184, 219, 221–5, *235*, 236, 247, 248, 260, 261, 287
  Winifred 260
Rav, Jan *See* Corvus
Recueil d'Arras 42
Redman, Robert 164
Regent 103
Regi, Domenico 283
Regnault, François 226
Resch, Conrad 103
Rest, Sir John 189
Resta, Sebastiano 59
Revelation 37, 127, 142, 143

Reynes, John 95, 118
Reynolds, Richard 252
Rice, John ap 242, 244
Rich, Sir Richard 212, 243, 244, 246, 249, 253
Richard III 2, 109, 189
Riche, Hugh 231
Rinck, Hermann 4
Risby, Richard 231
Ro: Ba: 272, 274
Robinson, Ralph 47
Rochford, George Lord 246
Roffensis *See* Fisher, John
Rogendort, Wolffgang 73
Rogers, John 144
Rome, English College 259
Roncalli, Cristoforo *See* Pomarancio
Roper family 174
  Margaret IV, *1*, 133, *169*, 170, 171, *174*, 175, 181, 182, 211, 225, 227, 228, 237, 242, 247, 248, 250–3, 257, 259, 267, 273, 275
  Mary *See* Basset, Mary
  Thomas 250
  William 20, 21, 32, *174*, 175, 211, 212, 218, 228, 243, 250, 251, 271, 272, 274–6
'Rosseus, Guilielmus' 119, 129
Rovere, Giuliano *See* Julius II
Roye, William 143, 150
Ruthall, Thomas 29, 30, 83

SS Collar 26, *27*, 176
Sack of Rome 199, 200, 213
St German, Christopher 163–7
St Michael, Order of 195
Salcot *See* Capon, John
Sampson, Richard 48, 127, 194
Sanuto, Marino 211, 218
Savinian, St 281
Savonarola, Girolamo 22, 41
Say, Henry 236
Schäufelein, Hans Leonhard 256
Schott, Johann 116, 150
Schumann, Valentin 127
Schwarz, Hans 73
Schwarzerdt, Philipp *See* Melanchthon
Schwertfeger, Johann 126
Scrope, Mary *See* More, Mary
Sebastiano del Piombo 75
Secundus, Johannes (Janus) 257
Segar, Francis 12
Segar, Sir William 12
Seneca 54, 270
Serbopoulos, John 92
Seusenhofer, Konrad 61
Shakespeare, William 109, 110, 275
Sharpe, Thomas 236
Siberch, John 95, 122
Sichardus, Johann 128
Sittow, Michiel 4
'Somersam, Richard' *See* Bayfield
'Some-say, Sir John' *See* St German
Soter, Johann 144
Soto, Pedro de 225
Southwell, Sir Richard 212, 243, 246
Sparchford, Richard 118

INDEX

Spelman, Sir John 246
Spenser, Robert 107
Spinelli, Niccolò *See* Niccolò Fiorentino
Spinelly, Sir Thomas 48
Spirito, Lorenzo (Gualtieri) 82
Stafferton, Richard 17
Stampfer, Hans Jakob 137-9
Stans puer 77
Stapleton, Thomas 98, 174, 228, 250, 263, 273, 274, 276, 281, 286
Star Chamber 232
Starkey, Thomas 191, 277
Steels, Johann 254
Steiner, Heinrich 256
Stokesley, John 161
Stow, John 276
Strong, Sampson 32
Succession, Act of 237-9, 242, 244
Suetonius 54
Suffolk, Duke of 198, 207, *208*, 237, 246
Suleiman I *213*, 221
Summers, Will 61
Supremacy 174, 208, 210, 211, 214, 235, 237-9, 242, 244, 246, 247, 249, 252
Symkys, Richard 236

Taylor, John 198
Terminus 87, 89
Theodore of Croyland, St 281
Theophylact 91
Thetford 193
Thevet, André 68
Theyer, John 79
Thomas, St, Apostle 227, 281
Thomas Aquinas, St 219
Thomas Becket, St 205, 250, 281, 282
Thomas à Kempis 226
Thorneton, William 242
Throckmorton family 286
Tilney, Edmund 275
Toledo, Fernando de 225
Topclyffe, Richard 1, 272
Torrentino, Lorenzo 270
Torrigiano, Pietro 1, 3, 5, 11, 214
Tottel, Richard 222, 260
Tramezzino, M. 269
Treason, Act of 244
Tregonwell, Sir John 249
Trent, Council of 216
Trogus Pompeius 110
Tunstall, Cuthbert 29, 30, 48, 54, *55*, 56-57A, 95, 111, 116, 118, 140, 187, 229, 264, 287
Twonson, N. 157
Tyndale, William 42, 119, 145, 146-9, 154, 157, 161, 165, 287. *See also* Bible

Urswick, Christopher 18, 20, 38, 41
Utopia, Island of *52*
Utrecht 76

Valderus, J. 180
Vautrollier, Thomas 224
Vele, Abraham 47

Vergil 227
Vergil, Polydore 107, 129
Veronica, St 33
Verstegan, Richard 259
Vespasian, Emperor 30
Vitalibus, Bernardinus de 24
Vives, Joannes Ludovicus 54, 185, 186, 268
Vocht, Jacob de 106
Vrelant, Paul van 62
'Vulgarius' 91

Walsingham, Sir Edmund 242, 243, 246
Waly, John 260
Warham, William 38, 111, 197, *204*, 205, 232, 287
Watson, John 236
Weiditz, Hans 256
Welschhaus, Johann *See* Bebel, Johann
West, George 179
Whalley, John 242, 244
White, Sir Thomas 174
Whitford, Richard 83
Whittinton, Robert 266, 267
Wickram, Jörg 255
Wiclif, John 126, 140, 143, 154
Wieland, Daniel 86
Wiericx, Anton 282
Willems, Conrad 155
Williams, John 278
Wilpurg von Erbach, Jodocus 69
Wilson, Nicholas 122, 235
Wilson, Richard 242
Wiltshire, Thomas, Earl of 246
Windsor, Andrew Lord 246
Winter, Thomas 191, 192
Wolsey, Thomas, Cardinal 32, 35, 38, 40, *42*, *43*, 48, 65, *67*, 71, 76, 111, 112, 116, 117, 120, 122, 150, 185, 187, 192, 194, 195, 197, 198, 207, 208, 216, 232
Wood, Anthony à 273
Wood, John à 242, 247
Woodville, Elizabeth 5
Worde, Wynkyn de 22, 266
Wriothesley Roll 111
Wyer, Robert 82
Wyngaerde, Anthonis van den 7

York, House of 27, 37, 216

Zangrius, Pieter 262
Zwingli, Huldrych 86, 123, *137*, 138, 139, 154, 157, 180

The nunne of Canterbury & her attaynder 1533. c. 25. of H. 8.
Kynge of malice & revenge coulde frinde no other matter as tou-
ye. nunne against B. fysher but that thei had harde by repo[rt]
others certen woordes y[t] y[e]. nonne had spoken agaynst y[e].
devorce & had not reueiled them to y[e]. kynge & his cou[ncel]
and so thei were attented (of misprision of highe treason
conceilment of thos woordes) in y[e]. bill drawen to attaynt y[e]. no[nne]
k. soughte allso to haue attaynted S[r]. Tho. Moore for talkin[g w]
her, & put in a bill into y[e]. higher howse to attaynt hym
misprision of highe treason. Sir Tho: Moore wroghte to
for a copy of y[e]. bill, but he wolde not sende it hym, & therefore
wroghte to y[e]. k. to purge hym selfe of it, & thereupon y[e].
discharged sir Tho: Moore, & attaynted neu[er] wrongfully [&]
by parliament makynge y[t]. an offence by acte whiche w[as]
before.   The k. caused al his bushopes sauinge y[e]. B. of [&]
to surrender al theire Bulles to hym, whereby they were ma[de]
bushopes, & they toke y[e]. k. l[ette]res Pat[en]tes to be bushopes
onley by hym.   The clargi of London were sworn[e]
y[e]. othe, & sir Tho: Moore y[e]. B. of Rochester & Doctor Wi[lson]
who had ben y[e]. k. confessor refused yt. & were therefore ymprisoned [in the]
Tower. The B. of Rochester sayd he wolde not swere to y[e]. othe [but]
I woll applie my selfe to y[e]. k. pleasure so far fourthe as I may w[ith] con[science]
lerninge, offeringe y[t]. he wolde be content to swere unto some
y[e]. othe, so y[t]. it were qualified either w[ith]. some condicions or excepcio[n]
other manner than it was there set fourthe. But y[e]. com[m]iss.
myslikinge y[e]. w[ith] his condicions & accepcions, as repugn[ant]

DATE DUE			
~~JUN 30 '79~~			
GAYLORD			PRINTED IN U.S.A.